P9-CEM-064

DATE DUE

NOV 27 2012	

POWER
AND
CONSTRAINT

POWER
AND
CONSTRAINT

The Accountable Presidency after 9/11

JACK GOLDSMITH

W. W. NORTON & COMPANY

New York • London

Copyright © 2012 by Jack Goldsmith

All rights reserved
Printed in the United States of America
First Edition

For information about permission to reproduce selections from this book,
write to Permissions, W. W. Norton & Company, Inc.,
500 Fifth Avenue, New York, NY 10110

For information about special discounts for bulk purchases, please contact
W. W. Norton Special Sales at specialsales@wwnorton.com or 800-233-4830

Manufacturing by RR Donnelley, Harrisonburg
Book design by Charlotte Staub
Production manager: Devon Zahn

Library of Congress Cataloging-in-Publication Data

Goldsmith, Jack L.
Power and constraint : the accountable presidency
after 9/11 / Jack Goldsmith. — 1st ed.
p. cm.
Includes bibliographical references and index.
ISBN 978-0-393-08133-6 (hardcover)
1. Presidents—United States—History—21st century.
2. Executive power—United States—History—21st century.
3. Separation of powers—United States—History—21st century. I. Title.
JK511.G62 2012
352.23'50973—dc23
2011048261

W. W. Norton & Company, Inc.
500 Fifth Avenue, New York, N.Y. 10110
www.wwnorton.com

W. W. Norton & Company Ltd.
Castle House, 75/76 Wells Street, London W1T 3QT

1 2 3 4 5 6 7 8 9 0

To Mom
with love

CONTENTS

Introduction

CHECKS AND BALANCES IN AN ENDLESS WAR

"IT'S GOING TO TAKE a long time to win this war," President George W. Bush told a group of Pentagon employees on September 17, 2001, six days after the terrorist attacks that marked a new era in global history.[1] "Americans should not expect one battle but a lengthy campaign, unlike any other we have ever seen," he said, three days later, at a joint session of Congress.[2] Bush was right. More than a decade after 9/11, Osama Bin Laden is dead and many of his top associates have been killed or captured. And yet the endless war against Islamist terrorists—already the longest war in American history—continues on several fronts, in several countries, with no end in sight.

An endless war, and an endless emergency too. "A national emergency exists by reason of the terrorist attacks at the World Trade Center, New York, New York, and the Pentagon, and the continuing and immediate threat of further attacks on the United States," Bush declared, three days after 9/11.[3] Bush renewed the emergency declaration every subsequent year of his presidency. President Barack Obama renewed it as well during his first three years in office. "The terrorist threat that led to the declaration on September 14, 2001, of a national emergency continues," he proclaimed. "For this reason, I have determined that it is necessary to continue in effect . . . the national emergency with respect to the terrorist threat."[4]

War and emergency invariably shift power to the presidency. Permanent war and permanent emergency threaten to make the shift permanent. George W. Bush's counterterrorism initiatives—warrantless surveillance, targeted killings, detention without trial, military commissions, limitations on habeas corpus, aggressive interrogations, and much more—were unthinkable on September 10, 2001. Bush succeeded in preventing another attack on the homeland, an accomplishment he described as the "most meaningful" of his presidency.[5] But many believe that his success came at an unacceptable cost to American legal traditions, and that he destroyed the constitutional separation of powers by violating scores of laws and snubbing Congress. "Decades from now," said Republican Senator Arlen Specter at the twilight of the Bush presidency, "historians will look back on the period from 9/11 to the present as an era of unbridled executive power and Congressional ineffectiveness."[6]

Barack Obama campaigned against the Bush approach to counterterrorism and came to office promising to repudiate it and to restore the rule of law. "As for our common defense, we reject as false the choice between our safety and our ideals," he said in his inaugural address.[7] But in perhaps the most remarkable surprise of his presidency, Obama continued almost all of his predecessor's counterterrorism policies. "Presidents don't tend to give back power on their own volition," remarked Princeton historian Julian Zelizer, nine months into the Obama presidency. "While there have been some changes it is difficult to conclude that the election made a serious dent in the strength of the executive branch."[8]

Spector and Zelizer—a mainstream politician and a progressive professor—reflect the widely held view that 9/11 was the death knell for the separation of powers and for presidential accountability. For many, James Madison's famous concern that "no nation could preserve its freedom in the midst of continual warfare" has been realized.[9] Books such as *Bomb Power*, *The Decline and Fall of the American Republic*, *Madison's Nightmare*, and *The Executive Unbound* argue that 9/11 brought a dramatic shift of power to the President.[10] These books differ in the details of their arguments and in their normative stance. But they generally agree with law professors Eric Posner and Adrian Vermeule, the authors of *The Executive Unbound*, that in military and national security affairs we live "in an age after the separation of powers, and the legally constrained executive is now a historical curiosity."[11]

The problem with the conventional wisdom about the expansion of presidential power is that it tells only half the story. The rest of the story, the one I tell in this book, is a remarkable and unnoticed revolution in wartime presidential accountability that checked and legitimated this growth in presidential power.

The U.S. Constitution creates a system of "checks and balances" that gives other institutions—Congress, the courts, and the press—the motives and tools to counteract the President when they think he is too powerful, pursues the wrong policies, or acts illegally. Far from rolling over after 9/11, these institutions pushed back far harder against the Commander in Chief than in any other war in American history. The post-9/11 Congress often seemed feckless, especially in its oversight responsibilities. But it nonetheless managed to alter and regulate presidential tactics on issues—interrogation, detention, surveillance, military commissions, and more—that in previous wars were controlled by the President. Congress was often spurred to action because the American press uncovered and published the executive branch's deepest secrets. It was also moved by federal judges who discarded their traditional reluctance to review presidential military decisions and threw themselves into questioning, invalidating, and supervising a variety of these decisions—decisions that in other wars had been the President's to make. Judicial review of the Commander in Chief's actions often left him without legal authority to act, forcing him to work with Congress to fill the legal void.

These traditional forces received crucial support from something new and remarkable: giant distributed networks of lawyers, investigators, and auditors, both inside and outside the executive branch, that rendered U.S. fighting forces and intelligence services more transparent than ever, and that enforced legal and political constraints, small and large, against them.

On the inside, military and national security lawyers devoted their days and many of their nights to ensuring that the Commander in Chief complied with thousands of laws and regulations, and to responding to hundreds of lawsuits challenging presidential wartime action. These lawyers' checks were complemented by independent executive-branch watchdogs, such as inspectors general and ethics monitors, who engaged in accountability-enhancing investigations of the President's military and intelligence activities. These actors were empowered by a culture of independence that had grown up quietly in the previous three decades. And they enforced laws traceable to 1970s congressional reforms of the presidency that most observers assumed were dead but that turned out to be alive and quite fearsome.

On the outside, nongovernmental organizations like the American Civil Liberties Union and the Center for Constitutional Rights connected up with thousands of like-minded lawyers and activists in the United States and abroad. Together, these forces—often, once again, invoking laws and institutions traceable to decades-old legal reforms—swarmed the government with hundreds of critical reports and lawsuits that challenged every aspect of the President's war powers. They also brought thousands of critical minds to bear on the government's activities, resulting in best-selling books, reports, blog posts, and press tips that shaped the public's view of presidential action and informed congressional responses, lawsuits, and mainstream media reporting.

The pages that follow will show that these forces worked together in dynamic ways to uncover, challenge, change, and then effectively approve nearly every element of the Bush counterterrorism program. There are many reasons why Barack Obama continued so much of the Bush program as it stood in January 2009. But the most significant reason was that almost all of this program had been vetted, altered, and blessed—with restrictions and accountability strings attached—by the other branches of the U.S. government. Obama and his White House team, sobered by a terrorist threat they fully appreciated only once they assumed power, refused to walk away from widespread political and legal support for aggressive counterterrorism actions. The institutions that pushed back against the Bush presidency did not cease to exercise their influence during Obama's presidency. Obama too felt the sting of checks and balances when he tried and failed to close the Guantanamo Bay detention facility and to prosecute 9/11 mastermind Khalid Sheikh Mohammed in civilian court.

Some of these checks on the presidency since 9/11 have occurred behind the scenes, but most of them have taken place in plain sight. And yet as a nation we have missed them, and their significance. We missed them because many came from distributed forces rather than from the institution traditionally conceived as the main check on the President during war, Congress. And we missed them because George W. Bush was seen as such a polarizing figure in a scary and unfathomable war, a perception ingrained by Barack Obama's rhetorically powerful campaign criticisms. When President Obama largely followed his predecessor's course, almost everyone assumed that the best explanation was that the presidency as an institution was out of control. In this book I sketch a different, and I believe more persuasive, explanation for the congruence. Two presidential administrations with starkly different views about executive power and proper counterterrorism tactics ended up in approximately the same place because forces more powerful than the aims and inclinations of the presidents and their aides were at work.

In telling this story about modern presidential accountability, I draw on my own experiences in the Bush administration, first in the Department of Defense in 2002–2003, and then in the Department of Justice in 2003–2004.[12] I also draw on dozens of interviews that I conducted with senior political, military, and intelligence officials in the Bush and Obama administrations, and with key representatives in the modern accountability regime for the presidency, including members of Congress and their staffs, federal judges, government lawyers and watchdogs, national security journalists and their editors, human rights activists, and academic experts. My aim in conducting these interviews was to capture a rich variety of perspectives on presidential accountability since 9/11, and to draw patterns and lessons from them.

The book unfolds in three parts. Part I recounts candidate Obama's criticisms of George W. Bush's counterterrorism program and his pledges for reform. It then describes the many ways Obama departed from these pledges and from the related expectations of his political supporters, and the few ways he did not. Part I canvasses reasons for the Obama administration's reluctant embrace of its predecessor's policies, including the efficacy of those policies, the reality of the terror threat, and the responsibilities of the presidency. But the main explanation it offers for the continuity between the two administrations is that the institutions of government and civil society pushed back against the early Bush policies, changed them, and then essentially blessed them in ways that Barack Obama found difficult to resist.

Part II describes in detail the regime of checks and balances that fostered continuity between the two administrations. Under the U.S. Constitution, a wartime president must take the initiative in meeting national security threats, and he exercises more authority with greater discretion and secrecy than in peacetime. The danger that war presents—a danger exacerbated in an indefinite war—is that the president may exercise these enhanced authorities imprudently or in his personal or institutional interest, at the expense of the nation. The response to this problem that has developed over the last decade lies with a number of variously motivated actors who constantly monitor the presidency, in public and behind walls of secrecy. These actors generate information about what the executive branch is doing; they force it to explain its actions; and they are empowered to change these actions when the explanations fail to convince.

The analysis in Part II moves beyond a traditional focus on the President, Congress, and the Supreme Court to examine some of the surprising lower-level forces, inside and outside the government, that have been so consequential in shaping presidential action. It shows how American human rights activists and their foreign counterparts worked with global media outlets and establishment figures to convince conservative Supreme Court justices to grant terrorists novel rights; how similar forces convinced lower courts to create a "citizen declassification" regime for closely held CIA and White House secrets; how a little-known investigator inside the CIA, working at the behest of Congress, discovered abuses in the high-value interrogation program and helped change them long before public knowledge of the abuses; how Republican senators, defying the President and their party, and working with generals supposedly under the President's command, helped to curtail the President's discretion over interrogation and detention; how faceless executive-branch lawyers micromanaged national security decisions; how elite journalists, aided by the Internet and bloggers around the globe, divined the government's deepest secrets, and why their editors published these secrets even when the President begged them not to; why every brigade in the army has a lawyer; and why General David Petraeus never went anywhere without one.

In describing how modern wartime accountability checks work in practice, Part II describes some of the costs and benefits of the system as they are seen by the people involved. Part III considers these costs and benefits more systematically. The main virtue of the system lies in its ability to self-correct: democratic and judicial forces change presidential authorities and actions deemed imprudent or wrong and constrain presidential discretion in numerous ways. These changes and constraints are part of a process that helps to generate a national consensus on what powers the President should exercise and how, a process that has largely legitimated the powerful post-9/11 presidency. One of the themes of Part III (and indeed of the entire book), and one of the important constitutional lessons of the last decade, is that constraints imposed by the watchers of the presidency can strengthen the presidency and render it more effective over the medium and long term in carrying out its national security responsibilities. Consensus and legitimate power are happy consequences of constraint. But as Part III also shows, they are inextricably tied to some unhappy consequences, including the harmful disclosure of national security secrets, misjudgments by the watchers of the presidency, and burdensome legal scrutiny that slows executive action. It is hard to know whether the virtues of the modern presidential accountability system outweigh its vices, or whether the particular counterterrorism policies it produced are the best ones, all things considered. Part III offers some tentative answers and a framework for analysis.

Arthur Schlesinger Jr.'s *The Imperial Presidency* is best known for its critique of the Cold War presidency. Few remember that Schlesinger was a fan of presidential power, or that he argued that the nation needed a strong presidency to protect its security and make the constitutional system work in a dangerous and complex world. Schlesinger thought the solution to the presidential pathologies he identified was not to cut the presidency down in size, but rather "to devise means of reconciling a strong and purposeful Presidency with equally strong and purposeful forms of democratic control."[13] The goal was to establish "a strong Presidency *within the Constitution*."[14] In the pages that follow, I make the case that in the last decade, in the most unusual and challenging war in American history, and at a time when the President exercises unfathomable powers, we have witnessed the rise and operation of purposeful forms of democratic (and judicial) control over the Commander in Chief, and have indeed established strong legal and constitutional constraints on the presidency. These forms of control are messy, and at the margins it is hard to know whether they go too far or not far enough. But they are deeply consequential, and they preserve the framers' original idea of a balanced constitution with an executive branch that, despite its enormous power, remains legally and politically accountable to law and to the American people.

POWER
AND
CONSTRAINT

Part One

CONTINUITY

Chapter One

THE NEW NORMAL

"TRAGICALLY, THE CURRENT ADMINISTRATION chose to respond [to the 9/11 attacks] with [a] series of unnecessary, self-inflicted wounds, which have gravely diminished our global standing and damaged our reputation for respecting the rule of law," said Harold Hongju Koh, two months before the election of 2008, in a Senate hearing on "Restoring the Rule of Law."[1] Koh was at the time the dean of Yale Law School. He was also the former Assistant Secretary of State for Democracy, Human Rights and Labor during the Clinton administration; a passionate leader of the human rights movement; and a leading critic of the Bush administration's counterterrorism policies. After summing up his indictment of Bush-era sins, the man who the following year would become Barack Obama's top State Department lawyer looked to the future. "As difficult as the last seven years have been," Koh said, "they loom far less important in the grand scheme of things than the next eight, which will determine whether the pendulum of U.S. policy swings back from the extreme place to which it has been pushed, or stays stuck in a 'new normal' position under which our policies toward national security, law and human rights remain wholly subsumed by the 'War on Terror.'" Koh urged the next President to reject the Bush paradigm and "unambiguously

3

reassert our historic commitments to human rights and the rule of law as a major source of our moral authority."[2]

This is precisely what Barack Obama had promised to do. As a senator and on the campaign trail, Obama had blasted the Bush approach to military detention, military commissions, interrogation, rendition, surveillance, and more, suggesting that the Bush tactics were un-American. "I will make clear that the days of compromising our values are over," said the then Senator Obama in a typical campaign speech, in 2007, at the Woodrow Wilson International Center. "We cannot win a war unless we maintain the high ground." Obama pledged that if elected, "[w]e will again set an example for the world that the law is not subject to the whims of stubborn rulers, and that justice is not arbitrary."[3] He reiterated these themes in his inaugural address on the first day of his presidency. "Our Founding Fathers, faced with perils that we can scarcely imagine, drafted a charter to assure the rule of law and the rights of man—a charter expanded by the blood of generations," he said to applause from supporters on the National Mall and around the country. "Those ideals still light the world, and we will not give them up for expedience sake."[4]

Obama moved quickly to fulfill these promises. Within hours of his inaugural address, he suspended military commissions and reversed some Bush-era secrecy rules. Two days later, and to greater fanfare, he signed executive orders that banned torture, closed CIA black sites, pledged adherence to the Geneva Conventions, promised to close the detention center at Guantanamo Bay (commonly referred to as "GTMO") within a year, and established a task force to give him new options for the "apprehension, detention, trial, transfer, release, or other disposition" of terrorist detainees.[5] "[O]ur ideals give us the strength and moral high ground" to combat terrorism, Obama said, just before signing the legal documents.[6]

These events created a conspicuous sense of dramatic change in the nation's capital—a sense that the American people had rejected the counterterrorism policies of the Bush era, and that seven years of aggressive tactics had come to a screeching halt.

"Bush's 'War' on Terror Comes to a Sudden End," announced the *Washington Post* the next day, in a typical headline. "With the stroke of his pen," the article reported, President Obama "effectively declared an end to the 'war on terror,' as President George W. Bush had defined it."[7]

But it was not to be. Contrary to nearly everyone's expectations, the Obama administration would continue almost all of its predecessor's policies, transforming what had seemed extraordinary under the Bush regime into the "new normal" of American counterterrorism policy.[8]

BUSH VERSUS OBAMA

In retrospect, what is remarkable about candidate Obama's criticisms of the Bush counterterrorism program is how much subtle wiggle room they left the future President. Once in office, the Obama administration exploited this wiggle room in some areas and departed from campaign pledges in others. The bottom line is that it copied most of the Bush counterterrorism program as it stood in January 2009, expanded some of it, and narrowed a bit.

War versus Crime. The Bush administration claimed that the United States was in a state of war with al Qaeda and its affiliates and that the President's full powers as Commander in Chief were in force. It claimed two sources of authority for these conclusions: the President's power as Chief Executive and Commander in Chief to respond to an attack on the country, and Congress's September 18, 2001, authorization for the President "to use all necessary and appropriate force against those nations, organizations, or persons he determines planned, authorized, committed, or aided" the 9/11 terrorist attacks.[9] Many of the Bush administration's most controversial policies—including military detention without trial, military commissions, and targeted killing—depended on this argument.

Candidate Obama said nothing concrete about this issue on the campaign trail. But many Obama supporters, including some who would serve in the Obama administration, disputed Bush's war powers characterization. They maintained that the criminal justice system's legal weapons—arrest, extradition, civilian trials, and the like—sufficed to meet the terror threat.[10] In its second month in office, however, the Obama administration embraced the war characterization, relying on the second Bush rationale. The September 18, 2001, congressional authorization "empowers the President to use all necessary and appropriate force to prosecute the war" against al Qaeda and its affiliates, Obama lawyers argued in a legal brief defending the detention without trial of a Guantanamo detainee.[11] They also copied the Bush administration in arguing that the President's power is "not limited to persons captured on the battlefields of Afghanistan."[12] Any such limitation, they argued, would "unduly hinder both the President's ability to protect our country from future acts of terrorism and his ability to gather vital intelligence regarding the capability, operations, and intentions of this elusive and cunning adversary."[13] The Obama lawyers additionally maintained, like their predecessors, that courts "should defer to the President's judgment" about the meaning of the congressional authorization.[14]

Military Detention. One of the most controversial Bush counterterrorism practices was the military detention of terrorist suspects without charge or trial. Candidate Obama criticized this practice on the ground that it did not give detainees adequate rights. But while some of his campaign advisers suggested that the practice should be abolished, Obama never did.[15] Nonetheless, Obama supporters who thought he would eliminate military detention were given hope when his initial executive orders mandated a task force review of the Bush military detention process. They were disappointed when President Obama, in a May 2009 speech from the National Archives, in a room where the Constitution and Bill of Rights are on display, stated that some detainees "who cannot be prosecuted yet who pose a clear danger to the American people" might not be released.[16] Eight months later, Obama's Guantanamo Review Task Force formally concluded that at least

48 detainees fit this category, though the number of people in military detention at Guantanamo Bay, Cuba, would remain closer to 175 because the task force's ambitions for transfers and prosecutions did not pan out.[17] After two years of deliberation, the Obama administration in March 2011 issued an executive order for periodic review of the GTMO detainees that was more generous to the detainees than an analogous Bush program. But it received the most attention for its official recognition, under President Obama's signature, of the indefinite military detention that many believed he would abolish.[18]

The justification for military detention without trial, President Obama explained in his Archives speech, is that some terrorist detainees who cannot be prosecuted "nonetheless pose a threat to the security of the United States."[19] This was the same policy rationale the Bush administration gave for military detention. Obama's lawyers also copied the Bush legal rationale. They argued that the September 2001 congressional authorization allowed the President to detain indefinitely, without charge or trial, members of al Qaeda, the Taliban, and "associated forces," even if captured outside Afghanistan.[20] This formulation was identical to Bush's except that the Bush lawyers extended detention power to those who "support" terrorist groups, while the Obama lawyers extended it only to those who "substantially support" these groups.[21] The Obama team's "broad definition of those who can be held . . . was not significantly different from the one used by the Bush administration," concluded the *New York Times.*[22] Federal District Court Judge Reggie Walton agreed, noting that the Obama refinements drew a "metaphysical difference" with the Bush position "of a minimal if not ephemeral character."[23] Later iterations of the Obama position drew fine legal distinctions that the Bush administration might not have drawn (we can never know), but these distinctions had no discernible impact on the scope of detention.

Military Commissions. In November 2001, President Bush authorized the establishment of military commissions to try suspected terrorists.[24] Commissions are courts run by the military to try enemy forces for war crimes and related offenses. They have special rules about evidence, secrecy, and other matters that make it easier to convict a defendant than in an ordinary civilian court. They also make it easier to convict than in a court-martial, the military court governed by the Uniform Code of Military Justice that is used to prosecute U.S. soldiers and is similar in most respects to civilian trials. The Bush commissions sparked controversy because they departed sharply from ordinary standards of civilian justice, and because President Bush announced their establishment without consulting Congress or his National Security Council. After years of litigation, the Supreme Court in 2006 invalidated the Bush commissions on the ground that they were inconsistent with a federal statute.[25] When President Bush sought to rectify the decision by getting Congress on board, Senator Obama voted against the subsequent bill, which he described as "sloppy" and not a "real military system of justice."[26] Obama was at the time open to, and voted to support, a military commission with greater defendant protections.[27] But by 2008, he seemed to reject the use of military commissions (as opposed to courts-martial) under any circumstances. "It's time to better protect the American people and our values by bringing swift and sure justice to terrorists through our courts and our Uniform Code of Military Justice," he said.[28]

Against this background, Obama's 120-day suspension of military commissions at the dawn of his presidency led most of his supporters to assume that commissions were dead. "Mr. Obama rightly denounced the tribunals during the campaign," and "we were delighted to see him shut them down so swiftly now that he is in the White House," cheered the *New York Times* editorial page. The *Times* presumed that the suspension rather than the termination of military commissions was "a legal nicety," for "[t]here is no good reason to restart these trials."[29] But it was not a legal nicety. After an intense review, the administration concluded that commissions were a necessary legal weapon in the Commander in Chief's arsenal. It reached this conclusion, Obama later explained, because commissions "allow for the protection of sensitive sources and methods of intelligence-gathering; they allow for the safety and security of participants; and for the presentation of evidence gathered from the battlefield that cannot always be effectively presented in federal courts."[30] This was precisely the Bush rationale.

Obama did seek additional reforms to commissions to disallow certain evidence obtained from coercion, to make it harder for the government to use hearsay evidence, and to give detainees more freedom to choose attorneys. Congress went along in the summer of 2009. The change on defense lawyers was practically no change at all. The change on hearsay maintained the flexibility to use it but placed the burden of proof on the government. The change on coerced evidence was real but not large because there was a high, and in practice probably insurmountable, bar to its use under the old rules.[31] Former chief prosecutor for military commissions Colonel Morris Davis exaggerated a bit when he noted that the 2009 reforms were nothing more than a "lightly revised version of the same" commissions that Congress approved, and Obama criticized, in 2006.[32] The 2009 reforms probably increased the reliability of commission adjudications at the margins. But Morris is right to suggest that these were not big changes from the 2006 baseline.

Moreover, even after the Obama reforms, the government still retained large advantages with the commissions compared to civilian trials or courts-martial—advantages that had made them repugnant to many during the Bush years. Unlike a civilian trial, where unanimity is needed for conviction before a civilian jury, in military commissions a two-thirds rule before a military jury prevails. A military commission need not read the defendant *Miranda* warnings to use his statements against him, and is not bound by the same rules of evidence or witness confrontation as in a civilian trial. Military commissions are also easier to close to the public than civilian trials.[33] These are some of the reasons why civil liberties groups declared, as Amnesty International put it, that Obama's embrace of commissions, even as revised, "backtracks on a major campaign promise to change the way the United States fights terrorism."[34]

Forum Discretion. Civil libertarians disappointed with adoption of military detentions and military commissions found solace when Attorney General Eric Holder announced in November 2009 that 9/11 mastermind Khalid Sheikh Mohammed would be lifted from the military commission where Bush had placed him (and where he had tried to plead guilty) and would be prosecuted instead before a civilian court in New York. This was not the radical departure from the Bush era that it was portrayed to be. The Bush administration prosecuted hundreds of terrorists in civilian trials, including 9/11 conspirator Zacarias Moussaoui, American Taliban John Walker Lindh, and alleged "dirty bomber" Jose Padilla. Holder underlined the broader continuity with the Bush era when he announced, in the press conference that revealed Mohammed's transfer to civilian trial, that a half-dozen other terrorists would be tried by military commission. Even more discouraging for those who hoped for change, Holder also said he would follow the Bush policy of holding Mohammed and other terrorists in military detention indefinitely if they are acquitted at trial or receive a short sentence. "I certainly think that under the regime that we are contemplating, the potential for detaining people under the laws of war, we would retain that ability," said Holder.[35]

The muted civil libertarian cheers that greeted Holder's announcement that he would try Khalid Sheikh Mohammed in a civilian court turned to cries of anger when Holder was unable to follow through. New York officials, Democrat and Republican, opposed a trial in the state. Congress eventually cut off funding for any trials of GTMO detainees in the United States, including Mohammed's. Holder tried to find ways to circumvent these restrictions, but he had little political support in the administration and he eventually gave in to political reality. In April 2011 he announced that Mohammed, who had spent the first two years of the Obama administration in military detention, would not be tried in civilian court after all. Instead, he would be sent back to a military commission, where he had been at the end of the Bush administration, trying to plead guilty.

Inherent in sending Khalid Sheikh Mohammed back and forth between different legal systems is yet another point of continuity between the two administrations. The Bush administration claimed the discretion to choose among three different venues—civilian trial, military commission, or military detention—for putting away terrorists. This discretion allowed it to place three 9/11 conspirators in three different systems: Zacarias Moussaoui was tried in civilian court; Mohammed al-Kahtani, the real twentieth hijacker, has been in military detention on Guantanamo Bay since 2002; and Khalid Sheikh Mohammed was first a high-level military detainee, then in the military commission system, then on his way to the civilian system, and now resides once again in the commission system. The Obama administration tried to articulate principled criteria for which terrorists should go in which system.[36] But it retained the discretion to use any of the three systems. "I don't think we can afford to limit our options unduly in an artificial way or to yield to sort of preconceived a priori notions of suitability or correctness," explained David Kris, the Justice Department's top national security lawyer, defending the right to use different systems. "[W]hen we look at the tools that are available to us consistent with our values, we've got to use the tool that is designed best for the particular national security problem that we find ourselves facing."[37]

Guantanamo Bay. Nearly everyone assumed that President Obama would follow through on his first-week presidential order to close the Guantanamo Bay detention facility within one year. But not former Vice President Richard Cheney. "I think they'll discover that trying to close [Guantanamo Bay] is a very hard proposition," he said in December 2008.[38] Cheney was right, and in late 2011, the island facility remains open and will be indefinitely. There were many reasons why Obama failed in his first-week pledge. Early administration hopes that the detainees could be prosecuted, transferred, or released proved fanciful. Foreign governments accepted fewer detainees than anticipated despite offers of money, presidential face time, and other favors.[39] And a lengthy and harder-than-expected review of detainee files indicated that many of them could not easily be prosecuted but were too dangerous to release.

This meant that GTMO could be closed only if some detainees were transferred to the United States for detention. But this proved an impossible task for which the administration—possessing limited political capital, and preoccupied with health care reform in 2009—never properly organized.[40] It didn't settle on a potential prison venue in the United States for the GTMO detainees until December 2009. But in order to hold terrorist detainees, the prison required significant alterations that would take months and perhaps years to implement because of a slew of complex environmental, fiscal, and government contracting laws. By that time Congress had turned sharply against any plan to bring detainees to the United States. Beginning in May 2009 and more firmly thereafter, it barred the administration from spending any money to transfer the detainees to the United States, effectively preventing the President from keeping a central campaign promise. "Obviously I haven't been able to make the case right now," President Obama said in April 2011, "and without Congress's cooperation, we can't do it."[41]

Habeas Corpus. Former law professor Barack Obama was an eloquent defender of habeas corpus, the judicial writ of freedom that permits any person in executive custody to ask a court to review the legality of the detention. "[R]estricting somebody's right to challenge their imprisonment indefinitely is not going to make us safer," he said in the Senate, explaining his vote against a law that eliminated habeas corpus for detainees outside the United States.[42] On the campaign trail, Obama rejected the "false choice between fighting terrorism and respecting habeas corpus," and described habeas corpus as the "foundation of Anglo-American law" and "the essence of who we are."[43] When the Supreme

Court in the summer of 2008 ruled that habeas corpus rights must extend to GTMO, Obama cheered.[44] The ruling was "a rejection of the Bush Administration's attempt to create a legal black hole at Guantanamo," he said. "Our courts have employed habeas corpus with rigor and fairness for more than two centuries, and we must continue to do so as we defend the freedom that violent extremists seek to destroy," Obama added.[45]

The Bush administration accepted the Supreme Court's 2008 decision but argued that habeas corpus should not extend to persons detained beyond Guantanamo, in places like Afghanistan, where hundreds of enemy soldiers were detained without charge or trial. Candidate Obama was silent on this issue, but his defense of habeas corpus and his description of places beyond the habeas writ as "legal black holes" led many to assume that he would reject the Bush position. But he did not. "Having considered the matter, the government adheres to its previously articulated position," an Obama lawyer in 2009 told Federal District Court Judge John Bates, who was considering the fate of some detainees in Afghanistan.[46] The Obama administration has "embrac[ed] a key argument of former President Bush's legal team," noted the *New York Times*.[47] When Judge Bates rejected the argument, the Obama lawyers appealed and won what the *Times* described as "a broad victory . . . in its efforts to hold terrorism suspects overseas for indefinite periods without judicial oversight."[48] The newspapers gave less attention to the fact that early on, motivated in part to fend off habeas corpus review in Afghanistan, the Obama administration had begun to raise the standards of the screening and detention procedures for suspects held in Afghanistan. These more rigorous procedures would be applied to a military detention population in Afghanistan that by 2011 had spiked to more than treble the size of the population under Bush.[49]

Global Targeted Killing. President Obama continued the Bush administration practice of targeting and killing enemy suspects in Pakistan and other places outside a traditional battlefield and inside countries with which the United States is not at war. But here one cannot charge Obama with any inconsistency, for he was clear on the campaign trail that he would target and kill members of al Qaeda and its affiliates wherever in the world they might be found. "The Bush administration has not acted aggressively enough to go after al-Qaeda's leadership," Obama said in a 2008 interview. "I would be clear that if Pakistan cannot or will not take out al-Qaeda leadership when we have actionable intelligence about their whereabouts, we will act to protect the American people. There can be no safe haven for al-Qaeda terrorists who killed thousands of Americans and threaten our homeland today."[50]

Obama fulfilled this promise in dramatic fashion with his approval of Operation Neptune Spear, the daring and dangerous operation that killed Osama Bin Laden in Abbottabad, Pakistan, on May 2, 2011. But in truth he had adhered to this promise long before then. In a dozen nations outside of Afghanistan and Iraq, the Obama administration "has significantly increased military and intelligence operations, pursuing the enemy using robotic drones and commando teams, paying contractors to spy and training local operatives to chase terrorists," reported the *New York Times* in August 2010.[51] The administration has been especially fond of using unmanned drones for "targeted killings" of enemy terrorists. It ramped up drone attacks quite a bit, using them more frequently during Obama's first year than Bush had in the previous seven combined. Many human rights groups criticized these attacks as illegal assassinations or "extrajudicial killings," and some accused the Obama administration of war crimes. But the administration has been unmoved. "[V]ery frankly, it's the only game in town in terms of confronting and trying to disrupt the al Qaeda leadership," said CIA Director Leon Panetta.[52]

Rendition. An important Bush counterterrorism tool was rendition, the practice of taking a person from one country to another, outside judicial process and against the person's will, for purposes of trial or interrogation. On the campaign trail, Barack Obama made it seem like he opposed this practice. "It's time to show the world that we are not a country that ships prisoners in the dead of night to be tortured in far off countries," Obama would often say.[53] Many people thought this meant that Obama would officially end the practice. But very early on, his administration made clear that it would keep renditions on the table. "Obviously you need to preserve some tools—you still have to go after the bad guys," said an anonymous Obama official in late January 2009. If rendition is "done within certain parameters, it is an acceptable practice."[54]

During his confirmation hearing for CIA Director a few days later, Leon Panetta made official that the new administration would keep rendition on the table, but he pledged that it would not render suspects for purposes of torture. Many saw this position as a rejection of the Bush practice. But Panetta also said, to less media notice, that the new administration would use the Bush-era legal test, which barred renditions only when it is "more likely than not"—that is, a greater than 50 percent chance—that the suspect "will be subjected to torture."[55] When Obama's Special Task Force on Interrogations and Transfer Policies recommended seven months later that renditions continue, it did not renounce this standard, but rather said it would "make recommendations aimed at clarifying and strengthening U.S. procedures" for evaluating "assurances" from the receiving country and for monitoring claims about torture.[56] Human rights groups did not see a change. "It is extremely disappointing that the Obama administration is continuing the Bush administration practice of relying on diplomatic assurances, which have been proven completely ineffective in preventing torture," said ACLU lawyer Amrit Singh.[57]

Because the public knows little about how (if at all) the Obama administration actually conducts renditions, it is unclear how (if at all) the actual practice has changed under Obama from the late Bush period. There have been reports that the administration has continued the later Bush-era practice of outsourcing rendition. In a practice that "began in the last two years of the Bush administration and has gained momentum under Mr. Obama," the *New York Times* reported in May 2009, the "United States is now relying heavily on foreign intelligence services to capture, interrogate and detain all but the highest-level terrorist suspects seized outside the battlefields of Iraq and Afghanistan."[58]

Black Sites. In its first week, the Obama administration dismantled the Bush system of secret overseas prisons for high-value detainees. This was a real departure from the Bush regime, but less of a departure than met the eye. For the last two years of Bush's presidency, the black sites were practically empty. During this period, the *New York Times* reported, only two terrorists were brought to the sites for a few months before being transferred to GTMO.[59] In addition, Obama's January 2009 order to close secret prisons contained two little-noticed loopholes: it applied only to CIA prisons (not military prisons), and it did not apply to facilities that "hold people on a short-term, transitory basis."[60] A possible implication of these loopholes became apparent when the *New York Times* reported in June 2009 that Obama's Department of Defense was holding detainees at a so-called "black jail" adjacent to the Bagram prison with no access to the Red Cross for "weeks at a time."[61] According to several reports, the detainees at this jail are sometimes subject to tougher interrogation methods than those approved for ordinary detainees, in accordance with Appendix M of the Army Field Manual.[62]

Surveillance. In the summer of 2008, candidate Obama voted to put President Bush's unilateral warrantless wiretapping program, which he had opposed as an abuse of presidential power, on a legally more defensible statutory basis. Obama supported the bill even though it gave telecommunication firms that cooperated with President Bush immunity from lawsuits, a provision Obama disliked. In office, President Obama has not renounced or sought to narrow any of the surveillance powers in use at the end of the Bush administration, and has not sought legislation to reverse the telecoms' immunity. This is perhaps unsurprising since Obama voted for the law. Obama did surprise many, however, when he successfully urged Congress to extend the PATRIOT Act and failed to take any steps to fulfill his campaign pledge to strengthen the Privacy and Civil Liberties Oversight Board, which oversees and protects civil liberties in intelligence gathering.[63]

Obama also enhanced the domestic role of the National Security Agency, America's powerful signals intelligence organization that operated Bush's controversial Terrorist Surveillance Program. Obama placed the NSA in charge of "Cyber Command," the new military combatant command in charge of coordinating America's offensive cyber weapons with its cyber defense of homeland critical infrastructure.[64] He approved the construction of a $1.5 billion, one-million-square-foot NSA data center at Camp Williams, Utah, that will provide "critical support to national cybersecurity priorities" and "intelligence and warnings related to cybersecurity threats, cybersecurity support to defense and civilian agency networks, and technical assistance to the Department of Homeland Security."[65] And his Justice Department sought and asserted additional authorities to make domestic wiretapping and record collection easier.[66] There is no reason to think that Obama is circumventing surveillance laws the way the Bush administration did in its early years. But there is also no reason to think he has backed away from Bush's later surveillance practices. If anything, Obama has expanded them.

Secrecy. Candidate Obama criticized "excessive secrecy" in the Bush administration, and on his first day in office President Obama pledged that "transparency and the rule of law will be the touchstones of this presidency."[67] During his first year Obama began ambitious initiatives on declassification and the Freedom of Information Act that promised more government openness, especially in national security.[68] But two years later the results of these initiatives were "embarrassingly modest," in the judgment of secrecy expert Steven Aftergood at the Federation of American Scientists.[69] Candidate Obama was also critical of secret Justice Department legal opinions concerning interrogation. Once in office he released these Bush-era documents, but he disclosed practically none of his administration's extensive secret legal work on other terrorism and war-related issues. The Obama administration also followed its predecessor in opposing legislation that would have expanded the President's obligation to notify Congress about certain intelligence activities beyond the so-called Gang of Eight—leaders of the Senate and House intelligence committees and senior congressional leadership.[70] In addition, it ramped up to unprecedented levels prosecutions of government employees who leaked classified information. "They're going after this at every opportunity and with unmatched vigor," said Aftergood.[71]

Perhaps no secrecy-related Obama practice was more surprising than the continuation of the Bush administration's assertions of the state secrets privilege. This privilege allows the government to prevent disclosure of evidence in civil cases that it thinks would endanger national security. Candidate Obama harshly criticized the Bush administration's use of this doctrine. But in its first few months in office, the Obama administration reconfirmed the doctrine in every pending case that challenged Bush-era counterterrorism practices, including cases involving rendition, surveillance, and allegations of torture. When the Justice Department in September 2009 announced new internal government procedures for the invocation of state secrets, the *New York Times* said that "new limits" had been imposed.[72] But when the Obama administration applied the procedures to pending Bush-era state secrets cases, they required no change in Bush-era practice, and many think that the Obama administration has asserted the privilege to the same extent as its predecessor.[73] For example, the Obama administration convinced a California federal court to throw out a suit alleging torture in black sites in what the *New York Times* described as "a major victory for the Obama administration's efforts to advance a sweeping view of executive secrecy powers."[74] And in the first major legal challenge to an Obama counterterrorism tactic, the ACLU suit challenging the alleged approval of a targeted killing of American citizen Anwar al-Aulaqi, the Obama administration argued that the state secrets privilege required dismissal of the case.[75]

Interrogation. The Obama administration's biggest and most important change from the Bush era concerns interrogation. The administration limited all U.S. government interrogation techniques to the relatively benign ones approved by the military field manual, and the CIA is now almost entirely out of the interrogation business.[76] In addition, President Obama described the most notorious Bush-era interrogation tactic, waterboarding, as "torture," and his Justice Department repudiated all Bush-era legal interpretations of the torture statute and related laws.[77] The administration also released hundreds of Department of Justice and CIA documents related to Bush-era interrogation programs, in part, President Obama said, to ensure that the practices would never occur again. And it reopened a preliminary criminal investigation of those involved in CIA interrogations that exceeded Justice Department authorization, and decided to pursue a full criminal investigation of two matters. All of these moves mark significant changes from the Bush years that invited loud criticism from national security hawks. Even these changes, however, were smaller than advertised. The main reason is that a 2005 statute, a 2006 Supreme Court ruling, and growing public opprobrium led the Bush team, by 2007, to narrow the range of CIA-approved interrogation techniques, especially as compared to 2002–2003.

Summary. "There is a very real danger that the Obama administration will enshrine permanently within the law policies and practices that were widely considered extreme and unlawful during the Bush administration," warned the American Civil Liberties Union in a July 2010 report. Acknowledging the Obama changes on interrogation and black sites, the ACLU nonetheless concluded that "there is a real danger . . . that the Obama administration will preside over the creation of a 'new normal.' "[78] This is basically what has happened. On the issues of whether terrorism is to be confronted as a war or as a crime, the legal basis for military detention, the discretionary approach to trials and detention, habeas corpus, the legal basis for rendition, state secrets, and surveillance, Obama's position is basically the same as the one that prevailed at the end of the Bush administration. Obama made small reforms to military commissions and he raised detention standards in Afghanistan. He also pulled back from late Bush administration practices on interrogation (though Bush himself had pulled back on this quite a lot from the 2002–2004 period) and secret prisons (again, Bush was not using these much in the end). Finally, Obama has ramped up targeted killing, and if anything the NSA seems more active in the homeland under Obama than under the late Bush administration.

NOT THE IVORY TOWER

Almost all of the Obama counterterrorism policies were in place by June 2009, when Harold Koh became Legal Advisor to the State Department. Many people inside and outside the government wondered how Koh, a fierce Bush administration critic, would abide the "new normal" that he had warned about the preceding autumn. Koh had long railed against the war framework for presidential powers. He criticized indefinite military detention and argued that the United States should abandon it.[79] He claimed that military commissions were "law-free courts" even after Congress had approved them, and he maintained that no matter what procedures commissions might employ, they were illegitimate and should not be used.[80] Koh further argued that the executive branch should treat the 9/11 plotters and other terrorists as "international criminals" and either "charge [them] criminally in civilian courts or find other countries who will accept them for criminal trial."[81] Otherwise, Koh asserted, alleged terrorists should be released or granted asylum.[82] Koh further decried "law-free practices" like extraordinary rendition and "law-free zones" like Guantanamo Bay, which he insisted must be closed.[83] He was also critical of the U.S. military invading "neutral countries without their consent" and of the collateral damage that resulted from Bush's bombing campaign in Afghanistan and Iraq.[84]

Koh was publicly silent on these issues during his first nine months in office. But in February 2010, he broke his silence in an informal public discussion at the Washington law firm of Arnold & Porter. At the end of Koh's presentation, a reporter asked him about a recent statement by Director of National Intelligence Dennis Blair that the Obama administration was targeting an American citizen with Predator drones outside the United States. A visibly uncomfortable Koh noted that the policy was still under review and that his job was to ensure that the United States complied with the international laws of war. And then he simply said, "If there ever came a point where I thought those rules were violated, I would resign. I am still here, so you can draw your own conclusions."[85]

It was unclear at the time whether Koh's terse statement reflected caution about discussing a covert operation or masked doubts about the policy itself. But his tepid defense of the "only game in town" for confronting terrorists halfway around the globe set off speculation in the legal academy and the government that he might not be on board for the Obama counterterrorism program, and might even be preparing to resign. It was thus with unusual anticipation, one month later, that the members of the American Society of International Law gathered at their annual meeting in the Grand Ballroom at the Washington, D.C., Ritz-Carlton hotel to hear Koh's keynote address, titled "The Obama Administration and International Law."

Most of the gathered international lawyers expected Koh to distance himself, at least somewhat, from the Obama policies that mirrored Bush's. What they heard instead was a vigorous defense of Obama administration counterterrorism policies, including the ones that mimicked Bush's. On the fundamental "war versus crime" question, Koh was now committed to the view that the "United States is in an armed conflict with al-Qaeda, as well as the Taliban and associated forces" and could exercise traditional military powers against these groups around the globe, consistent with international law. Koh argued that those military powers included detention without charge or trial for "the duration of the current conflict," something he specifically opposed while at Yale. He also supported military commissions, which he described as "appropriate venues" for terrorists who commit war crimes. He also defended the Obama administration's refusal to extend habeas corpus rights to detainees in Afghanistan. And in contrast to his performance a month earlier, he gave a robust defense of Predator drone strikes. "A state that is engaged in an armed conflict or in legitimate self-defense is not required to provide targets with legal process before the state may use lethal force."[86]

Many in the American Society of International Law crowd were stunned by Koh's speech. One audience member, Professor Mary Ellen O'Connell of the University of Notre Dame Law School, a self-proclaimed "old friend and great admirer of Harold Koh," began a question to Koh with the comment that "the Obama administration continues to see that there is such a conception as a global war on terror." An agitated Koh interrupted her. "I said a lot of things in my remarks; that is not one of the things that I said." But Koh never directly explained how or why such a fierce critic of the "extreme place" to which the Bush administration had pushed U.S. counterterrorism policies in the fall of 2008 was now on board with most of what Bush administration was doing at that time. Perhaps he thought he had already addressed that issue, earlier in his speech, in the prelude to his defense of detention, military commissions, and targeted killing. "The making of U.S. foreign policy is infinitely harder than it looks from the ivory tower," he said.[87]

Chapter Two

FORCES BIGGER THAN
THE PRESIDENT

BARACK OBAMA is not the first person to assume the office of presidency as a critic of executive power and then switch his position while on the job. President Thomas Jefferson, a fierce opponent of unilateral presidential war power before 1800, authorized military expeditions against Barbary Coast nations in the Mediterranean without congressional authorization. Congressman Abraham Lincoln opposed the broad presidential war powers that James K. Polk exercised in the run-up to the Mexican-American War. But as President during the Civil War, Lincoln would assert broader war powers than any President before or since. Woodrow Wilson believed in a strong presidency before entering office, but he also pledged an open and transparent one. When World War I came, however, he supported unprecedented secrecy restrictions. When Dwight D. Eisenhower became Chief Executive, he was determined to rein in the early Cold War presidency; instead he presided over the buildup of the modern secrecy system and the rise of covert action and executive privilege. Richard Nixon was a principled opponent of presidential power as a senator who saw matters differently as President. Candidate Bill Clinton berated George H. W. Bush's Haitian interception and detention policy but quickly embraced it as President.

President John F. Kennedy gave an eloquent explanation of the mismatch between pre-presidential beliefs and presidential actions during a television interview in the Oval Office in December 1962. Kennedy's "most penetrating answer on the President's attitudes and feelings about his job," as adviser Pierre Salinger later described it, was elicited by a question from ABC News White House correspondent Bill Lawrence.[1] "As you look back upon your first two years in office, sir, has your experience in the office matched your expectations?" Lawrence asked. "You had studied a good deal the power of the presidency, the methods of its operations," he noted. "How has this worked out as you saw it in advance?"

Kennedy shifted from side to side in a rocking chair but answered confidently. "I would say that the problems are more difficult than I had imagined them to be. The responsibilities placed on the United States are greater than I imagined them to be, and there are greater limitations upon our ability to bring about a favorable result than I had imagined them to be," answered the President, who in his short time in office had suffered through the botched Bay of Pigs invasion, a disastrous meeting with Khrushchev in Vienna, the Cuban missile crisis, and the Berlin crisis. "And I think that is probably true of anyone who becomes President, because there is such a difference between those who advise or speak or legislate, and between the man who must select from the various alternatives proposed and say that this shall be the policy of the United States," added the former senator. "It is much easier to make the speeches than it is to finally make the judgments."[2]

Barack Obama learned this lesson the hard way. He came to the presidency sincerely committed to bringing real change to America's counterterrorism policies. But he quickly encountered new information and significant limitations on his ability to bring about the result he had promised and that so many had expected. This information and these limitations reflected forces bigger than the pledges and inclinations of the President of the United States, forces that caused Obama to continue so many policies he once questioned or opposed.

THE VIEW FROM THE OVAL OFFICE

The first force hit Obama in the days before he became President, when credible threat reports indicated that Somali terrorists were sneaking into the United States from Canada to detonate explosives during his inauguration. As senior Bush and Obama aides scrambled to figure out how to prevent the threat and how to react to it if it materialized, Obama became "more subdued than he had been," recalled David Axelrod, Obama's closest political adviser. "It's not as if you don't know what you're getting into," Axelrod said. "But when the reality comes and the baton is being passed and you're now dealing with real terrorism threats, it's a very sobering moment."[3]

Sobering indeed, especially since the Somali threat paled in comparison to the larger threats the President-elect was reading about on a daily basis. Several Obama administration officials told me that reading these chilling threat reports led them to view Bush's counterterrorism policies differently. And it seemed to affect President Obama in the same way. "I want to end the politics of fear, the fever of fear," said candidate Obama, below an enormous "CHANGE WE CAN BELIEVE IN" banner, in a typical March 2008 campaign rally.[4] But when he was personally confronted with reports of Islamist terrorists hiding among civilians and plotting to use ever-smaller and more deadly weapons to disrupt our way of life, the "hope over fear" meme quickly gave way to "the threat is real" meme. "[A]n extremist ideology threatens our people, and technology gives a handful of terrorists the potential to do us great harm," said the President in a May 2009 speech that explained why he would continue military detention without trial and military commissions. "We know that al Qaeda is actively planning to attack us again. We know that this threat will be with us for a long time, and that we must use all elements of our power to defeat it."[5]

The reality of the threat was not the only new information the Obama team absorbed upon entering office. They also learned that the Bush policies were, in the words of Republican Senator Susan Collins, "better-thought-out than they realized."[6] The Obama team came to office wanting to end the Bush "state secrets" practice but demurred after studying classified CIA declarations that convincingly explained why the adjudication of lawsuits about rendition and the Terrorist Surveillance Program would damage national security. "The declarations were really well done," one senior Obama official said, adding that "they persuaded me."[7] The possibility of ending military detention without trial also foundered upon learning that the Bush administration was right that, in President Obama's words, there are terrorists "who pose a clear danger to the American people" but who "cannot be prosecuted for past crimes."[8] Similarly, the main impetus for the Obama continuity on military commissions, according to the *Washington Post*, was that the new administration realized, just as its predecessor had claimed, that cases against many terrorists "would fail in federal courts or in standard military legal settings."[9] And of course, closing Guantanamo was much harder than it looked from the outside, as the Bush administration had insisted all along.

Learning firsthand about the nature of the terror threat and the soundness of some of the Bush responses to it was a wake-up call for the young Obama administration. So too was the grim reality of presidential responsibility, which informed how these new facts would be interpreted. On January 20, 2009, Barack Obama went from a legislator and presidential candidate with no real national security experience or responsibility to the Commander in Chief whose counterterrorism decisions hold American lives in the balance. This intense, undelegable responsibility for the fate of the nation is "so personal as to be without parallel," said Harry Truman.[10] It is a responsibility the President has "no moral right to shrink" from, or "even to count the chances of his own life" against, said Abraham Lincoln.[11]

This new perspective had a profound impact on Obama, just as it does on every President. "[M]y single most important responsibility as President is to keep the American people safe," he said, three months into his presidency, sounding very much like George W. Bush. "It's the first thing that I think about when I wake up in the morning. It's the last thing that I think about when I go to sleep at night."[12] The personal responsibility of the President for national security, combined with the continuing reality of a frightening and difficult-to-detect threat, unsurprisingly led Obama, like Bush, to use the full arsenal of presidential tools. "He is a different man now," said Washington sage David Broder, explaining the psychological dimension that underlies Obama's Bush-copying policies. "He has learned what it means to be commander in chief."[13]

Another reason why Obama stuck with the Bush policies was that many of them were irreversibly woven into the fabric of the national security architecture. The Obama administration would not have faced the troubles of closing the Guantanamo detention facility if the Bush administration had not used the detention facility in the first place. And it would have had an easier time prosecuting some terrorist suspects in civilian courts had information about their crimes not been extracted through coercion (assuming, that is, that the suspects would have been nabbed in the absence of the information so gained). It is impossible to know how an Obama administration would have dealt with the manifold terrorist challenges beginning on 9/11, or how the world might look different today if the Bush administration had made different decisions. But some of the continuation of Bush policies no doubt reflects the fact that Obama inherited challenges traceable to decisions he might not have made had he been president in 2001.

The continuity between the two administrations also reflects a persistence in the interests and outlook of the national security leadership and especially of the national security bureaucracy.[14] Top national security officials are typically drawn from a small and relatively homogeneous pool of Washington, D.C.–based experts. Obama kept in place Bush's Defense Secretary (Robert Gates), his Chairman of the Joint Chiefs of Staff (Admiral Mike Mullen), his longtime FBI Director (Robert Mueller), his Deputy National Security Advisor for Afghanistan and Iraq (General

Douglas Lute), and his head of the National Counterterrorism Center (Michael Leiter). Obama's principal adviser for counter-terrorism, John Brennan, was a twenty-five-year intelligence vet-eran and George Tenet's chief of staff when the CIA established its interrogation program during the Bush years. Admiral Dennis Blair, Obama's first Director of National Intelligence (DNI), replaced another Navy man, Vice Admiral Michael McConnell, Bush's last DNI. And Obama's second DNI, James Clapper, was Bush's last Under Secretary of Defense for Intelligence.

Even when there is a departure from this pattern at the top, as when intelligence novice Leon Panetta took over the CIA, the underlying bureaucracy, with its administration-transcendent expertise and perspective, persists. During his first year in office, Panetta's principal deputy was Stephen Kappes and his general counsel was John Rizzo. Both men had been in the CIA for decades, and both had managed many controversial Bush-era counterterrorism policies. Alan Liotta, a career Defense Depart-ment officer who served as a deputy in the department's detainee affairs office under both Bush and Obama, was an important repository of institutional knowledge and continuity in vetting and helping to make release and transfer decisions about GTMO detainees. Similarly, career lawyers in the Department of Justice had been litigating state secrets cases for a long time, and had vetted and approved the Bush-era legal strategies, based on dec-larations prepared by career officers in the CIA and the National Security Agency. All of these officials had been working counter-terrorism problems for years and had experience and expertise that were hard for the new Obama appointees to discard or rebut. "Every new administration comes in with new ideas about how to reform the national security agencies," says Rizzo. "Each one realizes when they get inside that their options are much more limited by reality than they believed."[15]

The outlook and practices of the executive branch also pulled Obama toward Bush. Like everyone who becomes President, Obama assumed the institution's perspective. "He is . . . mind-ful as president of the United States not to do anything that would undermine or weaken the institution of the presidency," said Obama's lawyer, Greg Craig, in a February 2009 statement that would have been inconceivable a month earlier.[16] And despite the vitriol of the Bush years, many Bush counterterrorism policies reflected long-standing executive branch positions that Obama shied from rejecting. Every wartime President asserted the right to detain enemy forces without charge or trial. Many of them—including Washington, Lincoln, and Franklin D. Roosevelt—tried war criminals in military commissions. Presidents for decades had argued that habeas corpus does not extend to aliens detained outside the United States. The state secrets doctrine had been invoked by "every president in my lifetime," noted the then sixty-four-year-old Craig, defending Obama's use of the doctrine.[17] And rendition began under Clinton if not earlier, as the famous injunction by then Vice President Al Gore to "go grab his ass," in response to White House Counsel Lloyd Cutler's concerns about the legality of rendering a terrorist reminds us.[18] Seen in this light, it is no surprise that President Obama sought to maintain his inherited presidential powers. It would be a surprise if he had not done so, especially since, as Arthur Schlesinger Jr. once observed, "power always look[s] more responsible from within than from without."[19]

All of these forces—inside information about terrorist threats, the intense responsibilities of the presidency, the virtues of some Bush-era policies, the irreversible consequences of others, Washington's tight-knit national security culture, and executive branch outlook and precedent—pushed Obama to conform to his predecessor's approach much more than he had set out to do. But there was yet another force at work, an old force that appeared in a largely unnoticed new guise: the U.S. Constitution's checks and balances.

A Page of History

We have traveled a long way from the constraints that the constitutional framers placed on presidential war powers. The Constitution vests an undefined "executive Power" in a President institutionally distinct from Congress and designates him the "Commander in Chief" of the Army and Navy. But it divides military power by giving Congress the power to "declare war," the power to make rules for the regulation of the Army and Navy, and the power of the purse. This latter power was especially important for the framers, who believed the President could not start or conduct a war if he lacked the means to do so, and who thus sought to curb standing armies by limiting congressional appropriations for the Army to no more than two years. The framers also sought to control the President by insisting that he adhere to the law. The President "shall take Care that the Laws be faithfully executed," say the nine most important words of Article II. These words require the President to abide by the Constitution's division of war powers, as well as any valid laws that Congress makes to govern presidential conduct during war.

The framers did not think this written division of power would ensure that the President stayed in his constitutional lane. They assumed the opposite. "A mere demarcation on parchment of the constitutional limits of the several departments," Madison famously argued in *The Federalist*, "is not a sufficient guard against those encroachments which lead to a tyrannical concentration of all the powers of government in the same hands." Instead, Madison believed, "the interior structure of the government" must be organized so that "its several constituent parts may, by their mutual relations, be the means of keeping each other in their proper places." And to do this, each branch of government must be given "the necessary constitutional means and personal motives to resist encroachments of the others."[20]

These are the famous checks and balances that every schoolchild learns. The Constitution aimed to control excessive concentration of power in one branch of government by giving other branches and institutions the power and the incentive to push back. It makes Congress the primary counterpoint to the executive branch through its competing legislative authorities, its control over spending and executive appointments, its power of investigations and oversight, and, in an extreme case, through impeachment. The courts too were to play an important role by deciding cases that uphold legal restrictions against the President, including cases where courts deem the President to have exceeded his constitutional powers. The First Amendment's "freedom . . . of the press" was designed to ensure that journalists give voice to the people and expose secret or corrupt executive action. And all of these checks play a vital role in the informed exercise of the most important checking function of all—the presidential elections that the Constitution says must occur every four years.

For the first seventy years of American history, when the United States was a relatively weak military power with a small standing army that faced few outside threats, the system of checks and balances worked more or less as planned. Abraham Lincoln was the first to expand the military powers of the presidency significantly when he snubbed Congress and the courts and curtailed many civil liberties in response to the Union crisis. But Lincoln promised in his 1864 State of the Union address that executive power "would be greatly diminished by the cessation of actual war."[21] On cue, Congress reasserted itself with a vengeance and ran roughshod over Lincoln's successor, Andrew Johnson, and dominated the presidency for the next three decades.

The same pattern occurred during the two world wars. Woodrow Wilson exercised extraordinary powers in World War I, both at home and abroad, and curtailed free speech and assembly. But when the war ended, civil liberties re-emerged, the military demobilized, the Senate rejected the Versailles Treaty, and the voters returned the nation to "normalcy" by electing Warren Harding and initiating a dozen years of weak Republican presidents. In the run-up to and during World War II, Franklin D. Roosevelt exercised presidential authorities aggressively. But he followed Lincoln in promising, in 1942, that "when the war is won, the powers under which I act automatically revert to the people—to whom they belong."[22] The historical pattern of postwar congressional resurgence seemed to recur when the military began to demobilize after the war and Congress voted in 1947 to recommend the Twenty-Second Amendment's two-term limit on the presidency.

But then everything changed quickly—for the presidency, the nation, and the Constitution. The growing Soviet menace, the Cold War it spawned, and the possibility (after 1949) of nuclear destruction by the Soviets created a perpetual threat that led to permanent alterations in the nature of our government and the constitutional powers of the President. Rather than demobilize the military, as it had done after all previous wars and had begun to do in 1945, the government would maintain a large peacetime standing army that would range from two to four million soldiers for the remainder of the Cold War. The National Security Act of 1947 established new political and military organizations—including the Office of the Secretary of Defense, the Joint Chiefs of Staff, and the National Security Council—to manage the peacetime military bureaucracy, and the Central Intelligence Agency to gather information abroad. In 1952, Harry S. Truman, on his own authority, established the super-secretive National Security Agency to conduct "signals intelligence" and other technical collection activities.[23]

These new institutions concentrated enormous peacetime military authority in the President, which Truman quickly exercised. Truman alone decided to drop the atomic bomb in 1945, he alone decided to build the more powerful hydrogen bomb in 1950, and he alone retained the discretion whether and when to use these weapons. In March 1947 he unilaterally announced that the United States would support democracy and oppose the communist threat everywhere. The next year, without congressional consultation, the new CIA intervened in Italian elections, the first of eighty-one covert operations under Truman.[24] More momentously, in 1950 Truman dispatched American troops to defend South Korea from North Korean attack and announced his intention to send four divisions (about one hundred thousand men) to a NATO force in Europe, both without congressional consultation. Other presidents had sent troops abroad without congressional approval. But Truman was the first to do so on this scale, and the first to claim that Congress could not stop him. "Not only has the President the authority to use the Armed Forces in carrying out the broad foreign policy of the United States and implementing treaties," his State Department lawyers reasoned, but "this authority may not be interfered with by the Congress in the exercise of powers which it has under the Constitution."[25]

Some in Congress opposed these unprecedented presidential actions and the conception of presidential power on which they were built. But for the most part, and especially as the Cold War progressed through the Eisenhower and Kennedy administrations, the media, the academy, and the government saw the out-sized presidency as a necessary response to the Soviet menace. Underlying this view was the widespread belief in the decades after World War II that the presidency was more competent and trustworthy than Congress in military and foreign affairs, and better suited to make tough national security decisions for the nation. This "heroic" presidency dovetailed with the idea that traditional checks and balances were dead, and rightly so. "As Commander in Chief of the armed forces, the President has full responsibility, which cannot be shared, for military decisions in a world in which the difference between safety and cataclysm can be a matter of hours or even minutes," Arkansas Senator William Fulbright wrote in 1961.[26] The President and only the President had the information, incentives, initiative, and discretion to keep the country safe in a nuclear world; checks and balances were luxuries the nation could no longer afford.

Presidents from Truman through Nixon embraced this view. Compelled by crisis, responsibility, and opportunity, they arrogated more and more military and national security powers to themselves. And what they didn't take for themselves, Congress happily gave them, delegating all manner of national security powers to the President and steadily approving ever-larger military budgets to support ever-larger military forces at the President's disposal. Congress in the 1950s gave Eisenhower broad authorizations for war in Formosa (Taiwan) and the Middle East that he never used. When Congress, in the 1964 Gulf of Tonkin

Resolution, gave Lyndon Johnson discretion to take "all necessary measures" in Southeast Asia, the *New York Times* praised its breadth on the ground that "no one else [but the President] can play the hand."[27] As Arthur Schlesinger Jr. noted, "Every one of these innovations encouraged the displacement of power, both practical and constitutional, from an increasingly acquiescent Congress into an increasingly imperial Presidency."[28] They also encouraged displacement of judicial power. With the notable exception of the famous 1952 *Youngstown Steel* case (which was no more than a speed bump on the road to presidential enlargement), courts largely acquiesced in the rise of the imperial presidency, and for the same reasons as Congress.[29]

In the early 1970s, this conception of the presidency came crashing down as a result of presidential folly in Vietnam and the Watergate scandal. It was done in first by a new brand of aggressive investigative journalism, led by Seymour Hersh, who broke the story of the My Lai massacre and the CIA's illegal domestic operations; by Bob Woodward and Carl Bernstein, who broke the Watergate story; and by the *New York Times* and the *Washington Post* for whom they worked, which published their work and ran the Pentagon Papers story in the face of an attempted prior restraint by the government. These and many other stories revealed systematically mendacious and unethical government activity that finally jolted Capitol Hill from its slumbers. Congress held the Watergate hearings and authorized intelligence investigations by the Church and Pike Committees, and would go on to enact scores of historic reforms to check what it viewed as a war-prone, excessively secretive, non-law-abiding President. These laws included landmarks of presidential accountability such as the War Powers Resolution, the Foreign Intelligence Surveillance Act, the Presidential Records Act, the Presidential Recordings and Materials Preservation Act, the Ethics in Government Act, the Inspector General Act, a revised Freedom of Information Act, the Privacy Act, various laws to enhance congressional oversight of intelligence and covert operations, and more.

This "latticework of statutes," notes Andrew Rudalevige,

"aimed to imprison the president and strengthen the legislative hand in inter-branch relations."[30] Most people in the late 1970s believed Congress succeeded in this task. It was a time of the "Resurgence of Congress," as James Sundquist argued in his 1981 book of that title, a time when Congress had showed "a collective resolve—a firmness and unity of purpose extraordinarily difficult to attain in a body as diffuse as the Congress—to restore the balance between the executive and legislative branches."[31] For a brief period from the mid-1970s to the mid-1980s, these laws seemed so consequential that many worried, in Gerald Ford's famous words, that the presidency had become "imperiled, not imperial."[32]

But any imperilment seemed short-lived. Presidents seemed to skirt the most notable congressional reform, the War Powers Resolution, in small wars in Grenada, Lebanon, Iran, Libya, Panama, Haiti, Bosnia, Kosovo, and more. Another 1970s reform, the Independent Counsel statute, had teeth for a while, but it was put to rest in 1999 following Ken Starr's perceived excesses in investigating Bill Clinton. The other reforms were dull "inside government" fare that was mostly out of the news and seemingly not very consequential. Congress lost the political will and cohesiveness of the 1970s, and generally dropped the oversight ball in the 1980s and 1990s, with intermittent exceptions such as its investigation of the Iran-Contra affair. In the 1990s it did enact two domestic criminal laws—one prohibiting torture, the other war crimes—to implement international human rights treaty obligations that had taken on a new importance in the post–Cold War era.[33] But few at the time saw these laws as restrictions on presidential war power per se.

When George W. Bush took office in January 2001, most scholars of the presidency believed that the post-Vietnam, post-Watergate congressional reforms had failed.[34] This view seemed confirmed after the 9/11 attacks eight months later, which seemed to spark a radical, permanent, and unchecked expansion of presidential power confirmed by Barack Obama's embrace of the Bush counterterrorism program. As late as 2010, Garry Wills was arguing that the 1970s reforms achieved only "glancing" blows at executive power, and that Congress has largely capitulated to executive aggrandizement.[35] His ideological opposite, John Yoo, agreed. Presidents "worked around many of" these laws, he maintained, which "proved somewhat toothless."[36] Wills decried this state of affairs; Yoo admired it. But both men, as Richard Cheney knew, were wrong.

PUSHBACK

Cheney was in the White House as Gerald Ford's Chief of Staff when Congress imposed many of the novel restrictions on the presidency. He hated them then, and he never got over them. When others were bemoaning the failed congressional resurgence in the 1980s and 1990s, Cheney was railing against its continued impact. "[I]n 34 years [in Washington, D.C.], I have repeatedly seen an erosion of the powers and the ability of the president of the United States to do his job," Cheney told Cokie Roberts in 2002.[37] Cheney had spent his public career since the Ford days—as a member of Congress and as Secretary of Defense under George H. W. Bush—trying to reverse these trends.[38] When he became George W. Bush's Vice President, he convinced President Bush, even before 9/11, that the presidency had been diminished by Congress and needed to be "restored."[39]

After 9/11 it turned out that Cheney was right about the impact of congressional reforms on presidential powers. Many of the laws that scholars thought were dead or ineffectual were instead merely fallow, and they sprang to life with vigor in the first war for the nation's safety since their enactment. A central preoccupation of the war against hidden and undeterrable Islamist terrorists was finding the enemy before he strikes. In this type of war, "much of the primary action or 'engagement' with the enemy is more likely to occur in interrogation rooms and detention facilities, and across wires, and in vast computer reservoirs of stored data, than in bunkers and on traditional battlefields," note law professors David Barron and Martin Lederman.[40] But the collection of intelligence and the interrogation of detainees were two of the core areas of presidential discretion that Congress had extensively regulated in the previous decades. These laws seemed invisible before 9/11 because their constraints were relatively unimportant then. But after 9/11, when the government faced a novel type of enemy that it thought required novel tactics of information collection, these and many other previously inchoate restrictions on presidential power became very important.

When Congress authorized George W. Bush on September 14, 2001, to use "all necessary and appropriate force" against the perpetrators of 9/11 and their affiliates, the President, already swelled with power by virtue of the gargantuan peacetime military and intelligence bureaucracy under his command, became additionally invested with the full legal and military powers of Commander in Chief. But when Bush began to do things that past Commanders in Chief had done in wars with little if any congressional or judicial interference—surveil the enemy, target him, detain him, interrogate him, and try him before a military commission—he found himself hemmed in by legal restrictions imposed in the decades before 9/11. Many of these laws were premised on distinctions—between homeland and battlefield, civilian and combatant, crime and war—that the new enemy defied, making legal interpretations difficult. And many had never been construed before during a hot war, making their scope uncertain.

The Bush administration might have dealt with these difficulties by seeking assistance from Congress. But instead, as is well known, it settled on a strategy of aggressive executive unilateralism.[41] In the first year after 9/11, the administration determined that Geneva Convention protections did not apply to al Qaeda and the Taliban, it ignored the law requiring a warrant for spying on suspected terrorists from a secret national security court, it declared that the President was not bound by the torture law, and it argued that habeas corpus did not extend to prisoners detained outside the United States, including those in the detention facility on Guantanamo Bay. It also set up military commissions without consulting Congress. These early decisions—and the policies they gave rise to, such as the use of secret prisons, aggressive interrogations, and indefinite military detention—were the main focus of Barack Obama's campaign complaints, and the reason so many people think that Congress and the courts were feckless in the face of presidential power.

But a lot happened in the years after these policies were first implemented in 2001–2002. In fact, as the rest of this book will show in detail, the other two branches of government, aided by the press and civil society, pushed back against the Commander in Chief like never before in our nation's history. Congress altered and then approved, with qualifications, the Bush administration's early approach to military detention, military commissions, interrogation, and surveillance.[42] In some cases— most notably, with regard to military commissions—it did so because the Supreme Court enforced congressional restrictions against the President and left him needing Congress's approval. The Court also ruled that the Geneva Conventions applied to the conflict with al Qaeda, negating the President's contrary claim and causing a ripple of changes to counterterrorism efforts throughout the executive branch.[43] It also decided, contrary to the wishes of the President and Congress, that the constitutional right of habeas corpus applied to suspects held at Guantanamo Bay.[44] "Secret" programs for rendition and targeted killings were debated in public and Congress throughout the decade. Executive branch lawyers, interpreting congressional and judicial mandates, put brakes on some presidential initiatives and reversed others. Reforms from the 1970s that created inspectors general inside the executive branch and greater public access to internal executive branch documents helped to generate much of the information that made these reforms possible. So too did aggressive reporting by the press.

By the time Obama assumed office, Congress and the courts, with assists from other institutions, had vetted and altered the early Bush counterterrorism practices, sometimes quite a bit. In Part II, I examine the causes, operation, and consequences of these and other extraordinary accountability checks on the post-9/11 presidency. The point for now is that the changes to the early Bush counterterrorism program are the most fundamental reason Obama embraced so many Bush policies. When candidate Obama complained about GTMO, military detention, military commissions, warrantless surveillance, habeas corpus, and more, he was really complaining about early Bush practices, before the other institutions of government forced change on the presidency. "I would distinguish between some of the steps that were taken immediately after 9/11 and where we were by the time I took office," Obama said in March 2009, drawing a crucial distinction that escaped him before he became President.[45] When Obama and his task forces dove into the problem of rethinking U.S. counterterrorism policies, they found that most of them had already been rethought, changed, and largely legitimated. The Obama team, sobered by the challenges and responsibilities of the post-9/11 presidency they fully appreciated only once in power, refused to walk away from the political and legal support for counterterrorism actions represented in these changes.

PACKAGING

Obama continued the later Bush counterterrorism program, but he did so in a different way from his predecessor, with a different public attitude toward his powers. The Bush administration's early counterterrorism policies were often accompanied by expansive rhetoric about the Commander in Chief's untouchable powers and the administration's desire to leave the presidency stronger than it found it. This rhetoric, unprecedented in American wartime history, led many people to distrust the Bush administration and to worry that it was acting to increase its own power rather than to keep the country safe. Its main effect was to cause the press, Congress, and the courts to view Bush's wartime practices in a suspicious light. In its early years, the Bush administration failed to appreciate the ongoing need to convince the citizenry that the President was using his extraordinary war powers for the public good and not for personal or institutional aggrandizement. By the time the Bush administration began to act on this principle in its second term, it was too late; its credibility on these issues—damaged not only by its early unilateralism and expansive rhetoric but also by mistaken intelligence in the war with Iraq—was unrecoverable.[46]

If Bush invited a reputation as a lawless cowboy, Barack Obama invited the opposite reputation. He came to office a Bush administration critic, a former law professor, a civil liberties champion, and an opponent of the invasion of Iraq. Early on he placed in important positions throughout the government lawyers who were the leading intellectually committed opponents of the Bush counterterrorism program.[47] Against this background, Obama had enormous stores of credibility and trust when he began to speak as President about the dangers of terrorism and the difficulties of meeting the terror threat. His decisions to continue core Bush terrorism policies—after absorbing the classified intelligence and considering the various options—were akin to Richard Nixon going to China, establishing détente, and signing the Strategic Arms Limitation Treaty. "If an action is somehow out of character for a particular politician, then, for that very reason there are fewer external obstacles to that politician's performing it," notes Robert Goodin.[48] Because the Obama policies played against type and (in some quarters of his party) against interest, they appeared more likely to be a necessary response to a real terror threat and thus less worrisome from the perspective of presidential aggrandizement than when the Bush administration embraced essentially the same policies. This is one reason why so many policies that were controversial under Bush were much less controversial when Obama adopted them.

Obama's approach to rhetoric and public symbols in his counterterrorism policies bolstered his credibility for restraint and law-abidingness. Even as he was adopting many of the Bush policies, he broke from Bush in dropping "war on terror" language, in talking about the importance of adhering to constitutional values, in worrying publicly about terrorism policies going too far, and in suggesting that he was looking for ways to keep them in check. He has said nothing about the importance of expanding his power. His public efforts to close black sites and end CIA interrogations—especially in the face of loud criticism from the right—symbolized his commitment to the rule of law even if these practices were on the way out at the end of the Bush administration. The many smaller self-imposed restrictions were important public indications of restraint, especially when contrasted with Bush's early insistence on maximum presidential flexibility at all costs. They are yet more significant because the Obama administration seemed to embrace them on its own initiative rather than, as was so often true of its predecessor, under apparent threat of judicial or congressional scrutiny.

A typical example of these strategies in action is the Obama administration's "new" rationale for detaining enemy forces indefinitely without charge or trial. The administration took the same basic position as its predecessor but placed it in prettier wrapping. It eliminated the dreaded label "enemy combatant." It narrowed the scope of those who can be detained from persons who "support" al Qaeda and its affiliates to persons who "substantially support" them—a change without large practical consequences, but a change nonetheless. And it more explicitly grounded its authority to detain terrorists in Congress's authorization for the war and the international laws of war, showing that the President's detention powers were approved by bodies outside the presidency. This was the Bush position as well, but with an important difference: the early Bush administration had additionally argued, in the alternative, that it could detain enemy fighters on its own constitutional authority and without congressional support. The Obama administration dropped this argument (but did not reject it) and won favorable press coverage for its departure from the Bush position even though the change affected little in the President's power to detain.

One can view these and many similar Obama administration efforts as attempts to save face with supporters who expected bigger changes from the Bush era. But they also reflect a genuine ideological and intellectual commitment to a more limited conception of executive power and a more regularized conception of the rule of law. It is hard to explain some of the Obama administration's actions on any other ground. For example, one reason the administration has refused to work with Congress to get new military detention authorities is a fear that Congress might give it more power than it wants. Similarly, in a case challenging the President's power to target and kill an American citizen in Yemen, the administration in its legal briefs was grudging and even apologetic in making a perfectly appropriate state secrets claim.[49] The administration has also acquiesced, despite some helpful Article II authorities to the contrary, in Congress's unprecedented restrictions on the President's power to transfer enemy prisoners. Remarkably, none of these actions led the Obama administration to a place very different from its predecessor. But they do reflect a narrower conception of presidential power than the one that prevailed in the Bush administration.

Whether motivated by politics or genuine commitment—it was doubtlessly some of both—the Obama team early on developed a reputation for restraint and commitment to the rule of law in its counterterrorism policies. This reputation helped legitimate the extraordinary powers the President must exercise in the long war against Islamist terrorists. The President simply cannot exercise these war powers over an indefinite period unless Congress and the courts support him. And they will not support him unless they think he is exercising his powers responsibly, under law, with real constraints, to address a real threat. The Obama administration successfully conveyed this impression and was rewarded for it. The administration's superficial changes to the military detention rationale, combined with President Obama's reputation for commitment to the rule of law, helped to make military detention relatively uncontroversial to judges. New internal procedures for employing the state secrets doctrine brought no apparent change in the executive branch's employment of the doctrine. But it did help in the courts, one of which cited the procedures to support its conclusion that "the government is not invoking the privilege to avoid embarrassment or escape scrutiny" of its policies.[50] The small changes that Obama helped to foster in military commissions, combined with his robust embrace of them, put the commissions on a much stronger footing than they were under Bush. In these and other ways, the Obama administration's self-imposed checks combined with its reputation for law-abidingness and the rhetoric of self-constraint to strengthen—and validate—the core Bush counterterrorism program as it stood in late 2008.

But there were important downsides to the Obama administration's approach as well. These downsides reveal a great deal about how modern American checks and balances work in practice, and indicate another way these checks drove Obama to the same place as his predecessor.

One consequence of Obama's "rule of law" and "self-constraint" rhetoric, and of his few departures from the Bush-era policies, was that he opened himself up to charges of being weak on terrorism. Former Vice President Cheney, more than anyone else, exploited this opening. "[I]f they don't continue [Bush administration] policies, they will in fact, put the nation at risk," he said six days before he left office, laying down a marker.[51] Cheney turned up the heat after Obama became President. "When we get people who are more concerned about reading the rights to an Al Qaeda terrorist than they are with protecting the United States against people who are absolutely committed to do anything they can to kill Americans, then I worry," he said, two weeks into Obama's presidency. America's safety "depends [on] whether or not we keep in place policies that have allowed us to defeat all further attempts, since 9/11, to launch mass-casualty attacks against the United States," he added.[52] As the spring of 2009 progressed, Cheney charged that Obama's policies "made Americans less safe," raised "the risk to the American people of another attack," marked a return to the "law enforcement mode" that prevailed before 9/11, and represented a belief that "there's no longer a threat out there."[53]

Cheney no doubt meant every word. But almost every charge is based on the false assumption that Barack Obama had changed Bush's later policies—a false assumption indulged by some Obama administration officials in order to fight off criticisms from the left about continuity with Bush policies. As we have seen,

Obama explicitly committed himself to the war framework for the exercise of his powers, and he continued or expanded many Bush policies. Bush tried to close GTMO in his second term, and Cheney opposed those efforts; Obama tried harder to do the same thing before ending up in about the same place as Bush. Obama's few real changes from the Bush era—most notably, on interrogation policy and black sites—continued trends that began at the end of the Bush administration and that Cheney opposed while in office, although Obama did depart sharply from Bush in revealing reams of previously classified information about Bush-era interrogation practices. With this latter exception, Cheney's criticisms of Obama simply "repeated in public a lot of the same arguments he had been making within the Bush White House as the policy decisions went more and more the other way" during Bush's second term, as *New York Times* writer David Brooks correctly noted.[54]

But if Cheney was making essentially the same arguments against the Obama administration that he had made within the Bush administration during its second term, the arguments had a much different effect. The Cheney attacks knocked the young Obama administration on its heels and galvanized political forces that made the administration's rhetoric of constraint and its few genuine departures from its predecessor seem like weakness or unseriousness in fighting the war against terrorism. These political forces ultimately resulted in new restrictions on the Commander in Chief's exercise of his traditional powers.

Most notably, these forces killed Obama's first-week presidential pledge to close GTMO. The administration's release of Bush-era memoranda in March and April 2009 was greeted with fierce, Cheney-led, weak-on-terrorism attacks even though by that time Obama had embraced or expanded most Bush policies. The charges began to stick when the White House floated a plan in April 2009 to transfer from GTMO to northern Virginia some Muslim separatist Chinese Uighurs who had trained in terrorism camps but who, according to federal courts and the Obama administration, were not part of al Qaeda and thus not lawfully detained. The growing criticisms of the administration's national security competence and priorities came this time not just from Cheney and the Republicans, but also from Democrats like Virginia Senator (and military veteran) James Webb.[55] The Uighur plan accelerated a drop in public support for closing GTMO that had begun at the dawn of the Obama administration and would continue steadily for a year.[56] It also sharpened a decline in independent voter support for Obama.[57]

At this point, Congress, controlled by the President's party, did something it had never done in 220 years of American history. Every President before Obama had transferred enemy soldiers around the world, including to and from the United States, without any interference or even interest from Congress.[58] Franklin Roosevelt, for example, brought half a million prisoners of war to the United States during World War II without consulting or arousing Congress. But beginning with an overwhelming bipartisan 90–6 vote in the Senate in May 2009, Congress blocked Obama from bringing GTMO prisoners to the United States for military detention.[59] The same laws also barred him from transferring detainees to other countries without advance notice to Congress. These laws required the executive branch to submit a report fifteen days before any planned transfer or release of a detainee that specifies the detainee's name and destination, the risks he poses to national security, and the terms on which the foreign state (if any) is accepting the transfer. This requirement gives Congress significant leverage in making a heckler's veto if it thinks the President is about to release a GTMO prisoner who is too dangerous. And it puts the report's authors, and the executive branch more generally, on the accountability hook if something goes wrong. The effect of these restrictions is to slow to almost a halt the administration's exercise of a previously unassailed presidential power.

These restrictions also killed Attorney General Eric Holder's attempt to try 9/11 mastermind Khalid Sheikh Mohammed and his co-conspirators in a civilian trial in New York City rather than in the military commission where Bush had placed him. "I'm not scared of what Khalid Sheikh Mohammed has to say at trial and no one else needs to be afraid either," Holder said before the Senate Judiciary Committee, a few days after the trial announcement. "We need not cower in the face of this enemy," he added, insisting that "our institutions are strong, our infrastructure is sturdy, our resolve is firm, and our people are ready."[60] But Holder did not widely vet the decision and did not fully think through its security aspects. His announcement was met with anger and criticism around the country, first by Republicans, and then later by Democrats, especially ones from New York. The angry voices grew louder when, a month later, the administration decided to treat the Christmas Day "Underwear Bomber," Umar Farouk Abdulmutallab, as a criminal suspect with a right to counsel and full *Miranda* and related rights rather than as a wartime military detainee. It didn't help when Homeland Security Secretary Janet Napolitano claimed that "the system worked," and that the President himself said that Abdulmutallab was "an isolated extremist," when it turned out that he was in fact part of a conspiracy hatched by al Qaeda in the Arabian Peninsula.[61]

These criticisms began to have large political consequences for the Democrats. "Our Constitution and laws exist to protect this nation—they do not grant rights and privileges to enemies in wartime," said Republican Scott Brown on the night of his stunning January 2010 victory in the race for Edward Kennedy's Senate seat in liberal Massachusetts. "In dealing with terrorists, our tax dollars should pay for weapons to stop them, not lawyers to defend them," he added, repeating campaign trail themes.[62] The White House was devastated by the Brown victory not just because of its implication for health care reform, but also because polls showed that the most salient issue in the race was voter opposition to treating Mohammed and Abdulmutallab as ordinary criminals.[63]

The Brown victory on the heels of the "Underwear Bomber" incident emboldened many Republicans in Congress to propose legislation to prevent the executive branch from prosecuting Mohammed in civilian court.[64] These laws were never enacted, but by late January 2010, the White House was sending signals to Holder that Mohammed could not be tried in civilian court. "The White House had to deal with a political reality in Congress," explained the former number-two man in Holder's Justice Department, David Ogden. "And the situation was assessed as being politically untenable."[65] This political reality, eventually embodied in laws that prevented the President from transferring Mohammed and all other GTMO detainees to the United States for trial or any other purpose, led Holder in April 2011 to announce that Mohammed would be tried in a military commission in Cuba rather than a civilian court in New York. Congress prevented the Commander in Chief and his top lawyer from following through on a decision—whether and where to prosecute a war criminal—that previous Presidents had made without interference from Congress.

The fierce reactions to Obama's GTMO and civilian trial policies should be puzzling, for George W. Bush had pursued essentially the same policies with no controversy. Bush released hundreds of detainees from GTMO, many of whom returned to the battlefield. He pledged to close GTMO and made a bit of progress toward this end in his second term. And he prosecuted hundreds of terrorists in civilian courts, with full *Miranda* and related rights, including al Qaeda "Shoe Bomber" Richard Reid, who went to trial in a Massachusetts federal court in 2002 without a peep from Massachusetts's voters. The reason why Obama's actions were controversial and Bush's were not is the same reason why Obama has not been criticized much for his copying of policies that brought Bush so much grief. Bush's reputation for being very aggressive in protecting U.S. national security interests led the American people and their representatives to trust him when he made "soft" decisions to release detainees, to try to close GTMO, or to prosecute terrorists in civilian court. The opposite political forces were at work when Obama's reputation for restraint made people see similar "soft" actions as worrisome signs of weakness or a lack of seriousness in fighting terrorism.

"He who moulds public sentiment, goes deeper than he who enacts statutes or pronounces decisions," Abraham Lincoln wisely said in his first debate with Stephen Douglas, in 1854. "He makes statutes and decisions possible or impossible to be executed."[66] Public sentiment, and the law and politics through which public sentiment is expressed, combined to create the final, most fundamental, and perhaps least appreciated force bigger than Barack Obama's promises and inclinations to reverse the Bush program. Obama embraced most of Bush's counterterrorism policies because on the whole those policies as they stood in January 2009 reflected public sentiment about the right balance between safety and security. But the administration's fervent desire to close GTMO and try Khalid Sheikh Mohammed in civilian court collided with public sentiment and consequently failed. This is democracy and law in action. The same forces that pushed the too aggressive George W. Bush to be more solicitous of enemy soldiers had turned and prevented the too professorial Barack Obama from being more solicitous of enemy soldiers. The lesson—a lesson whose basis the next part of the book steps back to explore in much more detail—is that the Commander in Chief is deeply constrained by law and politics, even in this endless war.

Part Two

DISTRIBUTED CHECKS AND BALANCES

Chapter Three

ACCOUNTABILITY
JOURNALISM

"MY JOB WAS to decide what goes in the newspaper," says Leonard Downie Jr., describing his responsibilities from 1991 to 2008 as the executive editor of the *Washington Post*.[1] Downie is a soft-spoken Ohioan who by his own estimation is "shy" and "pretty boring."[2] He is a sharp contrast from his colorful Boston Brahmin predecessor, the hard-charging Ben Bradlee, who during the 1970s and 1980s transformed the *Post* from a sleepy regional newspaper to a major force in American journalism that "bristled with scoops—especially during Watergate—and was written with acerbic flair," as *Time* explained at the time of Bradlee's retirement.[3] The *Post* was a more subdued paper under Downie, perhaps reflecting his quieter personality, perhaps reflecting the times. But Downie's decisions were no less consequential than his predecessor's. As executive editor, Downie had the final say on which stories the paper pursued, which reporters covered it, where in the paper it appeared, the column inches it received, and what got cut from the reporter's draft. When the *Washington Post* focuses on the actions of the government of the most powerful nation in the world, these decisions can have huge consequences for American and global politics.

Many of Downie's hardest decisions about what to put in the

newspaper concerned the publication of classified information. Documents and programs become "classified" when a government official determines that their revelation would cause "exceptionally grave damage" (in the case of top-secret information) or "serious damage" (in the case of secret information) to national security.[4] Downie didn't feel bound by the secrecy stamp, which he, like most journalists, thought the government wielded promiscuously and self-servingly. " 'Highly classified' doesn't mean anything to me," he once explained. But while Downie disregarded labels, he did not disregard the potential effects of a story on national security. To the contrary, he tried hard to assess in advance both the national security impact and the public interest impact of a story. "The question is, is it important for the American public to know that its government is acting in its name in this particular way?" Downie said. "And then you weigh that against the consequences of publication, including national security harm."

To help him figure out the national security impact of a story, Downie had spoken to dozens of senior defense and intelligence officials during his years as editor. But he had never been invited to the Oval Office to hear from the President of the United States on the issue. Yet that is where he found himself, one morning in October 2005, seated at the end of a sofa covered in gold brocade next to a fidgety George W. Bush, who was seated in a blue-and-gold-striped armchair. In the chair next to the President was Donald Graham, CEO and Chairman of the Board of the Washington Post Company. Vice President Cheney, Director of National Intelligence John Negroponte, National Security Advisor Stephen Hadley, and *Washington Post* publisher Boisfeuillet Jones were sitting nearby.

The men had gathered to discuss a story being developed by the *Post*'s star reporter, Dana Priest. Since late 2002, Priest had written several pieces on the CIA's covert programs for rendition and interrogation of high-value terrorist detainees. After years of working sources in Washington and around the globe, she had discovered a secret CIA prison system for detaining and interrogating high-level al Qaeda captives that spanned eight countries, including Eastern European democracies.[5] In the course of her research on the secret prisons, Priest had also learned about some sensitive U.S. intelligence and counterterrorism operations with the allies that hosted the prisons but that were unrelated to the prison system. "Very early on," Downie later recalled, he and Priest decided that these collateral intelligence operations did not "raise any question" of public concern, and so information on them would not be published.

Priest had contacted the CIA to confirm the accuracy of her story and to ask if the CIA had particular concerns about its publication. The issue quickly reached Porter Goss, who had started his rocky tenure as CIA Director less than a month earlier. Goss sought a meeting with *Post* officials and soon greeted Downie, Priest, and Managing Editor Philip Bennett in his rectangular office overlooking the woods surrounding CIA headquarters in Langley, Virginia. With Negroponte at his side in front of a charred American flag pulled from the wreckage of the twin towers at the World Trade Center, Goss told Downie he would not confirm anything in Priest's story. But he made clear that the revelation of any hypothetical secret prisons program would gravely damage national security because it would require the CIA to alter its detention and interrogation operations; it would harm future intelligence cooperation with allies because it would show that the CIA could not keep important secrets; and it would end the useful collateral operations with those countries that had nothing to do with secret prisons. The first two reasons were "not a big concern of mine," Downie later recalled, "because that's their problem and it's not necessarily a national security problem," and in any event the government could "move those people to legal prisons, like Guantanamo Bay."[6] But the third reason, the risk of collateral damage from naming the countries, gave him pause. "We'll let you know when we're ready to publish," Downie said as he was leaving Goss's office.

A few days later, the White House invited Downie and his boss to meet with President Bush to discuss the Priest story. In the Oval

Office, Bush made essentially the same pitch as Goss. He gave an overview of the challenges in the war on terrorism, and while he wouldn't confirm Priest's story, he spoke hypothetically about the dangers of publishing it. Bush particularly emphasized the dangers of naming countries with which the United States had ongoing intelligence operations unrelated to the prisons. Hadley answered questions about the legality and efficacy of the program, once again in a vague and hypothetical way to avoid confirming its existence or providing new details. Vice President Cheney spoke only once, interjecting that the *Post* would be responsible for the resulting deaths if it published the story. The meeting was over in less than half an hour. Negroponte, whom Downie had known for decades, wrapped his arm around the executive editor's shoulder as he was leaving the Oval Office. "You aren't going to name those countries are you?" he asked. "I'll think about it," Downie replied.

Downie deliberated with Graham and Jones as they walked the five blocks up Fifteenth Street from the White House to the *Washington Post* headquarters, and then again in his office with his editors and Dana Priest. For Downie it was significant that Bush "never actually asked us not to run the story." Downie remembered when President Jimmy Carter asked Ben Bradlee not to reveal that the king of Jordan was on the CIA payroll, a request that gave Bradley pause but that he rejected.[7] "If the President of the United States makes an absolute, literal request" not to publish, Downie later noted, "it matters." Downie also believed that the "most serious consequences that would occur is that these places would be shut and the prisoners would be moved and interrogated someplace else," a result that did not seem like "irreparable harm" to him. But Downie had gone in to the meeting worried about naming the Eastern European countries. After both Bush and Negroponte had emphasized the danger of doing so, he came out thinking that naming the countries might "do irreparable harm to a number of other intelligence operations." The President and his aides "realized that they couldn't really stop the rest of the story," he later said, but "they didn't want this collateral damage, if you will."[8]

This is almost exactly how National Security Advisor Hadley saw the situation.[9] The President, Vice President, Director of National Intelligence, and Hadley "had a conversation before the meeting where we talked about our strategy," he recalls. They knew that the *Post* was going to run some version of the story. And they agreed that they could not stop it. "There's not much really that you can do," Hadley said. An appeal to the authority of the President and his right to decide what is classified would not work, because everyone in the press is cynical about overclassification. An appeal to patriotism would not work, since the press "basically has a view of patriotism that says, 'more information is better.' " And the courts would not grant an injunction for a prior restraint. And so the President and his advisers decided to put "whatever chits we had" on "the most important thing," and ask the *Post* to withhold the names of the European countries.

This strategy was, as Hadley later said, "largely successful." But it was successful only because the White House was asking for so little. What is really significant about the event is that the President and his aides couldn't stop publication of the rest of the story. The most powerful man in the world lacked any tools—other than a bit of implicit begging—to stop Leonard Downie from publishing the details of America's secret prisons that Dana Priest had gathered in part with the help of government officials who had violated their obligations not to disclose classified information. Instead, the decision was Downie's. "Under our constitutional system, those decisions cannot be made by the government," Downie explains. "That's unconstitutional. And it also would be dangerous to our democracy. It has to be left to editors and television producers to make these decisions."[10]

"CIA Holds Terror Suspects in Secret Prisons" was the headline of the Priest article that ran on the front page of the *Post* on November 2, 2005.[11] The 2,723-word story described "a covert prison system set up by the CIA nearly four years ago that at various times has included sites in eight countries, including Thailand, Afghanistan and several democracies in Eastern Europe, as well as a small center at the Guantanamo Bay prison in Cuba, according to current and former intelligence officials and diplomats from three continents." It gave details about how the program began, who was in the prisons, and how the government interrogated them. It also conveyed doubts within the CIA about the legality and sustainability of the program. And it explained why it did not name the Eastern European countries involved. "The Washington Post is not publishing the names of the Eastern European countries involved in the covert program, at the request of senior U.S. officials" who argued that "the disclosure might disrupt counterterrorism efforts in those countries and elsewhere and could make them targets of possible terrorist retaliation."

The *Post*'s story had a big impact. It bolstered pending legislation that would bar the government from inflicting "cruel, inhuman, or degrading treatment" on any prisoner anywhere in the world.[12] It caused outrage and recriminations among allies in Europe.[13] It led several countries to order CIA prisons closed. And it was almost certainly an important reason, in conjunction with complementary reporting by other journalists, why the Supreme Court the following summer ruled that the Geneva Conventions, including its ban on "humiliating and degrading treatment," applied in the war against al Qaeda.[14] By the fall of 2006, the controversy about high-level detainees stirred by the media had led President Bush to end the secret high-value detainee program and cut back sharply on authorized interrogations. These stories were paradigms of what Downie calls "accountability journalism," the idea that journalists should root out and explain the secret or unknown operations of powerful institutions so that citizens can hold these institutions to account for their actions. "When journalists use resourceful reporting and vivid presentation to hold the powerful accountable for their acts, they fulfill their highest purpose," he once wrote. "They help encourage the honest and open use of power."[15]

The secret prisons story is one of hundreds of astounding journalistic successes since 9/11 in disclosing deep governmental secrets. The press stumbled badly in its coverage of the weapons of mass destruction (WMD) rationale for the 2003 Iraq war. But in every other context it rooted out secret after secret about the shadow war that began after 9/11. This success is in part attributable to clever reporters and disgruntled leakers. But also very important were quiet revolutions in the bureaucracy of secrecy and the technologies of discovery that made it difficult for the government to keep important secrets, no matter how hard it tried. The press's many revelations about the government's conduct of the war were at the foundation of all of the mechanisms of presidential accountability after 9/11. They informed the public and shaped its opinions, and spurred activists, courts, and Congress to action in changing the government's course.

INTO THE SHADOWS

"We also have to work . . . the dark side, if you will," Vice President Cheney famously told Tim Russert on *Meet the Press* the Sunday after 9/11. "We've got to spend time in the shadows in the intelligence world."[16] Cheney was preparing the nation for a new type of war that would be fought differently from past wars. But his statement had an unintended resonance in the press. "If that's where the war is going to be fought, how are we going to cover it?" thought Philip Bennett, who at the time was the *Washington Post*'s foreign editor. "We cover wars in the places where they're fought. So either we're going to go into the shadows, or we're going to give up first-hand reporting about this war."[17] Cheney's assertion to Bob Woodward a month later that the war "may never end . . . in our lifetime" raised the stakes further.[18] "You might justify not sending reporters into the shadows for a month, or a few months, and then tell the story later about what happened, once it's all over," Bennett thought. "But it's not an option to give up independent coverage of the war forever."[19]

Secrecy is vital in wartime to avoid tipping off the enemy about government plans and operations and to promote candid deliberation inside the government about these plans and operations. And Cheney was right that the war against Islamist terrorists would, more than past wars, be fought in the dark world of intelligence and covert action, under the cloak of government secrecy. But when the government acts out of public sight, it is more prone than usual to mistakes and excesses, and it sometimes tries to keep these mistakes and excesses secret to avoid embarrassment. This is a big problem in a democracy, for citizens cannot hold officials accountable for these actions, and cannot redress them, if they do not know about them. The government does not have a good system for managing the trade-offs between secrecy and account-ability. In theory the executive branch is expert on what infor-mation might harm national security, but its self-interested and self-protective instincts cloud its judgment. In theory Congress and the courts could check these tendencies, but traditionally they did little in this realm (though as I explain in the next chapter, this has changed a lot in the last decade).

That leaves the press. The job of the so-called Fourth Estate, as Supreme Court Justice Potter Stewart once said, is to provide "organized, expert scrutiny of government."[20] Inspired by the First Amendment's protection for "freedom . . . of the press," national security journalists see their job as piercing the govern-ment's secrecy system to reveal what the government is doing and whether it is effective, so that the American people can decide whether they approve or want a change of course. "It's the fun-damental role of the press to hold individual government officials accountable for their actions, so that the electorate will have the necessary information in order to make wise decisions," explains the *New Yorker*'s Jane Mayer. "Secrecy, in the name of national security, has to outweigh the value of that basic democratic func-tion, in order to win out in any given story. It's a high threshold to meet."[21] Bill Keller, the former executive editor of the *New York Times*, agrees. "As journalists in a robust democracy, our respon-sibility is to publish information of interest to the public, and that includes publishing secrets when we can find them."[22]

This is a relatively new self-conception in the journalist's role. From the beginning of the nation the government has tried to keep national security secrets, and some in the press have tried, often with success, to expose those secrets.[23] But the press's adversarial relationship to the national security establishment is a mid–Cold War development. As recently as World War II, Franklin D. Roosevelt could, without irony, call on the "patriotic press" to self-censor "military information which might be of aid to the enemy."[24] In the two decades following the war, reporters had a benign view of the "heroic presidency." They had openly chummy relationships with powerful government officials, and largely reflected establishment national security views.[25] "Americans had been trained during the war and the post-war years to trust their Presidents," wrote David Halberstam in *The Powers That Be.*[26] The national security press in this era largely shared this attitude.[27]

The turning point can be traced to the May 1960 downing of the U-2 spy plane over the Soviet Union, when the Eisenhower administration was caught in multiple lies about the mission and White House involvement in it.[28] The press was embarrassed by this cascade of untruths, which for the most part it had faithfully reported. Journalists' anxiety about governmental co-optation, and their suspicions of the presidency, would grow throughout the 1960s and early 1970s. John F. Kennedy pressured the *New York Times* to tone down its pre–Bay of Pigs reporting on the planned invasion of Cuba.[29] When the operation proved a disaster, Kennedy complained to the *Times'* managing editor that "[i]f you had printed more about the operation you would have saved us from a colossal mistake."[30] Kennedy was posturing, for he soon urged the press to "heed the duty of self-restraint" in reporting on national security.[31] But the lesson that journalists began to draw was that the national interest demanded honest and independent national security reporting. That lesson would deepen with Lyndon Johnson's perceived perfidy over the Gulf of Tonkin incident, an event that convinced Congress to approve an expansion of the soon-to-be-unpopular Vietnam War. The President's "credibility gap" grew as information about the war's prospects, conveyed during government press conferences in Saigon and Washington, increasingly clashed with what journalists saw and reported from the ground. It also clashed with what Americans began to see on television, a relatively new medium that had seemed to enhance presidential power in the Kennedy years but that was now being used to great effect to expose presidential folly.

The clash of perspectives culminated in the publication of the Pentagon Papers, the Defense Department study of the Vietnam War that presented a darker picture than the government's public line about the conduct and success of the war. Daniel Ellsberg photocopied the papers and leaked them to the *New York Times* and later to the *Washington Post*. The government threatened criminal sanctions against both papers when it learned they might publish the documents. After heated internal debates, both papers defied the threats and published. The government then sought and received a lower-court injunction against publication. But the Supreme Court dismissed the injunction and affirmed the press's freedom, and even responsibility, to publish some classified national security secrets free of prior restraint. "In the First Amendment, the Founding Fathers gave the free press the protection it must have to fulfill its essential role in our democracy . . . [to] bare the secrets of government and inform the people," wrote Justice Hugo Black in the opinion that resonated most with the press. "And paramount among the responsibilities of a free press is the duty to prevent any part of the government from deceiving the people and sending them off to distant lands to die of foreign fevers and foreign shot and shell."[32]

The Pentagon Papers episode gave birth to accountability journalism. The press had placed itself in direct conflict with the government over the highest matters of state despite threats of jail for its editors and possible financial ruin for the newspaper companies. The executive branch used all of its tools of power to stop publication of the papers, but it was rebuked by the Supreme Court. And the secret official history of the war, once published, revealed that the government had been misleading the American people. American journalism emerged from the episode more controversial in the eyes of the public. It also emerged with a permanently skeptical attitude about whether the government was telling the truth, a realization of its power to defy the government even on matters of war, and a romantic self-conception of its role in American democracy.

The Pentagon Papers episode also undermined the legitimacy, in the eyes of the press, of the government's classified information system. At the dawn of the Cold War, President Truman authorized any executive agency to classify information deemed "necessary in the interest of national security."[33] By 1957, one and a half million government employees had access to the secrecy stamp.[34] Cold War America, frightened by the enemy within, wielded the secrecy stamp promiscuously, and overclassification was rampant. And then, after all of the confrontation and drama of the Pentagon Papers saga, it turned out that Ellsberg's lovingly photocopied "top-secret" Pentagon documents contained nothing that harmed national security and much that embarrassed the government. "The most celebrated leaker in American history revealed what appear in retrospect to be unnecessary secrets," notes Gabriel Schoenfeld, a critic of leaks.[35] Never again would the press take the secrecy stamp too seriously when deciding whether to publish sensitive national security information.

Then came the manifold lies of Watergate, lies by the President, his senior aides, and the Attorney General, many in the name of national security, many implicating criminal activity. The Watergate reporting by Bob Woodward and Carl Bernstein for the *Washington Post* brought down a President, provided information to the public that motivated Congress and the courts to fulfill their constitutional roles, and solidified the press's self-understanding that accountability journalism of secret government activity, even if related to national security, was among its most important tasks. This was the inherited legacy that led Philip Bennett and many other journalists to conclude after 9/11 that the press must relentlessly pursue the government's conduct of the war, even into the shadows.

FROM THE IRAQ DEBACLE TO SECRET PRISONS

"We have found a number of instances of coverage that was not as rigorous as it should have been," said the editors of the *New York Times*, in a mea culpa on May 26, 2004, for its erroneous and misleading coverage of the WMD rationale for the 2003 invasion of Iraq.[36] Some people see the press's skewed WMD coverage as emblematic of its failure to hold the government accountable for its secret actions after 9/11 in the broader "war on terrorism"— rendition, secret prisons, aggressive interrogation, surveillance, targeted killing, and the like. Journalists "have fallen short in our efforts to come to grips with how the government has fought and is fighting this shadow war," said Tim Golden of the *New York Times*, who did extensive reporting on detention and related issues in Guantanamo and Afghanistan.[37] But the truth is closer to the opposite: the press has been enormously successful in reporting on the shadow war during the past decade, even though the government put many hurdles in its way. The Iraq WMD episode is the exception, not the rule.

The main government hurdle to covering the shadow war was the classified information system. Government officials sign an agreement promising not to mishandle or disclose such information. An official who breaches the agreement and leaks classified information can be fired, sued for money, or prosecuted. These laws, and concerns about the impact on national security that underlie them, create powerful disincentives for government officials to talk about these programs. A different hurdle to reporting on the shadow war was that the press was preoccupied with other issues. In the first two years after 9/11, the press concentrated on how nineteen men wielding box cutters took a nation to its knees, why U.S. intelligence and defense agencies failed, why the Islamist terrorists and their allies so hated America, and the impact in America of the 9/11 attacks. It also focused on the continuing terrorist threat, which seemed much more palpable in 2001–2003 than today. Beginning in the fall of 2002, the press was further preoccupied with the run-up to and execution of the Iraq war, and then with the failure to find WMDs in Iraq and the growing difficulties of occupation. These stories swallowed journalists' energy and resources.

Even with these hurdles, the press did extensive early reporting on "secret" government activities. On October 21, 2001, Bob Woodward disclosed that President Bush authorized the CIA to go after al Qaeda with the "most sweeping and lethal covert action since the founding of the Agency in 1947."[38] On March 11, 2002, Rajiv Chandrasekaran and Peter Finn reported how the government since 9/11 had "secretly transported dozens of people suspected of links to terrorists to countries other than the United States, bypassing extradition procedures and legal formalities." They emphasized that the suspects had been "taken to countries, including Egypt and Jordan, whose intelligence services have close ties to the CIA and where they can be subjected to interrogation tactics—including torture and threats to families—that are illegal in the United States."[39] And on December 26, 2002, Dana Priest and Barton Gellman wrote about secret U.S. prisons for high-value al Qaeda detainees outside the United States "where U.S. due process does not apply." The story added that U.S. officials used painful "stress and duress" techniques in a "brass-knuckled quest for information, often in concert with allies of dubious human rights reputation, in which the traditional lines between right and wrong, legal and inhumane, are evolving and blurred."[40]

These and similar stories are remarkable in retrospect. Very soon after top-secret counterterrorism programs became operational, they were discussed in some detail on the front page of the *Washington Post* and elsewhere. In these stories, government officials unapologetically touted aggressive counterterrorism tactics that seemed to be at the margins of or beyond the law. "The gloves are off" and the CIA can do "whatever is necessary," one senior official boasted to Woodward.[41] It is "preferable to render a suspect secretly because it prevents lengthy court battles and minimizes publicity," diplomats told Chandrasekaran and Finn, adding that the renditions allow us "to get information from terrorists in a way we can't do on U.S. soil."[42] National security officials who spoke to Priest and Gellman "defended the use of violence against captives as just and necessary." One official told them that "if you don't violate someone's human rights some of the time, you probably aren't doing your job."[43]

While these stories described sharp departures from prior American practices, they did not cite concerns by human rights organizations or members of Congress that would be common a few years later. Nor did the stories lead to public outcry or push-back. "None of our early stories had legs, really," Dana Priest later said.[44] This was a time when the memory of 9/11 was fresh, the terrorist threat was palpable, and the country's basic view was that the attacks had occurred because the government had been "institutionally averse to risk," as the 9/11 Commission would put it in 2004.[45] In this milieu, government practices that would prove enormously controversial in a few years were greeted by the public with silence or a nod of approval. Accountability journalism "means holding things up to public inspection, and letting the public decide what the consequences ought to be," says Bill Keller.[46] The public inspected these stories and decided to do nothing. The government officials who operated these programs believed that they reflected the wishes, even the demands, of the American people, and that "the American public would back their view," as Priest and Gellman reported in 2002.[47] At the time, they were basically right.

This tepid public reaction has a complex feedback effect on the press. Journalists are supposed to resist conventional wisdom, but they are not immune to the social influences of the world in which they and their sources live. "If over time a story doesn't get traction, that may well be a signal that you should just report harder," says Keller. "But newspapers are put out by human beings, and the natural human tendency is, if you're not getting traction, maybe you should try something else."[48] Keller is speaking of the incentives that motivate journalists and their editors. If a line of investigative reporting doesn't produce a public reaction, even aggressive editors tend, over time, to move it deeper into the paper or give it smaller play. And investigative journalists who are rewarded in part by the prominence and consequences of their pieces become less enthusiastic about the issue, especially when there are so many other matters to pursue.

The public's reaction affects more than journalists' incentives. It also affects their sources. "We're to some extent captive of the bravery or lack of bravery of people in government" in the national security field, notes Keller.[49] And the bravery of these sources, or at least their beliefs and interests, reflect the social context. Government officials were especially secretive in the first few years after 9/11, making it hard for the press to find its way. When they spoke, they conveyed a limited and self-serving account of the secret war. There were few dissenting insiders in those days, no one who expressed concern to Priest, as many later would for her 2005 secret prisons story, about the "legality, morality and practicality" of the programs.[50] "A story can't survive in a vacuum, it needs to motivate sources and engage an audience," says the *Post*'s Philip Bennett. "Stories like these need a resonating chamber among officials and the public to stay alive, to surface new facts and to pump up the volume in the newsroom. The first rendition and prison stories didn't have that."[51]

A variation on this dynamic is part of the explanation for the relatively one-sided reporting on the WMD rationale for the Iraq war. The press may well have been unduly influenced by "jingoism," as Seymour Hersh asserts, and "groupthink," as Bob Woodward claims.[52] And some in the press, especially at the *New York Times*, were captured by opportunistic Iraqi defectors and selective access to classified information.[53] But another important cause was that most of the seemingly credible sources inside and outside the government (including senior Clinton administration officials) were signaling that Saddam Hussein possessed and might use WMDs. There were channels of dissent and uncertainty inside government, and more reporting about them than critics acknowledge.[54] But these stories had fewer and weaker sources making weaker claims than those beating the WMD drum. Walter Pincus's famously skeptical article published a few days before the invasion of Iraq, for example, claimed not that the Bush administration's WMD case was wrong, but rather that it was unproved. It cited for this claim only unnamed "official[s]" and "an individual who has regularly been briefed by the CIA."[55]

But if there were relatively few credible sources of information about the absence of WMDs in Iraq, there were plenty of such sources about the secret war against al Qaeda, and journalists pursued them relentlessly. On October 26, 2001, a 378-word story in the *News International,* a Pakistan newspaper, reported that "a source at the Karachi airport" had seen Pakistani authorities hand over a "suspected foreigner" to masked U.S. troops who placed the suspect in a U.S. airplane with the tail number N-379P scheduled for departure to Amman, Jordan.[56] This story "ricocheted among spy-hunters and Web bloggers as a curiosity for those interested in divining the mechanics of the new U.S.-declared war on terrorism," Dana Priest later reported.[57] The day it was published, a conservative website in the United States, freerepublic.com, posted it. Thirteen minutes later, a commentator on the site had searched Internet databases to determine that a plane with that tail number was owned by Premier Executive Transport Services, a Dedham, Massachusetts, firm. Another quickly speculated that Premier Executive might be like Air America, the secret Vietnam-era airplane fleet. Priest eventually picked up on this discussion (others had as well), and after analyzing corporate records in Dedham and public databases, and talking with sources inside the CIA, she was able to determine that Premier Executive and associated companies were CIA fronts.[58] This was one of several public clues that, together with Priest's sources and a lot of legwork, enabled her to unravel the secret prisons mystery.[59]

By 2004, Priest, British reporter Stephen Grey, the *New Yorker*'s Jane Mayer, and others were reporting detail after detail—some accurate, some not—on CIA renditions, secret prisons, the interrogation techniques being used in those prisons, and many examples of abuse. The mood of the country was changing by this time as the "war on terrorism" dragged on, the Iraq occupation went bad, President Bush's popularity waned, the Abu Ghraib pictures flew around the world, allegations of abuse grew, and controversial Department of Justice interpretations of the torture law leaked to the public. The synergy of publication that had failed to materialize in 2002 now began to work. Stories began to include criticism by human rights groups and politicians that was missing earlier. Officials who were increasingly worried about the CIA's shadow war activities began to leak their concerns, with new facts and classified documents, to the press. These disclosures led to fresh and more detailed reporting that was churned by politicians, blogs, cable news shows, and the foreign press. The cycles of disclosure, revelation, and recrimination ramped up, motivating domestic and foreign nongovernmental organizations (NGOs) to action and sparking dozens of public and private investigations. These events influenced the public and led Congress to pass laws and the courts to issue rulings that, as I discuss in later chapters, constricted the CIA programs.[60] By September 2006, the Bush administration had acknowledged the secret prisons, cleared them out, and cut back sharply on permissible interrogations.[61] By 2009, following the election of Barack Obama, the secret prisons had been closed and the CIA interrogation program terminated.

What the press uncovered about CIA prison and interrogation activities was just the tip of the iceberg. Beginning in 2005, it also got inside the secretive National Security Agency like never before, and turned the government's fragile signals intelligence regime inside out. Most notably, Eric Lichtblau and James Risen of the *New York Times* reported that the government was wiretapping without a warrant under the Terrorist Surveillance Program; monitoring terrorist-related international financial transfers; picking up international communications that "transit" through the United States; data-mining telephone and e-mail information; analyzing ATM transactions, credit card purchases, and wire payments; and cooperating with private telecoms in these efforts.[62] The press also reported in endless detail about highly classified military detention and interrogation practices at Guantanamo and in Afghanistan; about dozens of "secret" military and "covert" CIA operations around the globe, and the classified meetings and deliberations in Washington that supported them; and about thousands of other "secrets" of the shadow war against terrorism.

"There are a few operational things I have done that are as secret now as the day they were conceived," General Michael Hayden said in 2010, but only a "very narrow number of specific operational acts."[63] This is an astonishing statement, for Hayden presumably knew most if not all of America's important intelligence secrets from his perch atop the intelligence world after 9/11, first as Director of the National Security Agency until 2005, then as Deputy Director of National Intelligence from 2005 to 2006, and finally as Director of the CIA from 2006 to 2009. Thirty-four-year CIA lawyer John Rizzo has a similar judgment about the important secrets that have been made public in the last decade. He emphasizes that broad, continuous long-term operations involving many people tend to leak out, while short, discreet, one-off operations—like the one that killed Osama Bin Laden in May 2011—are more likely to remain secret.[64] These judgments comport with my own perceptions based on a briefer and less comprehensive view of the government secrecy system.

President Obama, who came to the presidency a credible critic of secretive government, was after two years expressing "great angst" over the regularity of harmful leaks.[65] His Under Secretary of Defense for Intelligence, Michael Vickers, testified in 2011 that unauthorized leaks of classified information were "one of the most serious problems" he faced. "The spate of unauthorized disclosures of very sensitive information places our forces, our military operations, and our foreign relations at risk."[66] It is impossible to prove these claims, and of course the public does not know what it does not know. But the claims are consistent with more objective markers about the scope of classified disclosures. The intelligence community reported hundreds of leaks of classified information in the decade prior to 2005, and at least 183 since then.[67] No doubt many hundreds more leaks were investigated within the intelligence community. The *New York Times* and *Washington Post* wrote hundreds of stories after 9/11 that self-reported disclosure of classified information. And many more stories that did not self-report classified disclosures nonetheless contained classified tidbits. We have become so used to the daily stream of revelations about the government's "secret" war activities that we are blind to the number, frequency, seriousness, and details of the disclosures, or how these disclosures operate as an important check on the presidency by spurring Congress, the courts, and civil society to action. We have also failed to appreciate how changes in government organization and technology undergird these trends.

THE BLOATED SECRECY BUREAUCRACY

In 2010, Dana Priest and William Arkin wrote a three-part series in the *Washington Post* called "Top Secret America." The story's bottom line was that "the top-secret world the government created in response to the terrorist attacks of Sept. 11, 2001, has become so large, so unwieldy and so secretive that no one knows how much money it costs, how many people it employs, how many programs exist within it or exactly how many agencies do the same work."[68] As of 2011, more than 4.2 million people in the public and private sectors—most located in or associated with the executive branch—held security clearances. Almost 1.5 million of them have top-secret security clearances.[69] These bureaucracies and firms create, collect, record, and analyze an unfathomable array of information that is classified and that, but for the occasional leak, is never made public. Untold millions of new national security "secrets"—in the form of facts, arguments, programs, policies, analysis, and the like—are created yearly on classified e-mail and Internet systems and in bug-proof rooms known as "Sensitive Compartmented Information Facilities" throughout the government. And then there are the millions of unclassified documents and records related to national security that remain undisclosed to the public because of executive privilege and a slow presidential publication process.

The sprawling, swollen national security bureaucracy generates and keeps more secrets than ever. Yet paradoxically, it has a harder time than ever keeping important secrets out of the public realm. "The classification system is not an iceberg, it's a volcano," says Steven Aftergood, who leads the project on government secrecy at the Federation of American Scientists. "It is not a static frozen mass, but a dynamic churning system that is constantly erupting. New material is absorbed into it at an astonishing rate, while other material is ejected—through a variety of authorized or unauthorized mechanisms—nearly as quickly."[70] Many of the ejections concern the government's most important secrets: the methods and means of its intelligence operations and covert actions.

One reason the system sheds so many secrets is that otherwise the government cannot explain its national security and foreign policies. "[P]ractically everything that our Government does, plans, thinks, hears and contemplates in the realms of foreign policy is stamped and treated as secret," noted *New York Times* Washington Bureau chief Max Frankel in an affidavit in the Pentagon Papers case that is as insightful today as it was four decades ago. Without the use of "secrets," Frankel explained, "there could be no adequate diplomatic, military and political reporting of the kind our people take for granted, either abroad or in Washington and there could be no mature system of communication between the Government and the people." Frankel described a partly cooperative, partly antagonistic relationship between officials and journalists in which the former conveys secrets discreetly to serve legitimate U.S. national security goals and the latter takes and uses them in the service of their readers and the public.[71]

Government officials also reveal classified information for less exalted reasons, as Bob Woodward's *Obama's Wars* illustrates.[72] The book opens with a detailed description of the first postelection intelligence briefing that Director of National Intelligence Michael McConnell gave to Barack Obama. Woodward describes the conversation, including the content of several classified intelligence programs and their code names, in great detail. Subsequent chapters reveal classified reports, memorandums, conversations, programs, meetings, and the like. Woodward unquestionably received much of this information from top government officials (just as he received classified information from top officials for his books about the Bush era). Most of these leaks had no conceivable justification in national security policy. They were, rather, attempts to create opportunistic spin, influence the President's Afghanistan decisions, show off to Woodward, and more than anything else, settle bureaucratic scores. Such open defiance and manipulation of the secrecy system at the top indicates a lack of seriousness about secrecy that inevitably corrodes the respect that lower-level officials give it in their discussions with journalists. The system then "becomes one to be disregarded by the cynical or the careless, and to be manipulated by those intent on self-protection or self-promotion," as Justice Stewart maintained in the Pentagon Papers case.[73]

Widespread disrespect of the secrecy system at or near the top of government emboldened the unusual number of whistle-blowers further down who gave information to journalists and others in the last decade because they thought the government was doing something illegitimate. The opportunities for perceived illegitimacy inside the government are unusually high in the novel and ideologically contested post-9/11 wars, especially since the tactics used in the wars are governed by criminal laws that weigh on officials' minds. Much of what Dana Priest eventually learned about CIA secret prisons came from people inside the government who were worried about the sustainability and legality of the program.[74] Anxiety about the perceived illegality of the Terrorist Surveillance Program is what led officials and contractors to tell the *New York Times* about it.[75] And military officials spurred journalists and human rights organizations to investigate interrogation abuses.[76] "I've been astonished at how willing many of those with close knowledge of these U.S. secret agencies had been to share their concerns," notes journalist Stephen Grey.[77] Officials involved in or even knowledgeable about activities they think are illegal or immoral often carry enormous emotional burdens. "You have this load of shit on your head, and you're going to take it off your head and put it on somebody else's," says Seymour Hersh, explaining why worried officials speak to him. "And so a guy like me, who is the last person in the world anyone would expect you to talk to, all of the sudden a guy like me, you might say, you know what, he's an asshole but he never burns anybody."[78]

The size of the national security bureaucracy made secrecy harder as well. Until the 1990s, a covert action was an intimate affair that required planning by a handful of people in the CIA, vetting by very few in the White House, a finding by the President, and reporting to the congressional intelligence committees. Today, a covert action typically requires multiple layers of vetting and review by dozens of lawyers and policymakers in the CIA, the Office of the Director of National Intelligence, the National Security Council, and the Departments of Justice, State, and Defense, before being presented to the President and his principals for a final decision and then being sent on to Congress. This much wider circle of eyes on covert action plans is a problem for secrecy because, as former CIA Director Richard Helms emphasized, "the probability of leaks escalates exponentially each time a classified document is exposed to another person—be it an Agency employee, a member of Congress, a senior official, a typist, or a file clerk."[79]

A similar phenomenon resulted from the post-9/11 push to expand the circle of government officials with access to secrets. Conventional wisdom after 9/11 was that U.S. intelligence agencies had held information about terrorist threats too tightly and had failed to share it with other intelligence agencies that, with a broader situational awareness, might have "connected the dots" before the attacks. Such "stovepiping" of information, charged the 9/11 Commission, "assumes it is possible to know, in advance, who will need to use the information," and further "assumes that the risk of inadvertent disclosure outweighs the benefits of wider sharing."[80] This arrangement reflected Cold War worries about spying that were outdated, the Commission concluded. It recommended that the " 'need-to-know' culture of information protection" be replaced with a " 'need-to-share' culture of integration."[81] The result was a massive push to share intelligence and related classified information across the government. But as this secret information got pushed to peripheries of the ever-expanding government, it became much harder, under the Helms principle, to keep it from leaking or being inadvertently disclosed to the public.

THE DIGITAL REVOLUTION

At the same time that information was being pushed to the periphery of government, the periphery was becoming much more porous because of advances in computer and telecommunication technologies in the decade after 9/11. It took Daniel Ellsberg months to copy the seven-thousand-page Pentagon Papers. Each day he would stuff a few volumes in his briefcase and sneak them out of RAND. He would then spend his evenings hovered over a then modern Xerox machine that took several seconds to copy each page.[82] "One hand picked up a page, the other fit it on the glass, top down, push the button, wait . . . lift, move the original to the right while picking another page from the pile," and so on, all night long, Ellsberg recounted in his memoirs.[83] Today the nation's most important secrets are stored in bits on computer systems. Someone who wants to steal or leak these secrets can in minutes copy over a million pages of classified information on to a memory device that can be concealed in an ink pen or a hearing aid, and later distribute the information, in encrypted form, around the globe.[84]

The WikiLeaks saga is the most obvious example of how secrets-in-bits are becoming hard for the oversized government to conceal. Julian Assange's "non-profit media organization" rose to prominence in 2010 with its stunning release of hundreds of thousands of classified American documents generated in the Iraq and Afghanistan wars, and a quarter-million classified diplomatic cables, among many other things. These documents were given to WikiLeaks by Bradley Manning, a twenty-two-year-old intelligence analyst with access to the Department of Defense's classified Internet system known as "SIPRNet." "I would come in with music on a CD-RW labelled with something like 'Lady

Gaga' . . . erase the music . . . then write a compressed split file," Manning explained to former hacker Adrian Lamo, who eventually turned him in. "[I] listened and lip-synced to Lady Gaga's 'Telephone' while exfiltratating [*sic*] possibly the largest data spillage in American history."[85] WikiLeaks, in turn, distributes and stores this data in heavily encrypted form on multiple computers around the world in what Assange describes as "an uncensorable system for untraceable mass document leaking and public analysis."[86] The government has taken aggressive steps to redress its lax security systems, disrupt WikiLeaks publication channels, and punish and deter future leak solicitors. Nonetheless, the digitalization of intelligence and the growth of the intelligence and military bureaucracies put the government in a much harder position to keep secrets than before.

And WikiLeaks is just the beginning of this trend. The year 2011 witnessed the rise of scores of WikiLeaks copycats, including many by traditional journalistic outfits. These organizations had different aims and technologies. But they are all designed to facilitate anonymous whistle-blowing, and as their numbers and innovations grow, so too will their threat to government secrets. The WikiLeaks model depends on a disgruntled U.S. government official like Manning pushing secret content out to the public. A different model is for outsiders to steal secret information from the government. The digital revolution facilitates that as well. Practically all U.S. government secrets are found, in some form, on computer systems. These hard-to-defend computer systems are under relentless exploitation by adversary nations and criminal gangs who can often hide their tracks, at least until after the damage is done. In the past few years, public and private hackers have broken into very sensitive government and defense contractor systems, where, according to Deputy Secretary of Defense William Lynn, they "acquired thousands of files from U.S. networks and from the networks of U.S. allies and industry partners, including weapons blueprints, operational plans, and surveillance data."[87] For self-interested reasons these spies usually don't publish what they find. But it is only a matter of time before hackers motivated by the same transparency imperative that inspired WikiLeaks start using this technique to steal and publish government secrets.

WikiLeaks is a piece of a larger technologically inspired trend that is relocating the center of gravity of U.S. national security reporting outside the United States. In March 2011, many non-U.S. newspapers reported on ties between Raymond Davis, an American arrested in Pakistan for shooting two civilians, and the CIA.[88] The *New York Times* had the story but temporarily withheld it because the Obama administration argued that disclosing his identity would put his life at risk.[89] The *Times* hesitated for the same reason that Leonard Downie Jr. withheld the location of the secret prisons. The American press considers U.S. national security interests in the publication balance, and it sometimes self-censors out of deference to U.S. national security. "We are on the team, but we can't be on the team," acknowledges Seymour Hersh, articulating the tension.[90] Non-U.S. media organizations, by contrast, give no weight to U.S. national security concerns. American journalists displayed "a willingness to work with us," says former CIA Director Michael Hayden. But with foreign media like WikiLeaks and Al Jazeera, "it's very, very difficult," he adds. "Other than perhaps making use of an allied relationship, you're kind of out of Schlitz."[91] The growing scrutiny of American military and intelligence operations by the technologically empowered global media, and its relative indifference to U.S. government pleas, are still further reasons why U.S. government secrets are harder than ever to keep.

Modern information technologies help defeat government secrecy in other ways. Without the devastating photographs of Abu Ghraib, subsequent written and verbal accounts of government abuse in Iraq, Afghanistan, and GTMO would have been looked at in a much different light. The technologies that made it possible to take and distribute the photographs—consumer digital cameras, JPEG compression files, electronic mail, and broadband Internet—came together in the 1990s but came into widespread

use only after 9/11. Before the Internet brought foreign newspapers to everyone's home, journalists in America and England
would not have come across an obscure Pakistan newspaper story
about a secret CIA flight. "Things that happen overseas are now
viewable to us in a different way," explains Dana Priest.[92] By 9/11
the intelligence community had also become dependent on electronic equipment that left clues about its activities and made it
harder to hide its tracks. Italian prosecutors used the signals from
cell phones to local transmission towers to track down and identify
the aliases, hotel locations, and phone calls to Langley of the CIA
agents who kidnapped al Qaeda suspect Abu Omar in Milan.[93]
Stephen Grey used the digital signals emitted by airplanes along
with online flight logs, flight-tracking databases on the Federal
Aviation Administration website, and data-mining software to
map out CIA flights and prisons.[94]

As this last example shows, the communication revolution
enables the creation and publication of giant public databases
on every conceivable topic that journalists and others can mine
with powerful computer search tools to reveal a lot about what
the intelligence world is up to. Such tools helped journalists see
through a poorly disguised CIA front company in Dedham, Massachusetts. And they led the *Chicago Tribune* to discover the names
of 2,600 CIA employees, many of them covert operatives, as well
as some of their home addresses and travel and work history. The
Tribune also gathered the locations of two-dozen secret CIA facilities around the United States, the names of twenty-six employees
at the CIA's Virginia training facility known as "The Farm," and
the ownership information and flight histories of seventeen different planes that landed there. "Cover is a complex issue that is
more complex in the Internet age," said CIA spokeswoman Jennifer Dyck. "There are things that worked previously that no longer
work."[95] The problem is more serious than Dyck describes, and
goes to the core of traditional human espionage. "In the Age of
Google, biometrics, and GPS, we have suffered a massive erosion
in our agents' abilities to travel and operate with false identities,"
notes a senior CIA official.[96]

The Age of Google also makes it easier for journalists to divine secrets from public information. "In many cases, the ultimate story I'm reporting is classified, but there are unclassified signs all around it," says *Time* (and former *Washington Post*) reporter Barton Gellman. Organization and bureaucratic charts, phone books, manuals and reports about equipment and methods, obscure reference works, conference speeches, and other government documents and technical information are readily available and searchable on government and government contractor websites, in academic databases, and other such places. These sources of public information allow Gellman to "guess, from little clues and emanations, what might be happening" behind closed doors, which in turn leads him to ask questions and draw inferences that eventually lead to a secret.[97] Informed guesses of this sort led Gellman to discover, among other things, the 2002 secret prisons story, the "shadow government" working in secret bunkers outside Washington, and the ring of nuclear sensors around the nation's capital designed to detect a nuclear or radiological bomb.[98]

Self-publishing and information-sharing tools like weblogs, listservs, photo-sharing, and related technologies also changed national security journalism. Information about war used to be channeled through elite newspapers and television networks that reflected a relatively narrow perspective and published only what could be squeezed into the allotted column inches and broadcast minutes. Untold government secrets were never discovered by the handful of reporters on the beat, and many that were discovered never made it to the public for lack of space or time. Digital tools break this chokehold and decentralize the collection, analysis, production, and distribution of information about U.S. military and intelligence activities. Today soldiers in the field—from privates to generals—are in daily e-mail contact with journalists, congressional staffers, academics, and bloggers, conveying otherwise unknown information about the war, much of which ends up in the public realm. Hundreds of "milblogs" written by current or former military or national security officials analyze and broadcast to the world information about ongoing military activity, and sometimes inadvertently include classified or sensitive information.[99] National security websites such as *Danger Room*, *Best Defense*, *Small Wars Journal*, and many more provide detailed expert analysis, often with reporting and commentary from people in the field. And expert bloggers pore over obscure documents and reports to discover secrets between the lines. Marty Lederman at the blog *Balkinization*, a prominent example, employed skills developed in the Clinton-era Justice Department to discern secrets in public legal documents, including the then classified fact that the CIA had secret prisons overseas.[100] He was also good at figuring out the secret import of ambiguities and loopholes in proposed legislation on surveillance and military commissions in ways that set agendas for the traditional reporters and congressional staffers with whom he frequently communicated.[101]

A great deal of commentary since 9/11 has analyzed the U.S. government's powerful surveillance capacities, and its attendant abilities to combine unconnected pieces of information to create a "mosaic" of revealing insights into otherwise invisible or secret activities.[102] What is less well understood is that these principles work in reverse. The technologies and institutions just described—WikiLeaks, e-mail, searchable public databases, data-mining tools, expert bloggers, listservs, digital photography, and more—have empowered the public to watch the government closely, and to build powerful mosaics of supposedly secret government activity. "Any private individual today can gain access to more intelligence capacity than could the most accomplished intelligence officer of a previous generation," notes Steven Aftergood.[103] Thousands of different eyes and minds around the world use this capacity to monitor, analyze, collaborate, and report on U.S. intelligence and military activities. What Dan Gillmor calls the "former audience"—people who used to merely consume news but who now participate in its creation—became national security reporters and analysts.[104] The new digital tools made traditional accountability reporting of war and national security much more robust than it otherwise would have been, and more importantly, added untold new sources of information and analysis about the government's war operations.

ACCOUNTABILITY JOURNALISM'S FUTURE

On February 11, 2011, the Associated Press published a story by Adam Goldman and Matt Apuzzo about the "haphazard accountability" that had been meted out over the years to CIA officials involved in the Agency's detention and interrogation program. Perhaps the most remarkable thing about the story was that the journalists purported to identify by first name (and in one case middle name) at least six current and former senior undercover CIA officers, as well as their former and (when relevant) current positions in the Agency. The story quoted a furious CIA spokesman who described the identification of these officials as "nothing short of reckless." The authors explained that using the names was important to establish the credibility of the story. And they assured readers that the Associated Press had taken steps to ensure that the agents' identities could not be discerned from the partial names in the story. "The AP determined that even the most sophisticated commercial information services could not be used to derive the officers' full names or, for example, find their home addresses knowing only their first names and the fact of their CIA employment," the story explained. "The AP has withheld further details that could help identify them."[105]

The Associated Press's assurances are extraordinarily naive. A cardinal principle of crowdsourcing is that thousands of eyeballs often can discern what only a few cannot. The fact that the Associated Press on an experimental basis could not infer the agents' identities from their names and CIA employment does not mean that others, using different techniques of discovery and adding different or later-discovered information to the mix, couldn't connect the dots. Terrorist organizations and foreign intelligence services surely began this task the day the story ran. After publication of the story the CIA must assume that there is a much greater likelihood that the agents' identities are compromised, with all of the bad implications for U.S. intelligence that assumption entails. So too must the agents themselves, who rely on anonymity and cover for their own safety and the safety of their families. Beyond the immediate concerns of personal harm are more diffuse but no less real concerns when secret agents read their names in the newspaper. As the spy novelist and former British spy David Cornwell (aka John le Carré) explains, spies who take refuge in secrecy can be more terrified about having their names in the newspaper than in the files of adversary spy agencies. "It may be pretty bad if the Russians find out about it, but it's terrible if the press finds out about it," he explains. "[T]he idea of having their faces in the newspaper—that's something [spies] wake up and sweat about in the middle of the night because there, somehow their identity and their security are being taken away from them."[106]

During the last decade, intelligence agents have seen their activities and identities exposed time and time again by journalistic revelations about top-secret covers, programs, and methods of intelligence. The depth and scope of public coverage of secret wartime activity has gone practically unnoticed amid the loud but misleading funeral cries for accountability journalism. "The future of accountability journalism is now at stake—along with much else—as a tsunami of economic, technological and social change washes over the news media," bemoaned Leonard Downie Jr. in a September 2010 lecture called "The New News."[107] Downie is referring to the collapse of the traditional revenue model that had supported investigative journalism budgets in newspapers large and small. When publication of information required heavy investments in printing presses, traditional newspapers were one of the few media outlets and thus were able to charge a high price for advertisements. These ads, in turn, supported investigative journalism. But the "commercial success of newspapers and their linking of that to accountability journalism wasn't a deep truth about reality," explains media theorist Clay Shirky. "Best Buy was not willing to support the Baghdad bureau because Best Buy cared about news from Baghdad," he says, referring to the electronics retailer known for its colorful newspaper ads. "They just didn't have any other good choices."[108]

With the rise of the Internet, advertising became decoupled from its accidental connection to the printing press as firms found better and cheaper ways to reach customers. Newspaper revenues plummeted as a result. Many newspapers have closed or only publish a few days each week, and those that did not close slashed their budgets, starting with budgets for investigative journalism.[109] The changing economics of newspapers have had a notable impact on accountability journalism budgets across the country. But as both Downie and Shirky emphasize, accountability journalism has suffered the most at the local and regional news level because newspaper coverage is most vital in local communities and local and regional newspapers have been hardest hit by the change in newspaper economics.[110] It has also suffered on television, which discovered that ratings are driven more by lively conversations with an ideological edge than by expensive investigative reporting.

National security and war journalism, by contrast, have thrived. In part this is because national security reporting has always been dominated by just a few traditional media players. Since 9/11 those players have been the *New York Times, Washington Post, Wall Street Journal,* and *The New Yorker.* There were only a handful of journalists from these and a few other traditional outlets covering the CIA and national security before 9/11. Today there is still a handful, though the handful is larger owing to the wars in progress. The big traditional players have not obviously reduced the resources they devote to covering war and national security. National security is a topic that is important and glamorous and central to their mission of covering national and international affairs. It a niche area where what these outlets say matters a lot and gives them unusual influence over the government. And their reporting has been supplemented by new forms of subsidized investigative journalism like what is found on ProPublica and the PBS show *Frontline.*

But even if the resources these traditional institutions devote to war and national security diminish somewhat, one must factor in the new sources of information and analysis made possible by the digital revolution that supplement and amplify these traditional sources. The last decade has shown that there is no end of non-traditional investigators, watchers, and content providers who are deeply interested in and motivated to cover national security and war. The combination of old-style journalism and the explosion of modern distributed information-collection and -dissemination tools, and their mutually beneficial collaborations, give the public extraordinary amounts of information about the day-to-day conduct of war, including war in the shadows. The publication of this information has been fundamental in the last decade in sparking efforts by Congress, the courts, and NGOs to check the President and change his course. But it was not just media institutions and their private-sector collaborators that were generating and publishing national security information so vital in a properly functioning democracy. As the next chapter shows, the government too was closely watching its spies, and often revealing what it found.

Chapter Four

SPIES UNDER A GOVERNMENT MICROSCOPE

DURING ALLEN WELSH DULLES'S TENURE as the longest-serving and most successful Director of the CIA, from 1953 to 1961, the Agency undertook nearly two hundred covert actions and made large strides in its ability to collect intelligence information, including important technological breakthroughs in overflight and satellite reconnaissance.[1] Secrecy was vital to the success of these endeavors, and Dulles was a famous keeper of secrets. But he was driven to distraction by incessant leaks of information to the media, which he viewed as a problem to be managed akin to the problem of Soviet spies. Both journalists and spies try to extract national security secrets contrary to the wishes of the American intelligence services. And both, if they succeed, inform the enemy about the government's national security plans and methods. "[I]n my own experience in planning intelligence operations, I always considered, first, how the operation could be kept secret from the opponent and, second, how it could be kept from the press," Dulles explained in his 1963 book, *The Craft of Intelligence.* "Often the priority is reversed," he added. "What good does it do to spend millions to protect ourselves against espionage if our secrets just leak away?"[2]

Dulles's complaints about leaks—which in his day paled in

comparison to the leaks of the last decade—would be echoed and amplified by all of his successors and the Presidents for whom they worked. But unlike his modern counterparts, Dulles didn't worry much about his business being known by others inside government. The courts played no role in monitoring CIA activities. Congress was more involved but not in a formal or serious way. The dominant congressional attitude was that CIA activities "had to be taken on faith," as Senator Richard Russell said in 1956, because of the need for secrecy, discretion, and ruthlessness in confronting the Soviet Union during the Cold War.[3] Dulles spent time on Capitol Hill talking to subcommittee heads with nominal authority over the CIA. But he told them little of substance about CIA operations. "I'll fudge the truth to the oversight committee, but I'll tell the Chairman the truth—that is, if he wants to know," Dulles once explained to a colleague.[4] The chairman usually didn't. "No, no, my boy, don't tell me," Senator John Stennis, the CIA's chief overseer, told CIA Director James Schlesinger, who had come to brief him, in 1973. "Just go ahead and do it—but I don't want to know."[5] Stennis's attitude was typical in the first quarter century of the Cold War. Congress would sometimes chastise the CIA for its mistakes after the fact, but meaningful oversight was, until 1975, entirely absent.[6]

Also absent was meaningful oversight within the executive branch. Eisenhower enthusiastically embraced covert actions as an inexpensive, quiet, and effective foreign policy tool against the Soviet Union and its proxies. He gave Dulles and his swashbuckling operators a long leash that resulted in (among many other things) famous coups in Iran and Guatemala. But the former five-star general also worried about CIA excesses and his lack of control over agency activities. Eisenhower required the CIA to report covert actions to the National Security Council, and established a board in the White House (today known as the President's Intelligence Advisory Board) to supervise the CIA. The board concluded in 1957 that the Agency was still operating "on an autonomous and freewheeling basis in highly critical areas involving the conduct of foreign relations."[7] But Eisenhower balked at imposing more control because doing so would require him to fire Dulles. "[W]ith all his limitations, I'd rather have [Dulles] as chief of intelligence than anyone else I can think of," Eisenhower explained.[8] Kennedy did fire Dulles after the Bay of Pigs debacle, but neither he nor his immediate successors imposed an effective chain of command over the CIA.

Lurking behind these Presidents' reticence to impose greater control over the CIA was a desire to deny responsibility for CIA actions gone bad. For the CIA's first quarter-century, the philosophy of "plausible denial" encouraged it not to tell the President everything it was doing, and discouraged him from wanting to know. And of course if the President couldn't know, neither could Congress. Tim Weiner concludes in his history of the CIA that intelligence secrets inside the government during this era "were shared on a need-to-know basis, and Allen Dulles decided who needed to know them."[9] This is an exaggeration, but not a large one. With various degrees of congressional and presidential approval and acquiescence, the CIA operated with remarkable autonomy from traditional checks within the executive branch or by Congress or the courts during Dulles's tenure and continuing through the mid-1970s.

During this regime of nonaccountability, the CIA's growing abuses, mistakes, and excesses—massive politically motivated surveillance of American citizens, domestic break-in programs, nonconsensual medical experiments, shady assassination plots, and much more—remained unpunished and uncorrected. The regime began to crumble on May 4, 1973, when CIA Director Schlesinger read in the *Washington Post* that Howard Hunt had broken into the office of Daniel Ellsberg's psychiatrist with the CIA's assistance.[10] Four days later, Schlesinger ordered every CIA employee to report to him any CIA activities conducted at any time in the Agency's history "which might be construed to be outside" the CIA's legislative charter. The resulting 693-page collection of illegal or inappropriate activities was known as the CIA's "family jewels." When some of the family jewels began to leak to the public, congressional committees led by Senator Frank

Church and Representative Otis Pike did top-to-bottom investigations of the activities of the CIA and its intelligence cousins throughout 1975.

The central conclusion of the Church and Pike investigations was that the intelligence community's pathological behavior was rooted in its excessive control of information and its inadequate accountability, both inside the executive branch and in its relationship with Congress. Congress was finally moved to impose real oversight on the intelligence community. The new regime that began in the mid-1970s revolved around governmental institutions—Congress, the courts, CIA lawyers, and independent executive branch investigators known as "inspectors general"—extracting and scrutinizing information about tightly compartmentalized intelligence activities, and taking corrective action. This system of placing spies under a government microscope—which Dulles never could have imagined, and would have done everything in his power to kill—grew slowly in the 1980s and 1990s. But in the post-9/11 period, and for the first time during war, they became vital mechanisms of accountability that forced unprecedented changes in presidential wartime tactics and profoundly altered the national security bureaucracy.

THE GRAND BARGAIN

In the fall of 1975, a young lawyer working in the Treasury Department named John Rizzo applied to the CIA for a job. Rizzo didn't know a thing about espionage or covert action. But he had been transfixed by the Church and the Pike Committee hearings the year before, and saw an opportunity. "Those guys are going to need lawyers," he thought at the time.[11] Before the public scandals of the 1970s, the CIA and other intelligence agencies didn't pay much attention to the law. As William Sullivan, a top FBI intelligence officer in the 1960s, explained to the Church Committee, "During the ten years that I was on the U.S. Intelligence Board, a Board that receives the cream of intelligence for this country from all over the world and inside the

United States, never once did I hear anybody, including myself, raise the question: 'Is this course of action which we have agreed upon lawful, is it legal, is it ethical or moral?' "[12] The few lawyers inside the CIA before the mid-1970s were not consulted when the Agency planned intelligence-gathering operations or covert actions. "The custom and usage was not to deal with General Counsel, as a rule, until there were some troubles," longtime CIA counterespionage chief James Angleton said in 1975. "He was not a part of the process of project approval."[13]

This attitude changed in the mid-1970s, and Rizzo, who got the job, was part of the change. In January 1976 he became the CIA's eighteenth lawyer (and the eighth hired since the Church and Pike hearings began the year before). Over the course of his thirty-four-year career, the CIA legal staff would expand nearly tenfold as the Agency transformed itself from being indifferent to the law to being preoccupied with it. During that period, Rizzo's brown beard would turn snow white as he evolved from a Church Committee baby to the "most influential career lawyer in CIA history," as the *Los Angeles Times* put it in 2009.[14] Rizzo became famous in the CIA for his natty dress, which tended to wide pin-striped suits, pastel ties and handkerchiefs, and Armani shoes. He also became invaluable as a trusted legal adviser to ten CIA Directors who knew how to keep his many CIA clients out of trouble as they pursued dangerous operations at the edges of an increasingly hazardous legal and political landscape.

At about the time Rizzo joined the CIA, Congress and the President were working out the initial stages of a "grand bargain" that would retain presidential control over intelligence but would impose three novel forms of accountability on the President and his intelligence agencies. Congress would prescribe legal limits on where and how the CIA and others in the intelligence community collected, analyzed, and disseminated intelligence information, as well as limitations on covert actions. It would eliminate the President's plausible deniability by requiring him to approve all covert actions in a formal "finding." And it would step up oversight by creating special intelligence committees in the House and

Senate and by requiring the executive branch to inform them of its activities.

The new regime broke sharply from the past, but it was relatively casual compared to what it would become. During much of this early period, Rizzo was the only CIA lawyer in the Directorate of Operations, the branch that ran spies and conducted covert operations (and thus tended to get in legal trouble). He had a "thrill a minute" facilitating the rescue of hostages in Iran from the Canadian embassy and the failed hostage rescue in the Iranian desert, early aspects of the CIA campaign against the Soviets in Afghanistan, early support for the Nicaraguan contras and the Solidarity movement in Poland, and many other covert operations in the Soviet Union, Central America, Africa, and Asia.[15] The executive branch reported these actions to the new congressional intelligence committees, but its internal scrutiny, especially in the early Reagan years, was relatively lax.[16] "There would be occasions," Rizzo says, "when [CIA Director] Bill Casey would hand carry the proposed presidential finding into the Oval Office for Reagan to sign, and no one else in the White House or the Executive bureaucracy saw it."[17]

Casey was inadvertently responsible for strengthening these accountability mechanisms. He was a fierce anti-communist, a believer in aggressive covert operations to confront communism everywhere, and a deep skeptic of congressional restrictions on the Agency, which he thought prevented it from doing its job. Acting on these impulses, Casey helped Oliver North and others on the National Security Council and in the CIA with their 1985–1986 plans to sell arms to Iran to help secure the release of American hostages, and then to use the proceeds to support the Nicaraguan contras. These adventures flew in the teeth of the grand bargain: they skirted laws, they were not supported by timely findings, and they were not disclosed to the congressional intelligence committees. The resulting Iran-Contra scandal and recriminations upended the covert action process, wrecked many careers, and sent a few to jail. (Rizzo avoided trouble because he had left the Directorate of Operations in 1984, "burned out" after years advising Casey's spooks; he was a congressional liaison during the Iran-Contra period, and was waiting outside Casey's office to prepare him for testimony before the Senate when the Director collapsed with a seizure from which he would not recover.)

The scandal also produced the modern intelligence accountability regime. In 1991, Congress closed many loopholes in the grand bargain and ramped up restrictions on the executive branch.[18] And a chastised executive branch created elaborate bureaucratic structures, monitored closely by lawyers and others, to ensure compliance with its grand bargain duties. One innovation was a requirement for the President to certify that a planned covert action would comply with American law.[19] To meet this command, many lawyers today at the CIA and under the Director of National Intelligence vet every proposed covert action.[20] If they approve, and if the intelligence officers deem the proposed action likely to succeed and worth the risks, the proposal goes to the White House. There it is elaborately reviewed again by lawyers and policymakers from the National Security Council and the Departments of Justice, State, and Defense. It is further vetted by the "Deputies Committee" (number-two officials in the relevant departments) and the Principals Committee (the National Security Advisor and the heads of relevant departments, including the Attorney General). If approved, it goes to the President for signature. In all, more than one hundred executive branch officials, including ten or so lawyers and often more, typically weigh in. Most proposed covert actions never make it through the process, frequently because they do not pass legal muster. And the ones that do are "lawyerized to death," says Rizzo. Presidential findings in the early 1980s used to be very short, but now they are typically many pages long, full of policy prescriptions and lawyerly caveats "written for the front page of the *New York Times*" because of expected leaks, he adds.

Once the President approves a finding, it is briefed to the Senate and House intelligence committees (or in "extraordinary circumstances" to the four congressional leaders and the top-four intelligence committee leaders).[21] The executive branch must also keep the committees (or, for very sensitive intelligence activities, their top-four members) "fully and currently informed" of other U.S. intelligence activities, including "significant anticipated intelligence activity."[22] It must additionally report intelligence failures, illegal conduct, large expenditures, and more. Nothing of significance happens in American intelligence without the intelligence committees, or some subset, knowing about it. (With a notable exception—the destruction of the CIA interrogation tapes—this was true even under the obsessively secretive Bush administration.[23]) In a morning staff meeting the CIA Director might learn about an asset arrested by a foreign government, an intelligence discovery about nuclear proliferation, a proposed financial investment in a new intelligence-gathering program, the consequences of a recent drone attack, and a botched operation in South America. The CIA reports all of this information to Congress in what one senior CIA official describes as an "incessant wave of interaction between the Agency and the intelligence committees."[24] In 2009–2011, the CIA sent Congress four hundred formal congressional "notifications" (short written reports); had more than seventeen hundred other engagements with Congress, including briefings, meetings, and hearings; and responded to thirteen hundred questions for the record and hundreds of less formal ones.[25] Contrary to conventional wisdom, CIA management loves to report to the committees because it wants buy-in for its politically risky actions. As a result of executive-branch reporting duties and congressional member and staff scrutiny, the intelligence committees probably know more about what the CIA is up to than any other congressional committee knows about any other regulated agency. They also know more than all but a handful of people in the CIA and White House.

The committees lack a formal mechanism to modify or veto the intelligence actions they are told about, but they do have significant effective power to do so. They sometimes leak a proposed operation to the public. They can (despite executive secrecy) take the proposal to the full Congress and seek legislation to stop it, as happened when Congress curbed covert action in Angola in

1975.[26] They can deny funding for the operation's implementation, as they did when Congress terminated funds for the Contras in the 1980s.[27] (This was the law Casey and North circumvented, to the Agency's detriment.) Or they can take a more direct route by raising a stink with the President, either with a formal vote or through informal channels. Ronald Reagan thrice signed but then rescinded proposed covert actions in response to committee unhappiness, and President George H. W. Bush pulled back on at least one.[28] More recently, in 2004, members of the intelligence committees reportedly objected strongly to a covert action finding to support U.S.-friendly candidates in an upcoming Iraqi election—then Democratic Majority Leader of the House Nancy Pelosi reportedly "came unglued" when briefed on the operation—and President Bush rescinded the finding.[29] Presidents usually relent in the face of serious objections because they know that a covert or intelligence operation is politically much riskier, and its success less assured, if the intelligence committees are not on board, and that the committees will retaliate in other intelligence contexts if the President departs too sharply from their wishes. Presidential subordinates spend a lot of time anticipating objections from the committee (and the committee's staff), and crafting executive branch intelligence policy to meet them.

The extensive reporting duties by the executive branch, when combined with these and other tools of congressional pushback, constitute the most extensive legislative oversight arrangement, by far, of any government in the world.[30] That does not mean that the oversight is great. The intelligence committees are supposed to "act as a board of directors who verify that secret executive actions serve the interests of the shareholders—the American people," says West Virginia Senator Jay Rockefeller, a longtime member.[31] But perverse political incentives usually keep them from serving this function well. Members receive few electoral benefits from time spent in secret oversight of intelligence because they cannot dole out intelligence goodies to wealthy donors and they cannot talk in public about most of what they learn and do. In addition, most of the members never develop the specialized expertise needed for real oversight (though their staffs, which here, as in other contexts, do most of the work, are deeply knowledgeable). Members also tend not to like responsibility for national security decisions. They like to know what is going on, and some are truly engaged. But in general they don't love to be on the hook for or against controversial intelligence activities, and the examples of pushback in secret that I just described are exceptional. Most of the time, members receive the information, ask questions, and sometimes make suggestions and criticisms; but they rarely signal overt approval. Thus, when a matter becomes public and controversial, with political implications, they can distance themselves from it, claim inadequate briefing, and then do engaged oversight.

These are some of the concerns that led the 9/11 Commission to describe congressional intelligence oversight as "dysfunctional" and to put it at the top of the list of problems in U.S. national security.[32] But even dysfunctional oversight has important "before-the-fact" disciplining and accountability effects. As the elaborate bureaucracy behind every covert action exemplifies, the duties to comply with the law and report activities to Congress, combined with political and legal and personal penalties for not doing so, spark valuable deliberation and care inside the executive branch. "[S]ome awfully crazy schemes might well have been approved had everyone present not known and expected hard questions, debate and criticism from the Hill," former Secretary of Defense Robert Gates once said, reflecting on the significance of the duty to notify Congress during his jobs in the CIA and on the National Security Council.[33] The hard questions and criticism are intermittent, but the intelligence community does not know when they will come, or what operations might blow up and spark criticism. And so they prepare for them, with the self-reflection that preparation entails, in practically every case. Having to tell another institution with different and often adversarial interests what it is up to forces the executive branch to reflect on its actions, and anticipate problems.

The congressional committees are not the only ones watching. We have seen how the press and public are better than ever at watching what the intelligence community does in secret. A crucial innovation of the grand bargain, and a partial substitute for more robust congressional engagement, was Congress's delegation of the accountability process into the executive branch itself. The requirements to collect and report information are part of this delegation. So too is compliance with the bevy of laws that Congress imposes and that the executive branch translates into more detailed executive orders, regulations, and directives, many of them classified.[34] The primary enforcers of these laws—what Michael Lipsky calls "street-level bureaucrats"—are the CIA's 150 or so lawyers.[35] That number is unparalleled in the world. "The British intelligence services have a handful of lawyers, and I've never met a lawyer from the French or German intelligence services," says Rizzo. "In most parts of the world the idea that lawyers would get involved in intelligence activities is an alien concept."

CIA lawyers, by contrast, are very involved. They often serve in component offices (such as the National Counterterrorism Center), side by side with operators to ensure that they comply with U.S. law. These operators spend their days and nights on deceptive and deceitful tasks that violate foreign and some international laws as well as everyday ethics. They are constantly reminded that whatever other rules and laws they must violate in their work, they must not violate U.S. law. In this environment lawyers are in great demand. "Watch your back and get a lawyer" is the attitude in the Directorate of Operations (now the National Clandestine Service), says Rizzo. Lawyers help operators sort through the cognitive dissonance that arises from the twin injunctions to violate some laws and norms but not others. And they provide comfort that whatever other fallout might occur from their CIA activities, operators needn't worry about violating what to them often seem like bewildering U.S. legal restrictions.

The obvious danger in this secret environment is that the lawyers will identify too closely with their clients' missions and not provide sufficiently detached legal advice. This sometimes happens in the CIA just as in other parts of the executive branch or any organization. But CIA lawyers have learned from bitter experience that poor legal advice will lead to scrutiny and calumny, and they are on the whole careful and precise in their legal judgments. They often say "no" to proposed intelligence or covert operations, or suggest changes to shape the operation to comply with the law. "[T]he lawyers assigned to the Directorate of Operations are not always perceived as part of a team by their clients but, rather, a hurdle that must be surmounted before the operators can do their jobs," Senator Bob Graham said in October 2002.[36]

The public rarely learns about these quotidian acts of intelligence accountability. It instead usually knows only about approvals of controversial actions that leak, often in misleading ways and usually in ways the Agency, because of secrecy restrictions, cannot explain or defend. Most in the public are also unaware that every CIA employee must tell the CIA General Counsel about a violation of laws or agency rules.[37] When senior CIA officials learn about a "possible violation" of federal criminal law from this or any other source, they must tell the Justice Department.[38] According to former CIA lawyer John Radsan, the CIA makes "several referrals to the Justice Department in a typical month."[39] The referrals are not signs of lawlessness, but rather of an accountability system working well. The very soft trigger of "possible" as opposed to "actual" violations promotes reporting of anything near the line so that the career lawyers at the Justice Department can decide the appropriate action in the first instance. CIA officials must also notify Congress and the President's Intelligence Oversight Board of unlawful action, and these bodies can also take action in response.

Democratic accountability for secret intelligence activities is one of the hardest problems in constitutional government because public debate and review of these activities are inconsistent with the intelligence mission. The American solution to this problem since the Iran-Contra affair has been to impose legal requirements on the intelligence community and then to give incentives to multiple decentralized and very different actors to scrutinize intelligence activities outside of public view to make

sure they are lawful and proper. Demanding reporting requirements, uneven intelligence committee oversight, large bureaucracies of compliance, lawyers everywhere, and a duty that
everyone report wrongdoing, taken together, significantly reduce
the secrecy *inside* the intelligence world that in Allen Dulles's day
was so vital to avoiding accountability for secret actions. The
CIA does controversial things and it makes its share of mistakes.
But everyone in the CIA knows that trouble follows from violating U.S. law. They also know that many people in the Agency,
as well as intelligence committee members and their staffers,
along with lawyers in the Justice Department, are watching for
violations and can impose various types of legal or political punishment if they find one. The most powerful and feared internal
government watcher, however, is not a member of Congress, a
lawyer, or a whistle-blower, but rather a man with the boring
title of "inspector general."

The Inspector General's Review

John Rizzo was the number-two lawyer in the CIA on September
11, 2001, but his boss, Robert McNamara Jr., retired two months
later, and for all but two of the next eight years Rizzo was the
CIA's top lawyer. Unfortunately for Rizzo, that meant that he was
the man the CIA leadership turned to for legal advice about the
CIA's secret program of detention and interrogation, and he was
the man to whom many of the infamous Justice Department legal
opinions approving controversial interrogation techniques were
addressed. As is now well known, the CIA cobbled together this
program quickly after the capture of senior al Qaeda leader Abu
Zubaydah in March 2002. The Agency believed Zubaydah possessed imminent threat information as well as actionable intelligence on future threats.[40] But it had little recent experience in
detention and interrogation, and it scrambled to put together a
program to extract that information. The program would be for-
malized to include ten authorized "enhanced interrogation tech-

niques," including sleep deprivation, cramped confinement with an insect, and waterboarding.

When Rizzo was approached to vet the inchoate program in the spring of 2002, he had no experience with interrogation or detention or the law surrounding it, and no insight into the efficacy of what was being proposed. He immediately knew that the potential fallout from the program was very high, no matter how the CIA proceeded. The Agency had just suffered its greatest intelligence failure, many of its leaders felt personally responsible, and the public imperative was for everyone in government, including lawyers, to be as forward-leaning as possible. Six months later, Senator Bob Graham would send the message that "lawyers assigned to the posts in the Directorate of Operations" must discard the "risk aversion" that had prevailed in the pre-9/11 period, but the CIA had received a similar message long before.[41] In this environment, Rizzo worried that the proposed interrogation techniques might look too passive if they failed to uncover information that would have prevented another attack. "If the techniques came to light in a recriminatory hearing after another attack, with all the restrictions and precautions and scrutiny by lawyers and doctors and psychologists, we'd look like a bunch of pussies," Rizzo thought. On the other hand, he and others in the CIA knew they were treading in dangerous legal and political waters, and that support for aggressive action would shift over time. "Would you rather get in trouble for being too aggressive in handling top al Qaeda guys or for not being aggressive enough when there are bodies in the streets?" was how Rizzo recalls the choice at the time. Given the failures on 9/11, the mood of the country, and prevailing threat reports, the CIA made the decision to be aggressive. "Ten years from now we're going to be sorry we're doing this," one CIA officer said in 2003, "[but] it has to be done."[42]

To maximize support for the program and minimize its fallout, Rizzo advised the CIA to tell as many people as possible. "I had a fairly developed sense of what might blow up in our faces, and I always tried to spread the knowledge as much as I could," he later recalled.[43] On September 17, 2001, the President had given the CIA a general "authorization for the CIA interrogation and detention program."[44] The CIA did not rest on this authorization alone. It made sure that the White House and the National Security Council, including the Attorney General, explicitly supported the new steps. The CIA would go back to these officials again and again over the years for reaffirmation "that the CIA program was lawful and reflected administration policy."[45] It also sought legal approval from the Justice Department. Rizzo had "mercifully never studied the torture statute" or related laws before 9/11, but he and his lawyers ruled out a few of the proposed techniques and then sent the others, which Rizzo thought were "close to the line at a minimum," for Justice Department scrutiny.[46] The Office of Legal Counsel responded to his request with the infamous and much-maligned legal opinions of August 2002 that narrowly interpreted the torture statute, broadly interpreted presidential power, and gave the CIA wide latitude for interrogation.[47] Rizzo did not rest on these opinions alone. He also told the Justice Department's Criminal Division and the FBI chief of staff about the plan to interrogate Zubaydah, and in general he kept the Justice Department in the loop.[48] The main departure from bureaucratic protocol was that State Department lawyers, at the insistence of the White House, were not shown the Office of Legal Counsel's legal opinions, though the Secretary of State was briefed on the program.

In September 2002, soon after the program was approved, the CIA also spent more than an hour briefing the top-four intelligence committee officials (Porter Goss, Nancy Pelosi, Bob Graham, and Richard Shelby) and some on their staff about the interrogation program and the just-approved techniques.[49] The White House's insistence on briefing this subset rather than the entire intelligence committees was technically compliant with the grand bargain, but in retrospect Rizzo thought that not getting broader and deeper committee buy-in at the outset was the Agency's biggest mistake. Nonetheless, the members of Congress originally told about the program raised few concerns. In fact, consistent with Rizzo's worries that the techniques might seem weak-kneed, two of the lawmakers "asked if the methods were tough enough," according to one CIA participant, and urged the CIA to push harder.[50]

There would be at least thirty more congressional briefings over the next few years before the program became public.[51] One member, Jane Harman, worried about the "profound policy questions" raised by the program and sought assurance that "the most senior levels of the White House have determined that these practices are consistent with the principles and policies of the United States."[52] But there was no pushback beyond this from members of Congress. When the program became public, many members ran for cover, claiming that they were inadequately briefed and that secrecy prevented them from doing anything in response. But these complaints rang hollow. The members could have (as they did in many other contexts) asked for more information and follow-up briefings. And as Nancy Pelosi's reported shutdown of the proposed covert action for Iraqi elections the following year showed, committee members knew how to push back against secret presidential actions when they wanted. The members briefed on the program did not push for more at the time because they, like those in the executive branch running the program in 2002–2003, were mortified by the threat information and disinclined to play it safe.

And so in sharp contrast to the go-go days under Allen Dulles and the still free-wheeling days under Bill Casey, the CIA carefully told officials throughout the executive branch and a few in Congress about what they proposed to do, and garnered their support in various forms. Contrary to Rizzo's hopes, this support would not protect the Agency when things started to go wrong. The trouble began in late November 2002, when James Pavitt, who led the Directorate of Operations, learned of a terrible incident at a CIA detention facility under his supervision.[53] (Years later, new reports maintained that the incident was the death by hypothermia of a detainee name Gul Rahman at a detention facility near Kabul known as the "Salt Pit.")[54] After consulting with CIA Director George Tenet and the new General Counsel, Scott Muller (who took over the top lawyer spot from Rizzo for nearly two years starting in the fall of 2002), Pavitt took two steps.[55] He dispatched his own team from the CIA to investigate the incident. And he informed John Helgerson, the CIA's inspector general, about it. Two months later, Pavitt told Helgerson that CIA officers had used unauthorized interrogation techniques, including a possible mock execution, on senior al Qaeda leader Abd al-Rahim al-Nashiri at a different foreign detention site. This time, Pavitt asked Helgerson to investigate the matter himself. At about the same time, Helgerson began to hear from "a number of individuals" that CIA activities in overseas detention sites "might involve violations of human rights," as Helgerson later put it.[56] In January 2003, Helgerson opened a full review of all of the CIA's detention and interrogation activities.

Inspectors general, or IGs, are watchdogs that have been sprinkled around the executive branch since George Washington named Baron Frederick von Steuben to be inspector general for the Continental Army. In 1978, as part of its post-Watergate resurgence, Congress gave them extraordinary functional independence within the executive branch and made them more beholden to Congress. These new "statutory IGs" are confirmed by the Senate and must report semiannually to Congress. They have access to all records and information inside the relevant agency and full power to launch investigations, issue subpoenas, and refer criminal wrongdoing to the Justice Department. The CIA was originally exempt from the 1978 inspector general law. But in reaction to the Iran-Contra affair, Congress closed this loophole in late November 1989.[57] The Berlin Wall had fallen three weeks earlier, calling the Agency's traditional mission into doubt; and now internal walls of secrecy within CIA had fallen as well.

The first independent CIA inspector general, a boisterous former CIA operations officer named Frederick Hitz, undertook over four hundred investigations and had a reputation as a "take-no-prisoners investigator," according to *Newsweek*.[58] His job is "to walk through the battlefield while the smoke cleared and shoot the wounded," Hitz would sometimes say, in a comment that still characterizes how many in the Agency view his office today.[59] Hitz was controversial in a CIA unfamiliar with independent internal scrutiny, especially since he was sometimes unsubtle about wielding his new powers. Through his high-profile investigations of CIA malfeasance, most notably the lax counterespionage safeguards that allowed Aldrich Ames to flourish as a Soviet mole, Hitz established the office's independence and cemented "a heightened awareness of the need for accountability" at the CIA, as he said at his retirement.[60]

John Helgerson became the CIA's third independent inspector general in May 2002. An earnest, genial man, Helgerson came to the job with three decades of experience in the Agency and impeccable credentials. He entered the CIA with a Ph.D. in political science from Duke University and grew up on the CIA's analytical side, the Directorate of Intelligence, where he focused on the Middle East, Africa, and Latin America before rising to lead the entire Directorate during the presidency of George H. W. Bush. Helgerson also ran the CIA's congressional affairs office in the 1980s, where he got to know Senate Intelligence Committee staffer George Tenet and the congressman most interested in CIA matters, Representative Richard Cheney. Helgerson additionally served as deputy director of the government's imagery and mapping agency and as the deputy to the second post-reform CIA inspector general, Britt Snider. CIA Director George Tenet thought so highly of Helgerson's analytical abilities that in August 2001 he put him in charge of the National Intelligence Council, the think tank for the intelligence community that produces national intelligence estimates. Early the following year Tenet had no qualms about recommending that the President nominate Helgerson to become inspector general. "John's breadth and depth of experience at CIA and throughout the Intelligence Community— as well as his sense of fairness and his absolute integrity—make him eminently qualified for this demanding and extraordinarily important position," he said at the time.[61]

Helgerson did not seek anyone's permission when he decided to review the full range of CIA detention and interrogation activities in January 2003. He simply informed the CIA's most senior managers what he was doing, put a dozen investigators, auditors, and inspectors on the matter, and plunged ahead. Helgerson came to the task with two attitudes ingrained by decades as a CIA analyst. First was what he once described as "the need to dig to get the facts and to accept nothing at face value, and to offer independent conclusions."[62] Second was a natural apprehension about the escapades of officials in the Directorate of Operations, whom Helgerson gently describes as "insular."[63] Helgerson in particular held a dim view of CIA involvement in the interrogation business. He was familiar with the CIA's doleful experience in that business in connection with its Latin American training programs in 1980s.[64] And he had cautioned senior Agency management about the pitfalls of getting involved in the interrogations in the spring of 2002, before he was confirmed as inspector general. "You guys have got to be sure you dig out the files and talk to the right people to learn of the problems the Agency ran into on these interrogation issues in earlier go rounds so we don't repeat them," he advised. "I don't want to spend my time as Inspector General looking into all interrogation stuff because that has the potential to take over everything."[65]

Helgerson had promised the Senate in his confirmation hearings to find and report the "unvarnished truth" in his investigations, and that is what he set out to do.[66] His team included career CIA officers as well as former FBI and other law enforcement investigators with little sympathy for the fraternity culture in the Directorate of Operations. They interviewed everyone of note involved in the program, including senior officials and the lawyers. Over a hundred people were questioned, often several times. Helgerson's team also requested and received more than thirty-eight thousand documents related to the program. And his team watched every one of the later-destroyed interrogation videos.[67] In theory Bush could have fired Helgerson, or George Tenet could have stopped his investigation to "protect vital national security secrets of the United States."[68] But either action would have been political suicide on Capitol Hill. The CIA inspector general's role is so well established that it never occurred to anyone to decline to comply with his many requests. "Our office received as good cooperation as could have been reasonably expected, given the far reaching and complex nature of the review," Helgerson would later say.[69]

Everyone cooperated, but few liked it. Helgerson says he received extensive encouragement for his investigation from the Agency workforce. "I could not walk through the cafeteria without people walking up to me, not to complain but to say 'More power to you.'"[70] He also says he received support from a few people involved in the matter under review. But most Agency officers subject to the review weren't so pleased. Those who engaged in unauthorized interrogation techniques or who were associated with detention deaths understandably worried about their fate and lawyered up. But Helgerson's rigorous and far-reaching review also scared the hell out of CIA management, operators, and most of the lawyers who had stayed within the four corners of legal and political guidance. These officials took no pleasure in running the detention and interrogation program. They had little sympathy for interrogators who acted beyond the strictures of their guidance. But they believed that Helgerson had a puritanical distaste for coercive interrogations that was leading him beyond his proper review tasks to second-guess the hard policy decisions that the President and the CIA Director had made in initiating the program. They complained that they were spending as much time responding to Helgerson's queries as they did fighting terrorists. Some came to view Helgerson's team as disorganized, mistake-prone, unfamiliar with the realities of counterterrorism, infected by hindsight bias, and prosecutorial in tone and approach.[71]

Meanwhile, there was still a war to be fought. Helgerson's menacing review began a little over a year after 9/11, when the threat from al Qaeda was still poorly understood and harrowing. Some of the hardest calls the CIA made about the operation of the detention and interrogation program—such as the aggressive interrogation of 9/11 mastermind Khalid Sheikh Mohammed in March 2003—took place practically under the critical gaze of the

Office of Inspector General. CIA officials trying desperately to prevent another attack would spend part of their days approving, monitoring, and analyzing interrogations and transfers, and other parts answering probing questions by Helgerson's team or digging for e-mails and documents that it requested. To make matters worse, Helgerson was at the same time, at Congress's request, conducting a critical review of senior CIA management for its failures in preventing the 9/11 attacks.[72] Many CIA officials would later take "strong exception" to the "focus, methodology and conclusions" of Helgerson's final 9/11 report, as CIA Director Michael Hayden stated in 2007. But in 2003–2004, Helgerson's simultaneous investigations of the 9/11 failure and the interrogation/detention program signaled to the leadership at Langley that the Agency was both too passive (before 9/11) and too aggressive (after 9/11). For the men and women still devastated by their failures to prevent the 9/11 attack and scrambling in the face of enormous uncertainties to prevent another, the seemingly contradictory messages, both backed by implicit threats of professional ruin or worse, were infuriating.

Helgerson completed his comprehensive 109-page report—blandly titled *Special Review: Counterterrorism Detention and Interrogation Activities (September 2001–October 2003)*—in May 2004. He presented it first to senior CIA managers and executive branch officials, and then a month later he gave it to the congressional intelligence leadership and briefed them on it.[73] The report made clear that the Agency was no rogue elephant, but rather had sought and received presidential approval for the program and legal guidance from the Department of Justice, and had repeatedly briefed the National Security Council and senior congressional leadership about the program, all without complaint. It noted that with little prior expertise and under intense time pressure, the Agency "invested immense time and effort to implement [the program] quickly, effectively, and within the law." It also noted that the program had "provided intelligence that has enabled the identification and apprehension of other terrorists and warned of terrorist plots planned for the United States and around the world," though it could not assess the effectiveness of particular interrogation techniques.

On the critical side, the report documented some ill-considered or illegal actions that had taken place prior to the establishment of the CIA's formal detention and interrogation program, and explained that many aspects of the program itself, especially in its early days, were poorly organized and managed. It chastised CIA lawyers for not obtaining comprehensive legal support from the Department of Justice. And most notably, it catalogued in detail two deaths (both of which occurred outside of the official detention program) and instances of "unauthorized, improvised, inhumane, and undocumented detention and interrogation techniques," including waterboarding Khalid Sheikh Mohammed 183 times, threatening detainees with unloaded weapons and power drills, blowing cigar smoke in detainees' faces, and forcing them into various stress positions. (John Rizzo thought the report was "balanced," but according to Obama's then CIA Director Leon Panetta, other CIA lawyers and Directorate of Operations officials disagreed with some of Helgerson's findings and conclusions.)[74]

Helgerson's independent review of the CIA's detention and interrogation activities in real time is without parallel in American wartime history. Before the review began, and in anticipation of it, CIA lawyers devised better training and approval guidelines.[75] (Most of the abuses Helgerson catalogued happened before these changes.) Helgerson's report made ten formal recommendations, eight of which the Agency adopted. The CIA conducted the program more cautiously after the review, and the waterboarding technique was never again used after 2003. There were many other consequences of the review, described below. The point for now is to recognize how important the inspector general has become as a fount of accountability inside the presidency's secretive national security bureaucracy. The leaders of the congressional intelligence committees lacked the political will to thoroughly examine the CIA program, as well as the time and resources of Helgerson's team. Moreover, in the early years after 9/11, separation-of-powers objections by the executive branch—classified information, executive privilege, attorney-client privilege, and the like—would have prevented them from anything close to Helgerson's full access to CIA personnel and documents as well as to Department of Justice and CIA legal memoranda. But by giving Helgerson a perch inside the CIA and comprehensive power to investigate, to collect information, to analyze it, and to send it to the Hill, Congress circumvents these hurdles and gets deep inside the presidency. Congress in effect delegates its initial oversight function to the inspector general, who can quickly gather a much more complete understanding of executive branch activity than Congress itself could have.

What Helgerson did inside the CIA is emblematic of the role that inspectors general across the government have played since 9/11. Glenn Fine, the inspector general of the Department of Justice, was just as forceful. On his own initiative he launched critical investigations into the FBI's roundup of illegal aliens in the panicked weeks and months after 9/11 and into its involvement with Defense Department and CIA interrogation practices in Guantanamo Bay, Afghanistan, and Iraq.[76] Like Helgerson, Fine saw his office "as an independent entity that reports to both the Attorney General and Congress."[77] But in truth, Fine, like Helgerson, acted more as an agent of Congress than of the President. In the post-9/11 period, Congress increasingly asked inspectors general to do national security investigations within the executive branch that Congress never could have done as quickly or effectively. Helgerson's investigation of responsibility for 9/11 was an example of this, as were Fine's reform-minded reports on FBI terrorist watch lists and the FBI's methods of obtaining personal and business records.[78] Since 2001, pursuant to a requirement of the PATRIOT Act, Fine also reviewed allegations of civil liberties abuses and dutifully reported them to Congress (and the public) twice each year, which then acted on them.[79] Congress also charged Fine and a team of inspectors general to do a "comprehensive report" of the controversial Terrorist Surveillance Program of warrantless wiretapping.[80] Congress continued this pattern in a 2010 intelligence law that created an independent inspector general for the Office of the Director of National Intelligence and gave inspectors general around the national security world many new tasks.[81]

In 1978, Jimmy Carter's Justice Department concluded that the placement of powerful independent inspectors general inside the presidency "violat[es] the doctrine of separation of powers."[82] Two decades later, and just three years before 9/11, a bipartisan group of distinguished experts described inspectors general as "congressional ferrets of dubious constitutionality."[83] Today, constitutional doubts about these congressional ferrets are largely gone. Inspectors general have grown in stature and power and have become an established, legitimate, and consequential mechanism of executive branch accountability, even in wartime. Despite presidential resistance, Congress has expanded their jurisdiction to every corner of the national security bureaucracy except the White House itself. It has steadily increased their size, power, and responsibilities over the years. And it consistently gives them political support in their clashes with the executive branch.

Many executive branch officials dislike or distrust inspectors general, sometimes with good reason. Inspectors general are not angels. Like all bureaucrats, they have biases, their competence varies, and they make mistakes. There is a genuine question, which I examine later, about who guards these powerful guardians. But on the whole, executive branch anxiety about inspectors general is a testament to their independence and effectiveness. What critics fail to appreciate is how credible independent inspectors general inside the executive branch can enhance executive power.

The 2008 amendments to the Foreign Intelligence Surveillance Act are a good example.[84] Beginning in 2004, lawyers inside the government, and then leaks to the press, and then a secret surveillance court, pushed back against excesses in President Bush's controversial Terrorist Surveillance Program. By 2008, President Bush needed new legislation to keep the program going, and Congress obliged with new surveillance powers that were viewed by some as a capitulation to presidential unilateralism. "A weak Democratic Congress passed a law giving the Bush administration virtually unchecked power to intercept Americans' international e-mail messages and telephone calls," charged ACLU Executive Director Anthony Romero.[85] But this characterization is wrong. The Democratic Congress was convinced that the pre-9/11 surveillance regime had been overtaken by technological developments and needed to be more flexible to redress modern terrorism and related foreign intelligence collection challenges. The consensus was that the executive branch should be given power to surveil persons reasonably believed to be outside the United States as long as it took careful steps to redact or eliminate conversations of innocent Americans.

The problems were that Congress did not trust the executive branch, especially the Bush administration, to use these new powers faithfully; and it did not trust itself to undertake the hard work of oversight needed to ensure compliance with its mandate. A major part of the solution to these problems was to empower inspectors general around the national security bureaucracy to regularly analyze the procedures used for targeting persons outside the United States and for redacting U.S.-person conversations, and to regularly report its results to Congress, which can then decide—after the hard information-gathering work has been done, inside the executive branch—if the law is being implemented as it wishes.[86] In explaining his vote for the law, the then senator and presidential candidate Barack Obama specifically referenced the inspector general guarantees that he believed "ensures that there will be accountability going forward."[87] (The new law also imposed other credible constraints, including advance review by a court of the legality of the procedures, and scores of legal restrictions on the executive branch that are enforced by "a bevy of lawyers crawling up their asses all the time," as one senior Department of Justice official said.)[88] The executive branch likely would not have received the modernized surveillance powers that are so crucial in the fight against hard-to-find terrorists if not for the existence of a credible inspector general that Congress could trust to monitor and enforce restrictions on presidential discretion in secret. In these and other respects, the institution of inspector general has empowered the presidency by constraining it.

OFFICIAL SCRUTINY

What John Helgerson uncovered and put in his report comprised the foundation of many subsequent government-wide investigations of the CIA detention and interrogation program, some of which are still going on today. No CIA program—including the ones that underlay the Iran-Contra scandal and the many investigated during the Church and the Pike Committee hearings— has ever undergone so much extended or critical scrutiny. In the process both the CIA and the accountability system governing it changed fundamentally.

Helgerson followed up the initial review with more focused investigations of the detention program and the CIA's rendition program as well.[89] He eventually referred twenty or so cases for criminal investigation by career Justice Department prosecutors.[90] One of these cases—Helgerson called it the most severe—resulted in a prosecution: CIA contractor David Passaro was convicted of assaulting Abdul Wali, who died in an Afghanistan prison in the summer of 2003.[91] Some saw a whitewash in the refusal to prosecute others in 2003, but the truth is more benign. "The fact that we do a crime report does not necessarily mean that we believe it should be prosecuted," Helgerson explained.[92] Congress required him to tell the Justice Department about "*any* information, allegation, or complaint" relating to a possible violation of federal criminal law, regardless of whether he thinks an actual crime was committed.[93] Prosecutors, by contrast, must convince a jury of a crime beyond a reasonable doubt. The career prosecutors who first examined the inspector general referrals concluded that they lacked sufficient evidence of criminal conduct, criminal intent, or the subject's involvement to bring charges.[94] A few cases were close calls, and would later be reopened. But after circling the globe to examine witnesses and evidence, the career prosecutors in 2004 concluded that they could not "probably . . . obtain and sustain a conviction," as Justice Department regulations require before bringing charges.[95] "The professionals at DOJ looked with considerable care at the various serious cases" and "spent countless hours in our work spaces," Helgerson later said, satisfied with their decisions.[96]

This was not nearly the end of the matter. After the Justice Department review came scrutiny before the CIA "Accountability Boards." An Accountability Board is an ad hoc group of CIA officials convened by the CIA Director to assess whether CIA officials failed to act "in a professional and satisfactory manner," and if so, whether they should be subject to disciplinary action ranging from a reprimand to termination.[97] Time before a CIA Accountability Board is a mark of dishonor that, during the review (which can take a long time), puts one's career on hold. Some CIA officials involved in detention and interrogation quit the Agency rather than face an Accountability Board.[98] Others went before a board and were sanctioned with "administrative penalties," including salary cuts and demotions.[99] One who was "reprimanded and reassigned" eventually quit the Agency but was later hired as a CIA contractor.[100] Some were pilloried in public even though they were cleared by an Accountability Board and had done nothing wrong. Others, including those allegedly involved in the death of Gul Rahman, were deemed to warrant no disciplinary sanction and were later promoted.[101]

Parallel to these CIA proceedings, the Justice Department's ethics office, drawing on Helgerson's work, spent nearly six years examining the opinions of the Justice Department lawyers who gave the CIA advice about the program in 2002. These opinions were written quickly and under intense pressure and fear of another attack and contained some widely documented legal errors.[102] The ethics investigators were looking into whether the errors were intentional or reckless, and thus amounted to professional misconduct. To answer this question they critically analyzed every draft of the opinion, every citation (and citation format) in each draft, every handwritten comment on each draft, and every e-mail and other communication related in any way to the drafts and the final opinions. They also conducted interviews, not only of the lawyers under investigation, but also of CIA lawyers (including Rizzo) and other Department of Justice lawyers (including me). No Justice Department lawyer has ever been subject to this sort of scrutiny.[103] The 261-page final report, issued six months after Barack Obama became President, contained dozens of new revelations about the origins and early operation of the CIA program and concluded that Jay Bybee and John Yoo, the authors of the legal opinions, committed professional misconduct.[104] A senior career Justice Department lawyer named David Margolis overturned this conclusion on the grounds that the ethics investigators themselves had done shoddy work.[105] But he too was critical of Yoo and Bybee, and the two lawyers' reputations were damaged by the episode.

Congress got into the investigatory act in March 2009, when the Senate Intelligence Committee launched a comprehensive inquiry into the origins and implementation of the CIA program, and the intelligence information it generated. The CIA provided unprecedented cooperation. In a nondescript secure building in the Virginia suburbs near the Beltway Loop, intelligence committee members and their staffers, with the assistance of half a dozen CIA employees, are able to peruse over four million pages of CIA records relating to its detention and interrogation program, including raw CIA cables, other operational documents, and e-mails.[106] Because this and related investigations require what CIA Director Leon Panetta modestly described as "large volumes of old information" and threatened to impose huge burdens on the CIA's "counterterrorism cadre," Panetta created a special "Review Group," populated by officers from across the Agency, to coordinate the response.[107] The investigation is still going on in December 2011, and its conclusions are now unknown. But it seems impossible that such a thorough ex post facto scrub of a repudiated program by a committee embarrassed by its poor oversight will not result in many findings adverse to the CIA.

There was also a multiyear criminal investigation of the CIA detention and interrogation program in addition to the cases referred to the Justice Department by Helgerson. In January 2008, Attorney General Michael Mukasey appointed career prosecutor John Durham to determine whether the CIA's destruction of ninety-two videotape recordings of its interrogation sessions was a crime.[108] (The House Intelligence Committee began a parallel investigation around the same time.) The head of the National Clandestine Service (formerly the Directorate of Operations), Jose Rodriguez, ordered the tapes destroyed on November 9, 2005, contrary to John Rizzo's advice.[109] Durham's investigation ranged far beyond the tapes to every corner of the program.[110] The CIA spent thousands of hours looking for and turning over hundreds of thousands of pages of documents. Senior and junior CIA officials, including many top lawyers, testified before a grand jury, often several times. Durham announced in 2010 that he would not bring criminal charges for the destruction of the tapes.

This was not the end of his work, however. In August 2009 Attorney General Eric Holder ordered Durham to reinvestigate a few of the CIA cases that prosecutors had previously investigated and decided did not warrant prosecution.[111] Holder's decision to reopen these cases—after the CIA had relied on the earlier decision not to prosecute as a basis for its own sanctions—was unprecedented and demoralizing to the men and women of the CIA who had been told that the matter was behind them after the inspector general, Justice Department, and Accountability Boards had done their work. Now they once again had to go through the distracting and psychologically draining process of lawyering up, spending dozens of hours refreshing their memories of seven- to eight-year-old events and documents, and preparing for and facing a grand jury under oath. Durham subsequently examined 101 instances of possible CIA involvement with terrorist detainees. He concluded that for all but two—involving deaths of detainees in CIA custody who were not part of the high-value detention and interrogation program—further criminal investigation was "not warranted."[112] Most in the CIA were relieved by this outcome. "It's good that he's narrowed things down to two cases," said one former CIA official involved in the investigation.

"On the other hand, he's been looking at these cases for two years and all he can say is they need more investigating? It's draining on people involved. On resources. We need some sort of finality."[113]

FOIA

The final form of official government scrutiny of the CIA interrogation and detention program was in many ways the most extraordinary. Throughout 2009, the Obama administration released to the public modestly redacted versions of the initial Helgerson report, the many Justice Department legal memos for the CIA program, papers discussing the value of intelligence gleaned from the program, scores of top-secret CIA communications, and many other highly classified documents related to the program. This opening of the CIA's most secret files, during war and so soon after the operation had ended, had never happened before. Nor had the disclosure of so many highly classified Justice Department legal memoranda.

The Obama administration took these extraordinary steps in the face of fierce criticism that it was jeopardizing national security. It did so, as President Obama vaguely said in March 2009, "as part of an ongoing court case," and as Leon Panetta said six months later, in "respon[se] to court orders."[114] The case in question was before New York Federal Judge Alvin Hellerstein, who had ordered the administration to process the documents for possible disclosure in response to a letter that a then thirty-one-year-old ACLU lawyer, Jameel Jaffer, along with his ACLU colleague Amrit Singh and four other human rights lawyers, wrote on October 7, 2003, to the CIA and the Departments of Defense, Justice, and State. "Please disclose . . . [a]ll records setting forth or discussing policies, procedures or guidelines relating to the torture or other cruel, inhuman or degrading treatment or punishment of Detainees," the letter asked.[115]

Jaffer, Singh, and their colleagues made this improbable request under the Freedom of Information Act (FOIA), a 1966 law designed to allow public access to government information.

FOIA requires the government to turn over requested documents, but it has many exemptions. If the government invokes an exemption, a judge can decide if it is valid, but the resulting litigation is often lengthy and expensive. In 1974, the reform-minded Congress narrowed one FOIA exemption from a blanket ban on disclosing classified information to one on disclosing "*properly* classified" information.[116] It also gave judges rather than the executive branch the final say on what is properly classified, and required agencies to produce the "segregable" portions of a document after deleting portions that are exempt.[117] At the time Senator Ted Kennedy stated in Congress that he hoped judges would use these provisions to redress "widespread abuses raging under the existing classification process."[118] But they did not, tending instead to defer to the executive branch representations that national security secrets must remain secret. FOIA was so ineffective in getting CIA documents that in 1992 a prominent court concluded that "we are now only a short step from exempting all CIA records from FOIA."[119] The hurdles to requests like the ACLU's grew higher still when the Bush administration issued new guidelines and orders after 9/11 making it harder for bureaucrats to reveal information in FOIA proceedings that touched on national security.[120]

These hurdles led most news organizations not to make FOIA requests in the early years after 9/11 in connection with highly classified matters. But Jaffer and his young ACLU colleagues had the right mix of idealism, smarts, and determination to give it a try. Jaffer was a relative newcomer to the world of national security law and human rights activism. He had come to the ACLU the year before from an equity derivatives practice at a New York corporate law firm, after a revelatory pro bono stint representing an innocent and frightened young Afghan man detained by the FBI in New Jersey soon after 9/11 had caused him to rethink his priorities. His senior ACLU colleagues expressed "enormous skepticism" when he filed the FOIA request, according to ACLU Executive Director Anthony Romero.[121] But Jaffer was not entirely naive. "I won't pretend that we thought we had a good chance of getting very much of this stuff," he later said. "In part we thought that filing the request would be a way of bringing attention to this issue and perhaps putting some pressure on the administration."[122]

Jaffer and others had grown frustrated over the tepid public and congressional reaction to press reports in 2001–2003 that the U.S. government was aggressively interrogating captured terrorists in secret and might be engaging in torture. "We thought these news stories were shocking, and were astounded that so few people were paying attention to them," Jaffer later said. He knew the FOIA case would be an uphill battle, but he hoped that a Bush administration refusal to release documents would "draw attention to the interrogation issue and raise the question of whether the administration's interrogation policies were legitimately being kept secret." Jaffer and his team also "thought the government might release useful information in the course of explaining why it was withholding some of the documents we'd requested."[123] If the government coughed up a few documents along the way, so much the better.

For many months after the ACLU sent its letter, the government—and especially the CIA and Defense Department—dragged its feet looking for the documents. But then the Abu Ghraib photos became public and gave credibility to the ACLU's concerns. Jaffer's team refiled its request and asked a federal court in New York to require the government to respond. The case was assigned to Hellerstein, an experienced judge with a reputation for fairness. Hellerstein is a proud former judge advocate general who was deeply offended by the Abu Ghraib photos and the allegations of abuse circling around the military and CIA. He did not bend over backward to help the ACLU, and his dozens of rulings in the case are models of judicial even-handedness. But he took the FOIA seriously and he was not cowed by the government's national security protestations.

"Ours is a government of laws, laws duly promulgated and laws duly observed," began his forceful 2004 opinion granting the ACLU's request. "One of our laws" is FOIA, and it, "no less than any other, must be duly observed." Hellerstein ordered the government to carry out its FOIA duty to search for the documents, identify them publicly (in a document called a "Vaughn Declaration"), and assert any exemptions from its duty to disclose. He noted that "[m]erely raising national security concerns cannot justify unlimited delay," and accused the government of displaying "an indifference to the commands of FOIA" and failing "to afford accountability of government that the act requires." And then he gave official voice to what many suspected when he said that "if the documents are more of an embarrassment than a secret, the public should know of our government's treatment of individuals captured and held abroad."

Some agencies quickly responded to Hellerstein's wake-up call. In late 2004 and early 2005, the FBI, seeking to distance itself from the growing scandal let loose by the Abu Ghraib photos, gave the ACLU documents in which its agents described abusive Defense Department interrogation techniques as well as FBI prohibitions on participating in them. These damning revelations from inside the supposedly unitary executive branch—the beginning of an avalanche of documents about interrogation excesses that would be revealed through the FOIA over the next few years—gave public credence to concerns that the Abu Ghraib abuse might be systemic. In contrast to the FBI, the more secretive CIA was not so forthcoming. Under Hellerstein's command it produced long "Vaughn Declarations" that identified documents covered by the ACLU request; but it declined to produce the vast majority of the documents, arguing that they were covered by FOIA exemptions.

Getting the CIA to cough up these secret documents would take the ACLU and its advocacy partners years of litigation, more than twelve thousand hours of legal work, over 250 legal briefs presented before Judge Hellerstein, endless hours scrutinizing every CIA exemption, and many-dozen important and innovative orders and opinions from Hellerstein duly enforcing FOIA's commands. The ACLU could devote these massive resources to the case because after 9/11 it had grown much richer. "Bush, Cheney, Addington, and Yoo were my best solicitors," says Anthony Romero, half-jokingly, explaining how his organization's membership nearly doubled and its budget more than tripled in the decade after 9/11.[124] The ACLU also had indispensable pro bono help from a New Jersey law firm. The rise of well-resourced advocacy groups that scrutinize government national security actions, supported by "free" legal help from even better-resourced private law firms, is one of the great accountability innovations of the last decade (and is explored more in Chapter 6). The resources and persistence of these institutions—subsidized and thus encouraged by the government itself, which reimburses FOIA plaintiffs for fees if they prevail—was vital in making FOIA work.

So too was Hellerstein's doggedness. "The case before Judge Hellerstein was one of the most difficult FOIA cases the government has ever faced, because he was exceptionally aggressive in pressuring multiple intelligence agencies to process FOIA requests for enormous amounts of extraordinarily sensitive records under a hellacious timetable," says Dan Metcalfe, a government-wide FOIA expert who from 1981 to 2007 ran the Justice Department's Office of Information and Privacy. "He held the government's feet to the fire as if it were negligently overdue in providing discovery responses."[125] By the fall of 2009, the "Torture FOIA," as Jaffer and his colleagues call it, became "a landmark case in every respect," in the words of secrecy maven Steven Aftergood.[126] By the summer of 2011 the ACLU had received more than 150,000 pages of previously secret documents related to interrogation from all corners of the government, many of them previously classified.[127] The Obama administration's 2009 document dumps received the most fanfare. But the flow had begun in late 2003, and during the Bush years they included revelations about prison conditions, prisoner abuse, and deaths in Iraq, Afghanistan, and Guantanamo Bay; a controversial Justice Department legal opinion on interrogation to the Defense Department; interrogation directives issued by Lieutenant General Ricardo Sanchez in Iraq; and much more.

The ACLU and the public also learned a lot from Vaughn Declarations, which forced the CIA to explain what it refused to produce. "The Vaughns are often as important as the documents themselves because they can reveal the existence of previously unknown documents (and thus, sometimes, of unknown activities), and can explain the context for other documents as well," says Jaffer. The CIA, for example, fought hard not to produce what it was nonetheless forced to describe as a fourteen-page "document signed by President Bush" on September 17, 2001, that gave "presidential authorization [to the CIA] . . . to set up detention facilities outside the United States, . . . the general authority for the CIA program."[128] There had been much speculation and reporting on this important indication of presidential responsibility, but no official government acknowledgment of it until the ACLU FOIA litigation.

The FOIA litigation before Judge Hellerstein became known by some in the CIA as a "citizen declassification" regime. The litigation propelled Jameel Jaffer from an unknown and inexperienced lawyer to a hero of progressive litigation, a man at the vanguard of the national security bar who used the courts and the FOIA in new ways to extract the government's darkest national security secrets. While Jaffer does not deny his team's accomplishments, he cautions against viewing them as evidence that the FOIA is an effective accountability tool. He points out that the ACLU received relatively few documents from the government's vast secrecy system, and that much remains out of public view. He also notes that the ACLU was fortunate to have drawn Judge Hellerstein, who enforced the FOIA more aggressively than other judges might have, and that if John McCain had defeated Barack Obama, fewer documents might have been released pursuant to Hellerstein's orders. Jaffer is right in some respects, but he misses the forest for the trees. The small but important fraction of documents about the Bush administration's secret program that the ACLU extracted had no precedent and large consequences. Jaffer is right that happenstance played a role in the ACLU's success (as it often does in court victories), but its lucky breaks would not have been possible without a FOIA system designed to do exactly what it did. The FOIA emerged from the decade after 9/11 a more salient and powerful accountability tool, buttressed by many successes that will make it easier for future Jaffers to get at secret government documents.

More important, the ACLU's historic FOIA litigation before Judge Hellerstein was merely a small point in a sprawling, vibrant post-9/11 "ecology of transparency," in University of Pennsylvania law professor Seth Kreimer's apt phrase.[129] The ACLU and other organizations bombarded the government with hundreds of other FOIA requests that resulted in analogous revelations about the post-9/11 roundup of Muslim immigrants, interrogation abuses, various surveillance matters, detainees and their review boards, and much more.[130] Many of these requests were based on media reports that themselves were based on official and unofficial leaks as well as the new technologies of discovery described in Chapter 3. The documents and Vaughn Declarations disclosed by the FOIA often referenced unknown documents and activities, and these revelations sparked new cycles of media and NGO scrutiny and new FOIA requests. Journalists were sometimes antagonists with the ACLU in seeking secret information, but they often worked with it, implicitly and explicitly, toward a common disclosure goal, and they both had had help from leakers and others inside the government. In addition, one of Hellerstein's most crucial rulings in the FOIA litigation was that the CIA could not invoke a statutory ban on disclosing its operational records because they had already been disclosed to Helgerson in his investigation.[131] The release of FBI documents pursuant to the ACLU's FOIA request triggered important inspector general investigations in the Justice and Defense Departments. Accountability powers that Congress had delegated to citizens, courts, and executive branch watchdogs worked together, and intersected with the transparency-forcing actions of other public and private actors, in unexpected and consequential ways. They also intersected with the efforts of foreign courts and investigatory bodies, which themselves engaged in unprecedented scrutiny and revelations about CIA prisons and renditions.

Human rights organizations, led by Human Rights First, packaged the manifold revelations about the U.S. government's secret interrogation practices into an aggressive advocacy campaign to shape public opinion and rouse politicians to action. The Republican-controlled Congress responded with dozens of hearings in 2004–2005 that further fed the ecology of transparency.[132] In the summer of 2005, Republican Senators Lindsey Graham, John McCain, and John Warner, outraged by the revelations in the press and the FOIA cases, and by Bush administration stonewalling, introduced a bill to limit permissible interrogation practices. McCain, a torture victim during the Vietnam War, sponsored an amendment to ban the CIA from committing "cruel, inhuman, or degrading treatment or punishment."[133] The Bush administration furiously opposed this bill and threatened to veto it, and Vice President Cheney made many trips to Capitol Hill. When Cheney's pressure made little headway, National Security Advisor Stephen Hadley took over negotiations for the White House and sought blanket immunity or waivers for CIA interrogators. The best he could get was a vague "defense" from prosecution for CIA interrogators who reasonably relied on legal advice. Facing a veto-proof majority and out of options, President Bush signaled support for the legislation, which then passed by huge majorities. A Congress controlled by the President's party had taken the extraordinary and unprecedented step of curtailing what the Commander in Chief believed was one of his most important wartime tools. "We've come a long way as a country since 9/11, and this development is a sign of that," said Tom Malinowski, Washington advocacy director for Human Rights Watch, just before the law passed.[134]

In popular lore, the White House at this point pulled a fast one when President Bush signed the legislation with the proviso that "the executive branch shall construe [the law] in a manner consistent with the constitutional authority of the President . . . as Commander in Chief."[135] This "signing statement" was widely interpreted to mean that the Bush had reserved the right to disregard the law when national security required. "[T]he President tried to publicly play McCain for a fool with the Commander-in-Chief version of 'I had my fingers crossed,' " noted legal blogger and later Obama administration official Marty Lederman, reflecting conventional wisdom.[136]

But what actually happened was quite different: McCain's 2005 amendment stopped the CIA program in its tracks. Hadley thought he had a deal that would allow the CIA program to continue, especially since the Justice Department had earlier concluded that the program was consistent with language similar to the McCain Amendment.[137] But Rizzo and CIA Director Porter Goss, oblivious to academic debates about signing statements, saw things differently. In a frosty meeting, Goss had briefed McCain on the CIA interrogation techniques. A shaking and angry McCain reacted that "it's all torture," Goss later told Rizzo. The senator believed his amendment banned what the CIA was doing, and he had rejected the CIA's efforts to soften the bill, creating what Rizzo describes as a "very perilous legislative history." Moreover, the vague protections for CIA agents who relied in good faith on legal advice gave only an uncertain defense at trial and did nothing to preclude years of traumatic, expensive, and possibly career-ruining investigations prior to trial. In light of the investigations already swirling by that time, the CIA was not prepared to continue in the face of such congressional disapproval. Rizzo drafted a memorandum for Goss informing the White House that the CIA was suspending the program until it received new and clear legal assurances. Law and accountability had spooked the spooks and led them to pull back despite White House wishes otherwise.

New assurances for the old program never came. Six months later the Supreme Court, responding to many of the same dynamics as Congress, invalidated the Bush military commissions and in the process announced that Common Article 3 of the Geneva Conventions governed the war with al Qaeda.[138] This meant that it was now a crime for any CIA official to commit "outrages upon personal dignity, in particular humiliating and degrading treatment." No one knows quite what this vague provision rules out, but it is more restrictive than the McCain Amendment, and it made reviving the original program impossible. President Bush decided to clear out the secret prisons and bring the high-value detainees like 9/11 mastermind Khalid Sheikh Mohammed to Guantanamo Bay. From then until Obama became President, the Bush administration reportedly held only two detainees in the secret prisons for a few months, and then both were transferred to GTMO.[139] New CIA Director Michael Hayden significantly narrowed the program to six heavily circumscribed techniques— dietary manipulation, sleep deprivation, facial hold, attention grasp, abdominal slap, and an open-fingered facial slap—in an attempt to make it politically and legally sustainable over the long run.[140] We do not know which if any of these techniques were applied to the two high-level detainees temporarily in secret prisons in the last two years of the Bush administration. But by the time the Obama administration, in its boldest break from its predecessor, put the program out of its misery in 2009, it had been dying slowly for a long time at the hands of the courts and Congress and the public in response to the revelations churned in the ecology of transparency.

Chapter Five

WARRIOR-LAWYERS

IT WAS THE AFTERNOON of September 29, 2009, and General David Petraeus was over an hour late for a ceremony to honor an Army colonel, Mark Martins, who was being promoted to brigadier general. Petraeus was stuck in the White House Situation Room in a drawn-out meeting with President Obama and his skeptical national security advisers over the Defense Department's request for forty thousand more troops in Afghanistan.[1] When the tense meeting finally ended, Petraeus jumped into his armored SUV and headed for the ceremony. Promotion ceremonies for baby generals routinely take place at the Department of Defense. But rather than turning right out of the White House gate toward the bridge that leads to the Pentagon, the Petraeus entourage headed down Pennsylvania Avenue to the Department of Justice. For Mark Martins is a military lawyer, and his promotion was being held in the Justice Department's Great Hall.

The Great Hall is a cavernous two-story room, bordered in imposing gray marble columns, where speeches, awards, and receptions take place. Because Petraeus was so late, Martins and his family formed a receiving line to buy some time. The line was long. Martins greeted classmates from West Point, where he graduated first in his class and in the general order of merit;

friends from Oxford University, which he attended on a Rhodes scholarship, graduating with First Class Honors; fellow officers and troops from his two years in the 82nd Airborne at Fort Bragg, where he led an infantry platoon; men and women with whom he competed in establishing his early soldierly bona fides by earning a Ranger Tab, Pathfinder Badge, Expert Infantryman Badge, Senior Parachutist Badge, and Air Assault Badge; classmates from Harvard Law School, where he graduated magna cum laude; scores of military lawyers with whom he worked in various teaching, learning, and service capacities before 9/11; and comrades of all rank and importance—soldiers, marines, sailors, airmen, and many civilians from several U.S. government agencies—with whom he deployed in Iraq and Afghanistan, for five years in total, after 9/11.[2] These men and women had gathered from around the globe because of their admiration for Martins, not for his sterling resume, but for what it represented: a fit, energetic, and proven infantry officer, a brilliant soldier-lawyer who had deployed in dangerous settings many times, an expert at the military profession of arms, an experienced and persuasive trial advocate, a modest but powerful leader by example, and an officer possessed with a steel will to accomplish difficult missions.

When Petraeus finally arrived, the Great Hall filled with the music of the national anthem and ruffles and flourishes as the four-star general, Attorney General Eric Holder, and Colonel Martins walked on to a stage flanked by two twelve-foot Art Deco statues, one of a scantily toga-clad representation of Lady Justice called *The Spirit of Justice*, and the other of a god-like, bare-chested man called *The Majesty of Law*. (Attorney General John Ashcroft famously covered the statues with drapes, which his successor, Alberto Gonzales, removed.) "I wonder whether he is a mere mortal or, indeed, a superhero," Holder said of Martins, after reviewing his extraordinary accomplishments.[3] And then, before the imposing statues, Petraeus, in full military dress, spoke. Mark "is one of those rare individuals who always seems to end up in the toughest assignments and who always performs exceedingly well in them," he said. "Indeed, there is no person in uniform I'd rather have on the team for a tough mission than Mark . . . , [who] has helped frame our thinking on, and develop the big ideas about, the importance of the rule of law and the role of JAG officers in the complex operations we are conducting today."[4]

It may seem improbable that the greatest American general of his generation would want a lawyer as a close partner in a tough mission. But Petraeus's encomium for Martins was not puffery. The two men had been friends and intermittent colleagues since they met in 1992, when Captain Martins, in his first job as a military lawyer, was assigned to the battalion of the 101st Airborne Division commanded by Lieutenant Colonel Petraeus in Fort Campbell, Kentucky. Before the post-9/11 "era of persistent conflict," they had worked together at the Joint Readiness Training Center (a realistic war-training ground) and in the rapid-deployment XVIII Airborne Corps. After 9/11, Martins had been at Petraeus's side for several of his toughest assignments, including his command of the Multi-National Force–Iraq in 2007 and 2008, which implemented "the Surge." Martins supervised 670 lawyers and paralegal staffers—which amounted to one lawyer or paralegal for every 240 troops on the ground—who performed all manner of legal services in support of the Surge.[5] But Martins was much more than just Petraeus's lawyer during the period. He was one of his trusted advisers who helped Petraeus conceive and execute his counterinsurgency strategy.

The Martins promotion ceremony was held in the Justice Department rather than the Pentagon because for seven months in 2009, between deployments, Martins had worked there, in offices a few feet from the Great Hall, on President Obama's Detention Policy Task Force. But the locale was also fitting because the ceremony represented one of the most important but underappreciated developments in modern warfare: the marriage of the military and the law, and the attendant rise of warrior-lawyers who are deeply integrated into military operations. Martins is the epitome of this evolution, but as Petraeus insists, with only a bit of exaggeration, he is "not by any means unique."[6] The U.S. military is filled from top to bottom with accomplished lawyers who work intimately with military commanders around the globe to ensure that they—the subordinates and agents of the Commander in Chief—comply with and are accountable to the maze of domestic, international, and foreign laws that govern every step of military activity, and to help them sort out political, diplomatic, strategic, and even tactical issues as well.

The Rise of Operational Law

Lawyers have been a part of the U.S. military since George Washington created the U.S. Army Judge Advocate General Corps for the Continental Army on July 29, 1775.[7] Until recently, however, lawyers did not play a large role in war-fighting. Through the 1970s, judge advocates during war did pretty much what they did during peace: traditional legal services like writing wills; advising soldiers on tax, marriage, and divorce issues; and doling out military justice for soldiers who misbehaved. They were not much involved in the planning and execution of military operations.[8] In World War II, generals ordered firebombings in the European and Japanese cities without consulting lawyers or considering legal implications.[9] President Truman received a great deal of advice about whether and how to drop the atomic bombs on Hiroshima and Nagasaki, but it did not come from lawyers advising him about the laws of war.[10] The same was true of Presidents Johnson and Nixon, and their generals, in the Vietnam War.[11] These military leaders had a sense that they should minimize civilian casualties when consistent with the military mission, but they were not advised by lawyers on the legality of their actions. Military planning and military operations were based on military strategy and tactics, diplomatic and political considerations, and morality. Lawyers played practically no role.[12]

This all changed after Vietnam, which left the U.S. military at its lowest point in American history in terms of effectiveness, reputation, and morale. When Mark Martins attended West Point in the early 1980s, "there was a real self-consciousness about ethical erosion and decay in the army," he recalls.[13] The officer corps responded to Vietnam with an elaborate regeneration strategy that involved development of "new doctrine, sophisticated new weapons, more rigorous approaches to training and the development of leaders, [and] large-scale changes to organizations and tactics," notes military theorist Andrew Bacevich.[14] The strategy also had a moral component. "For the officer corps," writes Bacevich, "the ultimate purpose" of reinventing the military "was to salvage the American profession of arms, thoroughly discredited and even dishonored in Vietnam by events such as the My Lai Massacre," where Lieutenant William Calley led a company of poorly disciplined American soldiers on a killing spree of hundreds of innocent Vietnamese civilians.[15] The military responded to My Lai and all it represented with a renewed emphasis on instruction and training in military honor, ethics, and morality, at West Point and other officer-training grounds. It also elevated the role of law and lawyers in military affairs.

Lawyers became a part of the solution because noncompliance with the law was seen as part of the problem. A very critical report about the My Lai incident by General William Peers concluded that a major cause of the massacre was that Calley's soldiers were poorly trained in their obligations to protect civilians under the 1949 Geneva Conventions and other international laws of war—laws that had long been "on the books" but not operationally influential, at least in the post–World War II era.[16] Army lawyers, stung by this criticism, took steps to address it. At their recommendation, the Defense Department in 1974 issued an ambitious directive that established a "Law of War program," ultimately run by judge advocates, to ensure that every member of the U.S. armed forces—from privates to generals—was thoroughly trained to comply with the laws of war in all their military operations. This program gave military lawyers an opening to communicate with commanders about operational matters, one that over the next quarter century would expand into extensive real-time counseling and influence in such operations.[17]

At first commanders abided by their rote law-of-war training responsibilities but resisted letting lawyers in on the military decision-making process. Over time, however, most of them came to see lawyers as essential to mission success. In part this was because of the changing nature of war. For the quarter century after Vietnam, most U.S. military engagements involved small, unorthodox military operations such as the invasions of Grenada, Panama, and Haiti, as well as "military operations other than war," the awkward 1980s term used to describe operations such as peacekeeping, drug interdiction, sanctions enforcement, humanitarian assistance, and the like. These forms of military engagement involved closer-than-usual contact with civilians and raised hard law-of-war issues—especially about detention, interrogation, and rules of engagement—that lawyers were vital in sorting out. Success in these contexts also involved complex relationships with international organizations that required extensive legal assistance. They also required commanders to work closely with locals and with private firms, which required contracts drafted by lawyers.

One of David Petraeus's earliest recognitions of the military value of lawyers came in 1995, when he was Chief of Operations to a UN force that intervened in Haiti. "It was peacekeeping, but we were doing real operations, including detention operations," he recalls. "It was a really somewhat chaotic environment and to get it going I would go out in a helicopter and find a plot of land that might be a good place for a forward operating base. We would land the helicopter, see who came up to us, and if the guy owned the land and could prove it, we'd contract with him on the spot." These two small slices of military operations exemplify the hundreds of things a modern military does in nonconventional operations that cannot be accomplished without legal infrastructure. "Lawyers had a huge influence on all that activity," says Petraeus.[18]

Success stories like these convinced commanders and lawyers alike that lawyers must not only review operational plans in advance, but also join soldiers in the field, especially since war plans go out the window as soon as the fighting starts.[19] The lawyers coined a new term—"operational law"—to describe the mix of domestic, international, and foreign law that they would apply in the field.[20] And they created an elaborate educational bureaucracy throughout the military to teach soldiers about the law. Every combat training center has lawyers who advise on legal issues during military exercises; and the Command and General Staff Colleges and War Colleges all have lawyers on their faculties.[21] Through years of teaching by and training with lawyers, the military establishment became acculturated to law and came to see legal compliance as serving the important post-Vietnam goals of restoring honor and discipline to the military.

The military establishment also came to see law as empowering. "To those in our military ranks, each of whom has sworn his or her oath to a government of laws and not of men, the rule of law is important because it legitimates violent conduct that otherwise would be both criminal and dishonorable," explains Mark Martins. Soldiers kill and maim and destroy property and unsettle lives, and American soldiers do so with high-tech weapons that often give them enormous advantages over their adversaries. Adherence to law, and especially to the laws of war that define when and how military force can legitimately be employed, is what justifies and excuses these otherwise-terrible acts, renders them moral, and enables a person of conscience and honor to undertake them.

Law in the post-Vietnam era was seen to do more than just empower and legitimate violence. It also, and increasingly, began to serve as a substitute for violence. Petraeus might have simply grabbed the land in Haiti by force, but doing so with a legal contract instead was easier and more effective. In the Grenada, Panama, and Somalia operations, U.S. forces might have confiscated adversary weapons by force, but instead they procured many of them through a lawyer-supervised "buyback" program.[22] Rather than destroying Afghanistan's ability to use commercial satellite imagery in the war that began in 2001, the U.S. military bought exclusive rights to the images with a contract instead.[23] A court injunction against a fund-raiser or a bank might be as effective in drying up terrorist financing as kinetic actions.[24] A law-heavy UN Security Council Resolution that imposes sanctions or threatens the use of force can send a message about political resolve and can sometimes coerce an outlaw nation's will more effectively, legitimately, and cheaply than an actual use of military force.[25]

At the same time that law was growing as a basis or substitute for military action, it was also increasingly constraining military action. When Donald Rumsfeld entered the Pentagon as Secretary of Defense in January 2001, a quarter-century after his first tour in that job in the Ford administration, one of the first things he noticed was many more lawyers. When he asked why, he was told that they were needed to interpret the mountain of new laws that had been imposed on the military since the 1970s. Between Rumsfeld's two Pentagon tours the Defense budget tripled.[26] But as Rumsfeld noted in his memoir, he was "astonished . . . to discover that the legislation authorizing the Department of Defense's budget had exploded from a bill totaling 16 pages in 1977 when I left the Pentagon to a whopping 534 pages in 2001."[27] In addition to these annual laws, each of which contains detailed and often cumulative restrictions on military activity, Congress also enacted hundreds of stand-alone laws during Rumsfeld's absence that had a major impact on Department of Defense operations.[28] These new laws are implemented with hundreds more pages of bureaucratic regulations. "The Defense establishment is tangled in its anchor chain," Rumsfeld wrote in a June 2001 memo that described this trend.[29] Lawyers are charged with divining the meaning of these rules, and with sorting out their ambiguities and contradictions. Their influence thus grew with the thickness and complexity of the anchor chain.

It wasn't just domestic law that was thickening the Defense Department's anchor chain—it was international law as well. The international laws of war were revised in the 1970s in two protocols to the 1949 Geneva Conventions. The negotiations for these treaties were contested, and while most nations eventually agreed to them, the U.S. government never has.[30] Nonetheless, the process of updating the Geneva Conventions led to the recognition of a sprawling and complex "customary international law" governing military conflicts. The U.S. military—with the guidance and encouragement of military lawyers—followed many aspects of this customary law, and wrote it down in ever-expanding legal and policy manuals that military lawyers interpret and apply. At the same time, control over the interpretation of the international laws of war was slipping from the Pentagon's grasp. The 1990s saw the birth of UN-sanctioned and U.S.-supported international criminal tribunals for the former Yugoslavia and Rwanda that began churning out authoritative opinions on the laws of war, some of which departed from the U.S. understanding of these laws. In addition, after the Cold War, the International Committee of the Red Cross and other NGOs like Human Rights Watch garnered global legitimacy as articulators of international military norms that were often more detailed and demanding than the ones the military adopted for itself.

International courts and NGOs made the international laws of war more complex and contested, and less friendly to U.S. interests. U.S. officials began to worry that these increasingly influential global institutions might apply these new norms to hold U.S. officials to account for legal violations. The 1990s also witnessed the creation of the International Criminal Court. The United States has not ratified the treaty creating this court, but the court nonetheless claims jurisdiction over any actions it deems a crime in any of the dozens of nations where the U.S. military has a presence. "Universal jurisdiction," which allows a foreign court to prosecute an official of another country for war crimes, also became a threat after an English court famously ensnared Chilean leader Augusto Pinochet in 1999. These laws and institutions made U.S. commanders anxious, not because they thought they would commit an actual crime, but because they worried about the possible anti-American biases of those interpreting and enforcing the law. For the military commander trying to win a battle in the fog of war thickened by the fog of international law, lawyers proved invaluable. They identified and helped circumvent legal landmines, and they provided an excuse, if their legal advice was followed, when something went wrong. Lawyers, in short, provided cover and comfort in the face of an increasingly demanding legal environment.

The information revolution was yet another reason for the rising importance of lawyers.[31] The growth of global television and the Internet in the 1990s made war observable everywhere, practically in real time. These technologies allowed people around the world to view mistakes in war—especially unintended civilian casualties—in ways beyond the ability of governments to control. They made the perceived fairness of how war is fought a matter of public evidence and global debate. For the U.S. military, this meant that the battle for hearts and minds—on the home front, on the battlefield, and in third countries—became more challenging and important. American adversaries exploited mistakes and even invited them by hiding in places guaranteed to generate civilian casualties if attacked. They also became very good at criticizing American mistakes and missteps in the language of law, which had become, as Harvard Law School professor David Kennedy has noted, "a vocabulary for judgment" and "a mark of legitimacy."[32] American commanders using the most precise weapons in history were forced to be much more prudent than ever in their selection of targets and, more generally, in how they conducted the war. Lawful action—and, also important, the perception of lawful action—had become more than a demand of honor or morality or something to abide to withstand legal scrutiny; it had become a military imperative.[33] And as legality moved to center stage as a military consideration, lawyers moved with it, for they could guide commanders to ensure that they complied with the law, and could defend the legality of controversial war decisions to the public.

All of these influences undergirding the rise of operational lawyers were on display in the two most extensive military engagements after Vietnam and before 9/11. Operation Desert Storm in Iraq in 1991 was the first war in which America's modern precision weapons and the CNN effect operated in tandem. It was also, not surprisingly, "the most legalistic war we've ever fought," according to Colonel Raymond Ruppert, who was General Norman Schwarzkopf's lawyer at the time.[34] Hundreds of military lawyers deployed in the field to counsel commanders about their operations. The most difficult issues arose from the Iraqi practice of placing military equipment near civilian targets (such as when the Iraqis parked jet fighters near the ancient temple of Ur), or of sending civilians into military targets (such as when civilians were killed in a Baghdad bunker that was also being used as a command and control center). But lawyers also advised on when private property could be seized, on contracts with local suppliers, on the taking of war trophies, on investigations of fratricide and war crimes, and on the complex legal limitations on an occupying power, among many others.[35] On the whole, the military elite viewed its lawyers as a positive force in the Gulf War, perhaps because the relatively straightforward war went so well and because the United States bested the Iraqis in the propaganda fight over casualties. Decisions in the war "were impacted by legal considerations at every level," said then Chairman of the Joint Chiefs of Staff Colin Powell, who added that "lawyers proved invaluable in the decisionmaking process."[36]

NATO's 1999 air campaign in Kosovo was a different story. It was politically and legally more controversial than the Gulf War because neither Congress nor the UN Security Council authorized it and because NATO pilots dropped "smart bombs" from high altitudes to minimize their risk. American lawyers were more involved than ever, especially in the elaborate vetting process to ensure that bombs targeted "military objectives," and that any damage to civilians was minimal. Lawyers did not prevent high-profile mistakes, including the bombing of a refugee convoy, a hospital, several civilian homes, a civilian train, and the Chinese embassy, all of which were roundly criticized by Yugoslav President Slobodan Milosevic, his allies, and war opponents as war crimes.[37] But the lawyers did slow down the targeting process, especially since the byzantine American procedures for approving targets needed to be replicated by every NATO government and its lawyers. Also throwing sand in the war effort were obscure congressional restrictions on military action that Rumsfeld would complain about a few years later. NATO Commander Wesley Clark explained in *Waging Modern War* how he overcame political hurdles to secure Apache helicopters for the conflict only to be greeted by lawyers telling him that Congress had placed restrictions on preparation of the Apaches for battle.[38]

"One of the most striking features of the Kosovo campaign was the remarkably direct role lawyers played in managing combat operations—to a degree unprecedented in previous wars," wrote Richard Betts, in his review of Clark's memoir. Betts concluded that "NATO's lawyers . . . became, in effect, its tactical commanders," and added that Clark's account of this process should "shock any student of wartime command."[39] It wasn't just lawyers inside the war room who were heavily involved in assessing the legality of the war. Outside adversarial courts were as well. The just-established International Criminal Tribunal for the former Yugoslavia later did a serious criminal investigation of NATO targeting practices during the Kosovo conflict, and several European countries faced litigation before the European Court of Human Rights on the same issue. This unprecedented judicial scrutiny of wartime actions troubled a military establishment that had been more careful than ever in deploying historically precise weapons under the watchful eye of more layers of fastidious lawyers than ever before. Although the investigation and lawsuit imposed no liability in the end, they did reinforce the sense among military commanders that the legal noose over their operations was tightening, and that consultation with lawyers was more important than ever.

After the 9/11 attacks, many commentators assumed that the legalisms of the Kosovo conflict would recede. "I believe the air campaign against Kosovo and Serbia may represent something of a high-water mark of the influence of international law in military interventions, at least in the near term," wrote General Charles Dunlap, an Air Force lawyer and scholar, in an influential essay published just after 9/11.[40] "The aftermath of that conflict, along with the repercussions of the terrible events of September 11th, seem to have set in motion forces that will diminish the role of law." Dunlap was writing in late 2001, when many believed that the United States had been too restrained in fighting the threat of terrorism, and that lawyers were responsible for this excess restraint. "Many Americans," Dunlap explained, "are exasperated with the law, especially when traditional applications of it proved to be an inadequate guarantor of basic security on September 11th." Dunlap was not advocating "taking off the gloves" in the war on terrorism, as some in the CIA had at about the same time. His essay was, in fact, a defense of the role of law in military operations. But he was predicting that the niceties of legalism that dominated relatively easy wars in Iraq and Kosovo might not survive the more extreme and intensive conflict with al Qaeda.

Dunlap's prediction did not pan out. The wars after 9/11 proved to be different from the ones of the previous quarter-century: the former were interminable conflicts with long deployments that involved intensive traditional war elements, heavy doses of disciplined counterinsurgency operations, and an unprecedented reliance on intelligence. But in these very different types of war, all of the trends that led to the rising influence of law and lawyers before 9/11—the need to legitimate violence and render it honorable, the growth in the number and complexity of domestic and international laws governing the battlefield, the rising influence of nongovernmental organizations (NGOs) and international and foreign courts, confrontation with civilians and private parties on the battlefield, the intimate scrutiny of the global press, public demands for just actions and actions perceived to be just, and the battle for hearts and minds, at home and abroad—would accelerate. As a result, military lawyers after 9/11 became more involved than ever in military training and more deeply integrated in military decision-making in line units and key staff organs. They also grew closer to the fight, with two to three lawyers deployed with every army brigade (about three thousand troops), and a lawyer deployed for many special operations forces down to the battalion level (five hundred to one thousand troops). In the process, lawyers garnered more experience, and yet more influence, in restraining and empowering military action.

TARGETING

The most obviously consequential action taken by the U.S. military in war is the use of firepower against its adversary. Fire can take endless forms, ranging from Hellfire missiles dropped from an unmanned Predator drone, to heavy mortars employed in conventional ground combat, to small arms like a pistol or grenade used in clearing a village of insurgents or in self-defense, and everything in between. The use of firepower can obviously bring advantage over an adversary. But less obviously, mistaken or disproportionate fire can bring major setbacks, especially in a war dominated by the battle for hearts and minds. Few events have harmed American war efforts in the past decade as much as collateral civilian casualties from attacks on military targets from the air; or erroneous fire based on mistaken identification from the air, in the field, or at security checkpoints; or disproportionate fire, such as when marines in Haditha, Iraq, killed twenty-four civilians in an overreaction to the death of a comrade by a roadside bomb. Such events are inevitable in wars on the scale and intensity of the ones being fought today. The U.S. military has an elaborate, multi-layered, lawyer-vetted process to keep them to a minimum—a process that, at the same time, ensures that soldiers throughout chain of command, from the President down, are accountable to law.

When General David Petraeus approved targets for fire, a giant bureaucracy of analysis and checklists would precede and underscore his decision. Greatly simplified, Petraeus gave guidance on goals, and the bureaucracy went to work and came back with target proposals. Intelligence experts collect and organize relevant information from human sources, intercepted communications, images from drones and satellites, and other sources about the identity of targets, their surroundings, and their likely movements. They also work with targeting and weapons experts to build "collateral damage estimates" that identify nearby civilians, schools, hospitals, mosques, water facilities, and the like. Often with the assistance of computer software, they assess the confidence with which particular weapons or payloads fired at particular angles on certain targets at particular times of the day will achieve the goal of the fire, with a range of estimates about expected casualties or other unwanted collateral damage. In the crucial battle of Sadr City in Iraq in 2008, to take one example, American forces fired guided missiles into a Shia militia meeting-place across the street from a hospital. "We had confidence that it would not cause collateral damage because the targeters correctly advised us that 'this is the circular error probable for the munition, this is how many we are going to shoot, this is what we think will happen, and we don't even think it will knock a window out across the road,' " explains Petraeus.[41] Collateral damage estimates are not, of course, always so rosy and are not always accurate. An important issue for the commander is how much collateral damage risk to accept, a calculus that requires an estimate of political, tactical, and strategic costs.

The collateral damage calculus—and indeed every other element of targeting—also involves extensive legal considerations. A targeting decision is the commander's decision, but lawyers like Mark Martins are involved at every step. They first of all ensure compliance with international law, which demands that fire be directed to military and not civilian targets (a tricky issue when the enemy wears civilian clothes or hides in a hospital or mosque); that it be calculated to not cause "unnecessary suffering"; and that the anticipated collateral damage to civilian life or property not be "excessive" when compared to the expected military gain of the attack (a difficult subjective judgment call). They are also involved in the crucial but law-intensive intelligence-gathering process that lies behind practically every use of force, as well as most detentions, in the military. Complex statutes, a long executive order known as "E.O. 12,333," and many Defense Department directives guide and restrict how the military recruits sources and procures, uses, and stores information. The operational lawyer must also ensure that the attack is consistent with other domestic laws (such as limits Congress has placed on the use of force), and with the rules of engagement and scores of other regulations, directives, and executive orders that apply on the modern battlefield. Making these decisions in battle requires the lawyer to be well trained as a warrior, and to have a thorough and realistic understanding of battle situations, intelligence-gathering techniques, and communications and weapons systems. "Soldier First, Lawyer Always" is the Army JAG Corps motto.[42]

In theory the military lawyer can veto a targeting decision at many points in the targeting process. "Lawyers will be very clear if there is a 'no kidding' red line that you are about to walk over," says Petraeus. "They will generally be firm and reminding you of that." Commanders heed such advice, but in fact they rarely approach a red line because lawyers have exercised much of their influence before the battle begins. Petraeus and his subordinate commanders had trained with lawyers for decades, and together with lawyers had already folded legal considerations into the rules of engagement and other battlefield directives.

When Petraeus led the 101st Airborne Division in the battle of Najaf, Iraq, in the spring of 2003, one of his battalions fighting toward the city center in tanks and armored personnel carriers was getting hammered by the Fedayeen Saddam using rocket-propelled grenades, small arms, and howitzers from civilian strongholds within and around the Shrine of Imam Ali, one of the holiest sites in Shia Islam.[43] The battalion fought back with artillery and air fire on targets around the shrine, taking the greatest possible care to minimize civilian casualties. "Our operations in Najaf in 2003 complied with the law because that is how we had trained, because soldiers had internalized the rules and commanders were setting the right tone, and because operational lawyers . . . were there in each headquarters down to brigade level to provide sound advice and supervise training on rules of engagement," he recalls.[44] Another factor kept the battalion far from any legal lines. Petraeus could have considered an attack on the holy shrine itself, which was shielding the enemy, at least if he determined that the military advantage from doing so outweighed the expected civilian damage. He didn't need a lawyer, however, to tell him this was a bad idea. "I didn't want a single round, not even a ricochet, to hit the dome," he says. "That was less about lawyers and more about the rule of land warfare and awareness of the cultural and religious importance of the shrine."[45]

Law and lawyers also help commanders in targeting and related decisions by acquainting them with the accumulated wisdom of the past. "Law embodies and summarizes human experience and wisdom about right action in a particular context," says Martins. The international laws of war contain principles that, along with their precedents of application, reflect centuries of experience and learning about the most effective way to conduct war. Rules of engagement and related Defense Department directives similarly reflect accumulated experience and learning. When the commander wants to take a militarily efficient action and the lawyer advises a law or regulation that suggests another course, the commander is forced to consider how others have thought in his shoes or might view his action from a different perspective—perhaps the perspective of Central Command in Tampa, or the Pentagon or National Security Council, or public opinion. "The law and written DoD or service policies can helpfully jog a tired brain to think through the second- and third-order effects of a decision— or the likely reactions to it at higher headquarters, in the public at large, or even by the enemy—thus resulting in the best sort of law-governed behavior, namely, actions resulting from principles that have been critically examined and deliberately accepted as wise ones," says Martins. When this process works, he adds, "legal advice does not constrain policy, but rather confirms it by forcing you to think about every aspect of the decision that time and circumstances permit before acting."

The military lawyer's value, and thus influence, come not just from the identification of and advice about laws, but also from advice on nonlegal matters. "Lawyers help you come to grips with the issues involved in a targeting decision, not all of which are legal issues," explains Petraeus. He is speaking of the military lawyer's role as "counselor" or, as some put it, "consigliere."[46] Lawyers are trained to think clearly, critically, and analytically, to find weaknesses in evidence or in causal inferences, and to consider the broader implications and effects of a decision. They are typically more attuned than most to the context, appearance, and political and moral implications of particular actions. "Sir, legally we can do this, but I just don't think it passes the CNN test; if this gets out, it'll look bad," is the way Andru Wall, a former lawyer for special operations, describes the phenomenon.[47] Lawyers also have a slew of precedents at their fingertips—not all of them legal precedents—to help commanders understand by analogy some of the hidden dangers of the situation at hand. They are also usually good staff officers who understand the military decision-making process well. In short, good lawyers have lots of relevant information, they think well, and they have good judgment. To the commander operating in what General George Marshall called the "chronic obscurity" of the battlefield, an experienced soldier with these qualities is indispensable.[48] This is why Petraeus uses lawyers "for a lot of other things" besides legal advice. It is yet another reason why they are so influential.

The lawyer's influence is replicated in this way up and down the chain of command in which targeting and related decisions are made, with variations appropriate to the level of decision. In 2010, the White House signed off on the targeting killing in Yemen of Anwar al-Aulaqi, the American citizen and senior figure in "al Qaeda in the Arabian Peninsula" who allegedly supported the "Underwear Bomber" Umar Farouk Abdulmutallab, and who was finally found and killed in October 2011. The locus of approval was the National Security Council in the White House Situation Room, where the Attorney General (on the advice of the Office of Legal Counsel) and other top government lawyers thoroughly scrutinized and signed off on the legality of the action, with conditions, under both domestic and international law. Other high-value targets outside traditional battlefields in Iraq and Afghanistan receive similar lawyer-heavy White House scrutiny. Lawyers are also involved in "targeting cells" lower down the chain from Petraeus, often down to the battalion level in the field, where they advise the commander on legality of weapons and targets, as well as on the prudence of various courses of actions. Modern "net-centric" information technologies—which allow in-time monitoring of and communication with soldiers on the battlefield—permit lawyers throughout the chain of command to dip into the operational realm with questions and advice.

Consultation with a lawyer before firing a weapon can obviously only go so far. A pilot in the sky or a soldier monitoring a checkpoint or clearing a village will not always have time to seek legal advice before using fire, either because an adversary poses a direct threat that requires an immediate response, or because he is fleeing. In these situations, commanders, with thorough assistance from (and often drafting by) lawyers, exercise control over the use of fire through rules of engagement, which are directives that delineate the circumstances when U.S. soldiers can engage enemy forces in particular combat operations.[49] Rules of engagement take into account legal restrictions as well as political, diplomatic, and tactical goals. They are often very elaborate, but then are simplified as appropriate and placed on a three-by-five card for soldiers to carry into battle. A typical rules-of-engagement card says that the soldier can act in self-defense, and indicates the steps the soldier must take to positively identify an adversary and assess his hostile intent, the circumstances in which levels of force can be used against the adversary, and the circumstances in which higher-level approval (sometimes all the way up to the President) must be sought and received before using force. There are many variations on this theme, depending on the goals of the operation.

Rules of engagement are mechanisms of law-informed discipline, but it can be hard to ensure that soldiers absorb that discipline. Mark Martins learned this lesson as a young infantry platoon leader in the mid-1980s charged with training four-dozen young men in their late teens and early twenties, most of whom lacked a college degree and some of whom got into the Army on a waiver because they had criminal records. "Discipline is the soul of an army," George Washington famously said. "It makes small numbers formidable; procures success to the weak and esteem to all."[50] Martins needed to instill in his young soldiers the discipline to hold together and fire, rather than flee, in the terrorizing face of an enemy. But he also needed to discipline them not to fire when doing so was unwarranted. "How am I really going to stop Staff Sergeant Schwartz from slugging an enemy soldier who is totally helpless after we've overcome the rest of his forces?" Martins wondered at the time. The answer, he came to realize after a few months with his troops, was not to tell Sergeant Schwartz, or to write down on a three-by-five card, that the laws of war banned firing on an enemy soldier out of combat. The answer was to thoroughly train soldiers how to act in real-life situations so that when they make decisions on the battlefield—tired, afraid, and stressed—their ingrained, law-compliant response would be second nature. Martins inculcated law-governed behavior not through cognitive learning about the laws of war, but rather through scenario-based training that focused on making the platoon a better fighting force. His soldiers learned to comply with the law without knowing it.

A decade later, as a lawyer, Martins applied this lesson in an influential military journal article that, along with the efforts of other young officers, changed the way the military trains soldiers to comply with the rules of engagement.[51] Martins's article identified the polar dangers that every rule of engagement must navigate. "The first danger is that troops will respond tentatively to an attack, thereby presenting harm to themselves, to fellow soldiers, or to some mission essential facility," he explained. "The second, opposite danger is that troops will strike out too aggressively, thereby harming innocents." The first danger seemed to some observers to reach a crisis point in Afghanistan in 2010, when General Stanley McChrystal, hoping to significantly reduce the number of civilian casualties, issued super-strict rules of engagement that required near-certain identification of the adversary before using force, limited air support, and forbade U.S. troops from firing on an identified enemy soldier if a civilian is nearby or if the enemy soldier drops or hides his weapon.[52] U.S. troops were even deterred from acting in permissible self-defense for fear that the inevitable after-action review would find that they miscalculated the threat. Taliban soldiers, aware of these constraints from press reports, exploited the rules of engagement by firing at soldiers and then dropping their weapons, and by carrying human shields. "The bad guys know our hands are tied: They hide behind women or children, or where they think women or children might be, and they know we can't shoot back or call an airstrike," a staff sergeant in Afghanistan told the *Los Angeles Times*.[53] The predictable and indeed anticipated result was that the number of civilian casualties dropped but the number of U.S. soldier casualties rose.

When David Petraeus took over for McChrystal in Afghanistan in the summer of 2010, he ordered a thorough review of the rules of engagement. One of the things he found was that each level down the chain of command was tightening them, just a bit, out of fear of violating them, to ensure that red lines were not crossed.[54] The result was that the rules on the ground looked different, and more restrictive, than the ones issued by McChrystal. Donald Rumsfeld calls this process "taking a tuck." He and the Joint Chiefs of Staff would send rules of engagement down the chain of command; the combatant commander, not wanting to violate them, would "take a little tuck"; they would go to the country commander, who, not wanting to break the rules, would also "take a little tuck"; and so on. "You end up with four or five layers down there taking tucks and you end up with some rules of engagement that don't look like what the chairman of the Joint Chiefs or the Joint Chiefs of Staff or even the combatant commander intended," explained Rumsfeld.[55] Petraeus encountered a similar phenomenon in Iraq in 2007 with "escalation of force" rules that soldiers use at security checkpoints. The soldiers had grown tentative as a result of restrictions generated in part by a similar chain-of-command cascade that responded to events like the global media storm and the attempted prosecution in Italy of a

U.S. soldier who accidentally killed an Italian intelligence officer at a security checkpoint in 2005.[56]

Tuck-taking extends beyond rules of engagement.[57] Tentativeness and risk aversion are present throughout the law-dominated world of the U.S. military. Some lawyers—especially inexperienced ones—will say "no" to an action or will provide ambiguous advice simply to avoid dirtying their hands in a controversial but lawful military action. Some skittish commanders use legal uncertainty as an excuse for not taking a perfectly lawful but risky action. More broadly, everyone in the military is constantly reminded, and fearful, of legal limits and obligations, and knows that accidents, mistakes, or excesses of any kind will likely result in extensive military "after-action reviews" or "post-incident investigations." Even when damage or injury results from fire that is undoubtedly legitimate, an investigation is required. Pilots know that these reviews and investigations will often include audio and video recordings of their firing decisions and associated verbal exchanges.

The reviews are sometimes friendly, and are merely designed to compile "lessons learned" or to establish a record to tamp down public criticism or to clear the soldier of misplaced charges or concerns. But they can be unfriendly as well, and some result in courts-martial for violations of the Uniform Code of Military Justice. Whether friendly or unfriendly, all retrospective reviews are stressful; soldiers live in anxiety that they might inadvertently cross the line. Some frontline soldiers—often in their teens or early twenties, and mostly ignorant of how the law works—are more afraid of after-action review than enemy fire. And of course after-action military review is not the only form of review soldiers face. They are also concerned, to some degree, by the press, domestic and international courts, and NGO critics, all of which perform their own forms of scrutiny.

Surrounded by law and under the gaze of many potential retroactive critics, it is entirely rational for soldiers up and down the chain of command to hesitate before acting. Such hesitation can be costly. In October 2001, a Predator drone identified a convoy believed to carry Taliban leader Mullah Omar and followed him to a building that looked like a mosque. General Tommy Franks, who headed Central Command, had the call, and he sought Secretary of Defense Rumsfeld's approval, who sought and received President Bush's. When Franks got the go-ahead, he ordered a strike on a vehicle outside the building rather than on the building itself. He did so in part on the advice of a military lawyer who expressed caution because of the probable presence of civilians inside the building.[58] Omar escaped. This pattern of lawyer-induced hesitancy to strike top al Qaeda or Taliban leaders would repeat itself ten times in the first month of the war in Afghanistan, and would persist throughout the decade after 9/11.[59] "I wanted commanders making go or no-go decisions on targeting with the advice of lawyers—not the other way around," complained Rumsfeld in his memoirs. "The legal impulse by nature was to be restrictive and risk-averse, which was not always compatible with waging an effective war against vicious fanatics."[60]

Some military officials, too, think lawyers have too much influence over command decisions. "Lawyers are much too involved in the execution of our operations at war," says Jack Keane, an influential former four-star general who, among his many accomplishments, was one of the intellectual architects of the Surge. "They manage to embed themselves right in the middle of our operational considerations and this process is fundamentally flawed. General guidance in rules of engagement is fine but the specifics of what we're getting down to not only constrains the leaders who are executing the mission on the ground and in the air, in terms of close combat, but it also, I think, has a limiting effect on operational and tactical commanders in restraining them."[61] Even General Petraeus, who admires and relies heavily on lawyers, cautions that they can "constrain the initiative [that is] essential to military success." Lawyers can be " 'surprise, surprise,' overly legalistic," he says, adding that "operators sometimes have to remind lawyers that these are binary decisions for our troops and they involve decisions that have to be made in the blink of an eye—either life or death for that individual and potentially for the folks that are at the far end of what it is the individual is about to launch down-range."[62] Martins too recorded the hazards that lawyering poses to initiative and effective fighting in his influential rules-of-engagement article, and he frequently underlines the point.

Risk aversion, loss of initiative, and intrusion on the commander's prerogative are undeniable costs of a law-dominated military. But there is another side to the story: a properly run, law-dominated military also garners enormous power from the constraint of law. Just as Martins's infantrymen could not accomplish much without the discipline of rules, neither can the U.S. military more generally. The Department of Defense is in many ways the largest organization on the planet. It requires many laws and directives to function, to ensure weapons and personnel arrive on time, with the right equipment, at the right place, and are employed effectively on the battlefield. It also needs laws and directives to ensure that the commands of the President and Secretary of Defense, and the requirements of statutes and treaties, work their way throughout the bureaucracy to the other side of the world, where Sergeant Schwartz follows and implements them. Accomplishing purposeful and constrained behavior in wartime in a large military organization is very hard to do. But it is more vital than ever. For in an era of global media and instant criticism, what Sergeant Schwartz does on the other side of the world can have devastating effects on the entire war-fighting effort. Law and lawyers, when they work properly, keep these events to a minimum.

Rumsfeld is right to worry about the adverse consequences of "restrictive" and "risk-averse" lawyers who counsel commanders not to fire on legitimate targets when in fact firing was appropriate. But we call the same lawyers "too permissive" when they say "yes" in a way that results in unnecessary, war-damaging civilian casualties. And we call them "prudent" and "disciplined" when they help to avoid or minimize civilian casualties that might have led to strategic setbacks in the war or other reprisals against the troops. Everything depends on outcomes. In assessing the overall value of law and lawyers in the military, one must consider outcomes in all three dimensions. One must also take into account the broader benefits of soldier discipline and restraint that are induced by law, and not just the costs of hesitation and risk aversion.

While it is hard to demonstrate how these costs and benefits cash out, the continued rise in the influence of lawyers in the post-9/11 era reflects a judgment by the military establishment that having the lawyer in the targeting cell is a net-plus on balance. "I accept the costs of law and lawyers, acknowledge them, and want to minimize them as much as possible," says Martins. But on the whole, "we still have a lot of initiative, we still have forces that can win, we're still very effective, and we're made more effective by the legitimacy that comes from being law-governed; and that requires lawyers out and about." Martins is not giving a brief for the status quo. Crafting wise laws and directives and interpreting them in ways that strike the right balance between initiative and restraint require good judgment and constant calibration in light of experience. The reason warrior-lawyers like Martins are in huge demand in the military is that they strike this balance well, finding ways for commanders to accomplish their objectives on the law-heavy and open-to-the-world battlefield with minimal strategic, political, or legal fallout.

FROM ABU GHRAIB TO ROLFF

Neither law nor lawyers prevented the abuses at Abu Ghraib. This "nonbiodegradable event," as General Petraeus described it, was the greatest military defeat the United States suffered after 9/11, and it still colors how U.S. counterterrorism operations around the globe are perceived and judged.[63] We now know that the Abu Ghraib abuses happened as a result of wanton criminal acts, and more broadly as a result of poor military doctrine, planning, and training for detention prior to the invasion of Iraq; failures to supervise or enforce proper discipline in Iraqi detention facilities; an inappropriate mixture of detention and interrogation operations; confusing and contradictory legal and policy guidance emanating from many quarters of the executive branch; and poor leadership.[64] A less pondered question is how the U.S. military, which for decades had been so sensitive to the tight connection between lawful action and military success, and had devoted so many organizational and training resources to ensuring lawful action in targeting and in rules of engagement more generally, had allowed itself to be relatively unprepared for detention operations.

The answer to this depressing question is that the wars the U.S. military had been fighting and preparing to fight in the decades prior to 9/11 led it to downplay detention operations. After Vietnam the Defense establishment, burned by its failure at irregular warfare, and as part of its resurgence strategy, focused its doctrinal, organizational, and training energies on defeating state militaries in high-end, high-intensity conflict. This focus seemed to pay off in the successes in Operation Desert Storm in Iraq in 1992 and in Kosovo in 1999. Both conflicts—and indeed every military operation of any scale in the 1980s and 1990s—involved difficult and high-profile targeting operations that reinforced the perceived need for intensive training and lawyerly supervision in that area. Detention issues in these conflicts, by contrast, were not as prominent. Operation Desert Storm produced a relatively short and conventional POW scenario that the Army handled easily with few new lessons learned. The Kosovo conflict, and the military's many "operations other than war" in the 1990s, presented smaller but trickier detention issues. Nonetheless, most military leaders did not think the detention aspects of warfare—normally a small aspect of a conventional military operation—warranted new doctrine, resources, or training. Before 9/11, detention was thus relegated to the relatively small military police branch, and within that branch it was a second- or third-tier priority that was—as in Abu Ghraib—typically handed over to poorly trained reserve units. Humane and effective detention of many thousands of people for extended periods of time is very hard work in a traditional war, and is significantly harder in overcrowded, makeshift prisons in an occupied country marred by insurgency. The Defense Department didn't anticipate or prepare for this contingency, and military and civilian leadership did not adjust in time.

This was a monumental mistake, because it turned out that detention, no less than targeting, implicated the amalgam of law, legitimation, public diplomacy, the CNN effect, and human rights that together are such decisive elements in modern warfare.

The U.S. military responded in two ways to the Abu Ghraib catastrophe and to analogous problems with detention early on in Afghanistan. First, it conducted intensive investigations and trials to hold individuals accountable. In contrast to the CIA, whose internal investigators issue secret reports and farm out the criminal process to the Department of Justice, the U.S. military has a more open investigative process and, in a tradition that predates the Constitution, conducts its own trials in its respected military criminal justice system. After Specialist Joseph Darby gave the Criminal Investigation Division at Abu Ghraib a compact disk of photographs of abuse at Abu Ghraib in January 2004, and months before the photos were made public, the system kicked in. Eleven very critical investigations within the Defense Department, many of which included critical analyses of senior officers, would publicly document the various causes of the abuses and recommend reforms. In addition, at least a dozen soldiers were court-martialed, with punishment ranging from ten years (for Charles Graner, a central figure in the abuses) to a formal reprimand (for Lieutenant Colonel Steven Jordan, who was acquitted on charges related to improper supervision but who was convicted for disobeying orders).[65] Beyond that, dozens of others in the military were subject to nonjudicial punishment or adverse administrative action growing out of detention abuses in Iraq, including career-ending actions for many officers. Many others saw their military careers end as a result of association with the Abu Ghraib scandal even though they suffered no formal sanctions.

Critics continue to charge that higher-ups like General Ricardo Sanchez, commander of the Multi-National Force–Iraq in 2003, or Defense Secretary Donald Rumsfeld (who took responsibility for the abuses, ordered numerous investigations, and twice offered his resignation to the President) should have been formally punished in some way. But there is a sense among most people in the military that it doled out meaningful accountability for Abu Ghraib and that, having many wars to fight, the continuing debates about the past are less important than the second response to Abu Ghraib: correcting systemic shortfalls in detention, making sure the abuses don't recur, and improving military effectiveness more generally. This the military has done, in extraordinary and underappreciated ways. Beginning in 2004, and continuing throughout the decade, the U.S. military made large changes to its organization, training, personnel, and leadership development to ensure that it complied with relevant U.S. and international law governing military detention and interrogation of enemy soldiers in its continuing hostilities in Iraq and Afghanistan. It was moved to make these changes by the dishonor of Abu Ghraib, Supreme Court rulings and congressional statutes analyzed in the next chapter, and pressure from the press and human rights groups that began earlier. But also driving these changes, and leading the U.S. military to conduct itself in its detention operations far beyond the dictates of what the law required, was a larger doctrinal change known as "COIN."

Military doctrine is an authoritative account of how the military should fight its wars that drives more specific decisions about organization, training, materiel, and the like. It is an essential element of military success that aims to ensure that the military acts purposefully, guided by lessons learned, new information about national security threats, and other acts of self-reflection. After the Abu Ghraib abuses became known, every branch of the military made dozens of doctrinal changes related to detention that were embodied in various revised "field manuals." The most famous and influential changes came to the Army's revised 2006 Counterinsurgency (COIN) Field Manual. Counterinsurgency is a battle by governments or their allies against insurgent forces in rebellion. The Army largely put its head in the sand about fighting counterinsurgencies after it failed at the one in Vietnam. Its subsequent focus on preparing for conventional battles left it largely unprepared to fight the insurgent wars—one component of which is the detention of insurgents—that immediately followed the easy conventional victories in Afghanistan in 2001 and Iraq in 2003.

David Petraeus became famous after 9/11, and quickly moved up the chain of command, because he took the lead to fix this problem. Petraeus had written his Ph.D. dissertation at Princeton in 1987 on the lessons of Vietnam. One lesson—contrarian at the time—was that "prudent preparation" for likely future wars should "lead the military to recognize that significant emphasis should be given to COIN forces, equipment, and doctrine."[66] Petraeus lived this prescient analysis in 2003 when, as commander of the 101st Airborne Division, he defeated insurgency forces during his occupation of Mosul, the second largest city in Iraq. The lessons he learned in Mosul, in his 1990s experiences in "operations other than war" in Bosnia and Haiti, and in his 2004 command in Iraq training Iraqi security forces and police were reflected in the new 2007 COIN Manual that Petraeus helped to develop at the "Doctrine Division" of the U.S. Army Combined Arms Center at Fort Leavenworth, which he commanded between Iraq deployments.

The central tenet of COIN doctrine is that a counterinsurgency is a battle with insurgents for the control and support of the civilian population. In COIN operations, killing and defeating insurgents is a secondary goal to winning over the hearts and minds of the population. "The more successful the counterinsurgency is, the less force can be used and the more risk must be accepted," explains the COIN Manual.[67] Collateral or accidental civilian damage may be lawful, but it is a setback in the counterinsurgent's efforts to gain legitimacy in the eyes of local civilian populations. This is why McChrystal's rules of engagement, and many other elements of counterinsurgent warfare, are more restrained in the use of force and other military activities than the law demands.

The same COIN philosophy applies to detention operations. Both U.S. and international laws permit the U.S. military to capture enemy soldiers and dangerous insurgents in Iraq and Afghanistan and detain them until the conflict ends or as long as they remain a threat. The Geneva Conventions, designed primarily with traditional wars in mind, require very few procedural safeguards to ensure that the right person is detained and has a chance to know and contest the facts of his detention. They leave matters like evidentiary rules and burdens of proof and the procedural rights of the detainee more generally to the discretion of the detaining government. As a result, notes University of Texas law professor Robert Chesney, they "place little pressure on militaries to engage in law enforcement-style methods of collecting and preserving evidence," and leave soldiers in the field and their commanders to focus on their traditional concerns of finding and killing the enemy and protecting the forces.[68]

COIN upends this traditional approach to detention. Its goal is not simply to incapacitate bad guys, but rather to do so in a fair process based on evidence presented publicly to the extent feasible in order to make detentions just and appear to be so before the civilian population. The COIN Manual provides general guidance on this task by summarizing the law that all soldiers must follow; by explaining who can be detained and for how long; by insisting on a separation of detention and interrogation personnel; by requiring that military detention be done by "specially trained, organized, and equipped military police units in adequately designed and resourced facilities"; and by urging the turnover of these activities as soon as feasible to the host-nation.[69]

This philosophy was implemented, painfully but largely successfully, during the COIN-inspired Surge in Iraq during 2006–2007. When President Obama chose General Stanley McChrystal to implement COIN in Afghanistan in 2009, McChrystal made improved detention operations a priority. "Detention operations [are] critical to the success of counterinsurgency operations," he wrote to Secretary of Defense Robert Gates in the summer of 2009.[70] In theory the detention option should allow the military to remove dangerous insurgents from Afghanistan's many areas of armed conflict and garner human intelligence about where the next insurgent attacks might come. But when McChrystal took over in 2009, detention operations in Afghanistan—which had developed a foul reputation in the years following Abu Ghraib and had become a source of friction between the U.S. and both its allies and the Afghan government—had ground nearly to a halt. U.S. soldiers and marines frequently complained that they lacked meaningful recourse to one of the most important facets of COIN doctrine. McChrystal described the detention problem to Gates as a potential "strategic liability."[71]

Because Mark Martins had garnered significant experience in COIN-related detention operations as David Petraeus's chief lawyer during the Surge, he was chosen in 2009 to help lead detention and related rule-of-law efforts in Afghanistan. His promotion at the Justice Department to brigadier general, in fact, was done in anticipation of his assignment to serve under Vice Admiral Robert S. Harward Jr. in the newly established Joint Task Force-435 (JTF-435) for Afghanistan, which was charged with conducting "detention, corrections, judicial sector and biometrics operations" in conjunction with the Afghan government, U.S. civilian authorities, and international partners.[72] The assignment was an unusual one, for Martins would not serve as Harward's lawyer, but rather as the initial JTF-435 commander while Harward was being confirmed in the Senate and then as Harward's deputy commander.[73] He would use his military and legal training and experience not to advise clients, but rather to command thousands of troops in an effort deemed critical to mission success in Afghanistan.

A big piece of changing detention operations in Afghanistan was architectural. Before 2009, most U.S. military detainees in Afghanistan were held in an old Russian airplane hangar on the Bagram Airfield. This decrepit facility, a locale of early prisoner abuses, had no windows and no natural light. It was widely despised by detainees and had a terrible reputation in Afghanistan. In 2009, the U.S. military opened a high-tech modern facility with large cells and plenty of natural light, five miles away, in Parwan, Afghanistan. What happens inside the Parwan facility is more important than its architectural features. "There are more insurgents per square foot in corrections facilities than anywhere else in Afghanistan," McChrystal wrote in 2009. "Unchecked, Taliban/Al Qaeda leaders patiently coordinate and plan, unconcerned with interference from prison personnel or the military."[74] They also recruit from within the facility. The response in Parwan to this "insurgency inside the wire"—a response that built on and learned from similar efforts in Iraq—was twofold. The first was to segregate "irreconcilable" hard-core radicals from reconcilable "accidental guerillas." The second was to fight the insurgency raging in prison cells by offering the detainees, especially the reconcilable ones, serious educational and vocational training as part of detention operations. Detainees are taught to read so that they can see for themselves what the Koran says about jihad. And they are taught practical skills such as tailoring, baking, and farming, both to assist them in living constructive lives once released and to send a credible signal of goodwill to the Afghan population.

One focus in JTF-435 was on creating a process to ensure that the right people ended up in Parwan in the right way.[75] Within seventy-two hours, a soldier must explain to his commanding officer and a military lawyer why a captured suspect meets a detention definition that derives from Congress's September 2001 Authorization for Use of Military Force.[76] Suspects are often released at this stage because the standard is not met or the evidence is too thin. If they are not released, they must be transferred within fourteen days to the detention center in Parwan, where the International Committee of the Red Cross meets with them and where they are notified that a "Detainee Review Board" of three officers will assess their case within sixty days. A neutral officer presents the case to the board and must proffer "all relevant evidence." Each detainee is also assigned a "personal representative"—another U.S. military officer—to "act and advocate in [his] best interests." The personal representative must present all reasonably available information "in the light most favorable to the detainee," and cannot disclose detrimental information learned from the suspect. A suspect can attend the hearing that determines his fate. So too can human rights organizations, Afghan government officials, and the media. Various forms of testimony—live and written— can be presented. Some classified evidence—usually involving information that would reveal sources and methods of intelligence collection—is presented in a closed session that the personal representative, but not the suspect, can attend. The suspects a board sees in a typical day can include a man who gave landmines to the Taliban, one who discarded a hand grenade approaching a military checkpoint, another captured with bomb-making materials in the home, another with links to insurgent commanders, and yet another captured among a group of insurgents.[77] The board uses a "preponderance of the evidence" standard and can release the suspect, detain him, or turn him over to the Afghan government for trial or rehabilitation. If the suspect is detained, he must be given another hearing within six months.

In addition to its elaborate procedures, the military goes to extraordinary lengths to collect, process, and present credible evidence.[78] The Department of Defense defines forensics as the "application of multidisciplinary scientific processes to establish facts," and that is precisely what soldiers in the field, backed up by professional forensics experts, increasingly do. Soldiers in Afghanistan trained in "detention operations" carry elaborate "forensics" or "site exploitation" kits into battle among the many items in their heavy pack. After they clear a house or a building of insurgents, or capture someone, they often stay and take actions designed to prepare for the detention review process and a possible criminal trial down the road. They collect witness statements and photographs of the scene. They do a forensics sweep for evidence such as weapons, ammunition, cartridge cases, cell phones, cameras, documents, photos, cups, bottles, clothing, and components of improvised explosive devices. They harvest fingerprints and DNA evidence, scan retinas, collect other biometric data, and perform chemical tests for evidence of explosives. They are trained to triage this material (so that only the most probative is sent in for analysis), to package it properly to minimize degradation and cross-contamination, and to complete properly chain-of-custody forms. The soldiers turn over all of this evidence to one of several Joint Expeditionary Forensics Facilities in Afghanistan, known as "JEFFs." The forensics experts in the JEFFs are trained to the same standards used by the U.S. Army Criminal Investigation Laboratory for criminal trials, and they use identical processes, protocols, and techniques for the processing, analysis, and identification of evidence. In short, soldiers are not just warriors in the field, but police investigators as well, backed up by a CSI-like laboratory that uses processes rigorous enough to satisfy a military trial of a U.S. soldier.

Nothing close to this level of due process and proof has ever been provided in military detention operations. But human rights organizations that monitor Detainee Review Boards insist on yet higher standards of process and proof. They complain, in the words of Jonathan Horowitz of the Open Society Institute, that "the rules are a far cry from the regular system of courtroom checks and balances."[79] Horowitz is right to say that U.S. detention operations in Afghanistan do not meet the standards of criminal trials. But military detention during war has never held itself to the standards of regular judicial systems. What Mark Martins and his JTF-435 colleagues implemented in 2009–2010 is the fairest and most rigorous battlefield detention process in military history. It is also a process that compels U.S. soldiers to take risks different in character from those taken by prior generations of troops. One such risk is that soldiers sometimes spend extra time in dangerous locales to collect evidence.[80] Another is that soldiers release people they believe are terrorists or insurgents, or fail to pick them up, because they also believe they lack conclusive evidence that will stand up before fellow soldiers sitting on Detainee Review Boards or before ordinary Afghans.

In these senses, the constraints of the more rigorous military detention system—both the procedure and proof requirements, and the constraints of critics who are invited in to monitor the system—are like the targeting constraints found in the rules of engagement. They force soldiers to hold back, to accept additional personal danger, and sometimes to lose the opportunity to incapacitate a suspected militant. But in the Afghanistan insurgency context, the more traditional and less constrained military detention operations posed risks to soldiers as well, including the inability to detain many suspects for lack of legitimacy and hostility from the local population that made victory difficult. The detention system implemented by JTF-435, like constrained targeting rules and rules of engagement, reflects a COIN-inspired judgment that the costs of enhanced restraint are an appropriate price for a more legitimate and defensible detention system. And at least from the perspective of detention effectiveness, that judgment seems to have been confirmed by experience. U.S. detention operations in Afghanistan have largely been "detoxified," as Martins puts it, and soldiers and marines have a meaningful option—now largely supported by the Afghan government—to detain insurgents who would otherwise continue to terrorize the Afghan population. By the summer of 2011, the United States was holding more than three times as many detainees in Afghanistan as in 2009 with many fewer complaints from the Afghan government or U.S. allies. Human rights groups, unsurprisingly, were alarmed by the increase in numbers.[81] But the evidence and process supporting these many additional detainees were undoubtedly more powerful than the evidence and process supporting the smaller numbers two years earlier. The U.S. military, and the Commander in Chief whom it serves, were empowered by constraint to take many more insurgents off the battlefield with less controversy than before.

Constrained U.S. detention operations are an important element of Afghan counterinsurgency strategy. But the ultimate goal for the U.S. military is, as McChrystal told Gates, to get out of the detention business in Afghanistan altogether.[82] Unfortunately, in many parts of Afghanistan, there are no police, no courts, no prosecutors, no prisons, and thus no government provision of justice. Even in the places where there is an Afghan government presence, it is often ineffective or corrupt. To make matters worse, the remnants of the Afghan justice system are under systematic attack. "Taliban fighters have mounted a concerted campaign to eviscerate the fragile Afghan judicial system by systematically assassinating hundreds of judges, lawyers, and prison guards," the *National Journal*'s Yochi Dreazen reported in 2011.[83] The Taliban also provides its own corruption-free but often brutal and repressive "shadow courts" to dispense Islamist justice, and in many parts of Afghanistan the Taliban's justice system is more popular and effective than the government's. The government's failure to provide effective local justice was a primary cause of the rise of the Taliban two decades ago and remains an impetus for the insurgency. In the battle for the hearts and minds of civilians that characterizes counterinsurgency operations, helping the Afghan government improve its justice system is a primary strategic goal of U.S. forces. "We must support the Afghan government in its efforts to establish basic dispute resolution in key districts in order to facilitate improvements in security, to create the conditions that foster the reintegration and reconciliation of former insurgents, and to combat corruption that undermines trust in the Afghan government," noted Secretary of Defense Robert Gates in a speech at NATO headquarters in 2011.[84]

Gates is referring here to the "build phase" of counterinsurgency operations. The basic tasks of counterinsurgency forces are first to clear a city or village of insurgents through military force, then hold what they cleared, and then build the political and legal institutions necessary for security and order after the soldiers leave.[85] The third phase of counterinsurgency operations requires soldiers to be "nation builders as well as warriors," as David Petraeus said in his foreword to the COIN Manual. When the government fails to provide essential justice services, the COIN Manual instructs, "counterinsurgents may need to undertake a significant role in the reconstruction of the [host-nation] judicial system in order to establish legal procedures and systems to deal with captured insurgents and common criminals." The manual adds that "during judicial reconstruction, counterinsurgents can expect to be involved in providing sustainment and security support" and "can also expect to provide legal support and advice to the [host-country] judicial entities."[86]

These passages from the COIN Manual about building justice and rule-of-law capacities during the "hold" and "clear" phases of COIN operations were drafted by Mark Martins in 2006 for his friend David Petraeus. Martins lived his own words in an unusual new command that he assumed in Afghanistan in September 2010 known as the "Rule of Law Field Force," or ROLFF. The goal of ROLFF is to revive governance in southern Afghanistan, where the insurgency is strongest, during the "hold" phase of COIN operations after an area has been cleared of insurgents. Martins and his soldiers—most of whom are lawyers, engineers, criminal justice and forensics experts, and security forces— enter an area immediately after it is cleared to begin rebuilding before the insurgents can reconstitute. Working with the Afghan government and U.S. civilian authorities, they refurbish courthouses, detention facilities, and prisons; build secure housing for investigators, prosecutors, and judges, as well as the occasional forensic lab; train and organize the police, prosecutors, judges, and other Afghan officials who use these facilities; and provide the security, communication, transportation, and procurement infrastructure needed to make the facilities work. Much of this work focuses on establishing "rule of law green zones," which are secure compounds where, as Martins explains, key players in the justice system (and, often, their families) can be protected from intimidation and attack and provided with basic facilities and services. "We're trying to create a secure place, a safe place, for spreading the rule of law," notes Martins's colleague, General Amir Mohammad Jamshid, the head of Afghanistan's Central Prison Directorate.[87]

Martins and other senior military officials believe that rule-of-law green zones and related efforts to improve the Afghan justice system are a key element to winning over Afghan hearts and minds and thus defeating the Taliban insurgency. "When fighting an insurgency, a government that protects the population and upholds the rule of law can earn legitimacy—that is, authority in the eyes of the people," notes Martins. "Individuals deciding whether to support or oppose a government will be attracted, other things being equal, to a government that adheres to law."[88] Many are deeply skeptical of the ROLFF approach. They doubt that the bottom-up provision of security and justice in a country that lacks a trustworthy national government or a rule-of-law tradition, and that has been wracked by decades of war and corruption, can succeed. They are especially doubtful that ROLFF's progress in the last few years in building up the capacity of Afghan officials to dispense effective and legitimate justice will survive after U.S. forces wind down their support or leave altogether. Martins is not a wild-eyed optimist about rule-of-law green zones. He acknowledges that the success of ROLFF depends a great deal on the ability of U.S. troops and, ultimately, the Afghan government to provide security. But he has a realistic sense of the goals of ROLFF, and believes those goals can be reached. "This is not a game of perfect," he often says. "We only need to help the Afghan government be better, on balance, than Taliban groups that dispense motorcycle gang justice."

It is too early to tell whether ROLFF or more ambitious, COIN-inspired governance and development programs will succeed. But even before that evidence is in, ROLFF stands as a remarkable testament to how war has changed, and to how integral law has become to war. A decade ago many believed that law should, and would, become less salient in the global wars against Islamist terrorists, and many of the controversial early Bush programs can be seen as efforts to break free of legal restraints. But the roles of law and lawyers in military operations have grown significantly since 9/11. Within the military, legal restraint is seen as more vital than ever to the success of military operations. And as the rise of ROLFF and similar programs and operations show, law has become much more than an empowering restraint. General Martins's troops are fighting to bring Afghan citizens criminal justice capacity, dispute resolution services, and other legal institutions, all with the aim of promoting the legitimacy of the Afghan government and defeating the insurgency. By the end of the first decade after 9/11, and only a few years after the Abu Ghraib catastrophe, law has literally become both a weapon of warfare and what the war is about.

Martins himself would spend a year racing around Afghanistan against the political clock trying to make ROLFF succeed. But on September 15, 2011, one decade and four days after Khalid

Sheikh Mohammed's improbably successful plot to wreak havoc on the United States, Martins assumed a new assignment that would require him to use law as a weapon of warfare in a different way. On that date, he became chief prosecutor in the Office of Military Commissions, where his most important duties would be to prosecute Mohammed and his coconspirators at Guantanamo Bay, Cuba, and to revitalize and legitimate a military commissions institution and process that had been damaged by a decade of political and legal mistakes and false starts. "Like our field duty in Afghanistan's contested provinces and districts, this will be another assignment to strengthen the rule of law," Martins said upon learning of his appointment.

Chapter Six

THE GTMO BAR

MICHAEL RATNER NEVER IMAGINED he would spark a judicial revolution that would bring the Commander in Chief to grief over terrorist detention. Ratner is the bald, bespectacled, sixty-eight-year-old president of the Center for Constitutional Rights (CCR), a far-left legal advocacy organization founded in the 1960s by the self-described "radical" civil rights lawyer William Kunstler and other civil rights attorneys.[1] Over the years, the CCR represented the Attica rioters, the Chicago Eight, Puerto Rican National Liberation members, the Nicaraguan contras, Black Panther Minister of Justice H. Rap Brown, and assorted other "violent radicals, Communist front-groups, cop-killers, and sworn enemies of the United States," in the words of conservative critic Marc Thiessen.[2] Ratner and the CCR lost most of their cases, but they won a few, sometimes setting landmark precedents. "What's the purpose of going along with the status quo?" Ratner would ask. "The government has enough paid people to do their dirty work."[3]

Reading the *New York Times* in his Greenwich Village apartment on the morning of November 14, 2001, Ratner learned that President Bush had issued "Military Order Number 1."[4] He was stunned to read that the Commander in Chief had unilaterally created military commissions and asserted the power to detain any noncitizen deemed a terrorist. But what outraged him most was an obscure provision near the end of the order providing that a detainee "shall not be privileged to seek any remedy or maintain any proceeding [in] any court of the United States." Ratner thought this provision illegally abolished habeas corpus, the ancient writ protected in the Constitution that allows a prisoner to challenge the legality of his detention before a court. "I felt as if there had just been a coup d'etat in America," Ratner thought at the time. "It was a watershed moment for a country that I still thought had some semblance of a democracy and some adherence to the principle that Presidential authority was under law."[5]

Ratner had made a career out of representing unpopular clients, and he immediately thought that the CCR must represent the first person detained under the order. But when he and his staff met later that morning at CCR headquarters just twenty blocks from the still-smoldering 9/11 ruins, they hesitated. "We were all extremely concerned that we might be representing the conspirators who were involved in 9/11," Ratner later recounted.[6] Some in the CCR worried about the effect on fund-raising. Some worried how representing terrorists would serve the CCR's aims of using law to promote progressive social change. And some worried that it might be personally dangerous to represent the terrorists. After a week of intense deliberation, the organization decided to go forward and seek clients. "The issue of denying habeas corpus was so fundamental that no matter what, we had to do the case," Ratner later explained. The CCR president had bucked himself up and rallied his troops by reminding everyone of the organization's refusal to represent Yusef Salaam, one of five young black men arrested in 1989 for raping Trisha Meili, the white Central Park jogger. CCR had declined Salaam as a client because the case was too controversial, but it was later embarrassed when DNA evidence exonerated all five men. "Look at what happened in Salaam's case," Ratner told the CCR lawyers. "You just don't know. You just have to have these cases tested in the courts because you just can't trust the executive."

But getting the cases tested in court was easier said than done. "Zero, absolute zero" was how Ratner rated his chances of con-

vincing the courts to review the detentions of the GTMO clients that the CCR began to gather in the winter of 2001–2002.
Ratner had good reason to be skeptical. The country was seeth-
ing with anger and hungry for vengeance. In previous wars in
American history, Presidents had captured and detained enemy
soldiers without judicial interference. And the Supreme Court
seemed to have already decided the issues that Ratner would be
raising in seeking the detainees' release. "We started looking at
the precedents, and we're staring *Quirin* and *Eisentrager* right in the
face," he recalled. In the *Quirin* case the Supreme Court approved
Franklin D. Roosevelt's World War II military commissions and
in the process noted that the President had the power to detain
enemy soldiers until the end of the war. *Eisentrager* was a post–
World War II Supreme Court case that denied a foreign enemy
soldier detained outside the United States judicial relief under the
writ of habeas corpus. "We are cited to no instance where a court,
in this or any other country where the writ is known, has issued
it on behalf of an alien enemy who at no relevant time and in no
stage of his captivity has been within its territorial jurisdiction,"
reasoned Justice Robert Jackson for the Court. "Nothing in the
text of the Constitution extends such a right, nor does anything in
our statutes." Taken together, these decisions seemed to allow the
President to detain terrorist soldiers on Guantanamo Bay without
judicial supervision as long as the war with al Qaeda and the
Taliban lasted.

The *Quirin* and *Eisentrager* decisions were part of a broader
historical tradition of judicial deference to the executive branch
during war. "Never in American history had the [Supreme]
Court tried in any way to interfere with a war in progress," noted
Arthur Schlesinger Jr. in 1973.[7] Ratner knew firsthand about this
tradition. In the 1980s and 1990s, he and his CCR colleagues,
deeply involved in the antiwar movement, filed lawsuits challenging the legality of U.S. military and paramilitary action in
Cambodia, El Salvador, Nicaragua, Grenada, Iraq, and Kosovo.[8]
They lost every one. Ratner also had a bitter personal experience
with Guantanamo Bay. For a decade before 9/11, presidents had

used the island as a detention facility for "undesirables" precisely because it was outside of U.S. sovereignty and thus beyond judicial review.[9] In the early 1990s, Ratner and the CCR represented a group of HIV-positive Haitians that President George H. W. Bush and then President Clinton had ordered detained on the island naval base after they were intercepted trying to come to the United States. They secured the Haitians' release after a legal battle with the government.[10] But they suffered many defeats along the way that heightened Ratner's pessimism about his chances with the 9/11 detainees. "I had learned that the United States could win some legal arguments that Guantanamo, because it was offshore, was a law-free zone; that the refugees we represented were not protected by the Constitution; and no court could hear their cases or protect their rights," he later said.

In spite of these obstacles, on February 19, 2002, the CCR filed its first GTMO lawsuit on behalf of Shafiq Rasul, a British citizen picked up in Afghanistan. It was one month after the detention facility at GTMO first opened, and just two weeks after the Bush administration declared that none of the prisoners there would receive legal rights under the Geneva Conventions or access to any court. Almost no one noticed Ratner's lawsuit. "Few people or reporters seemed concerned with efforts to gain a hearing or winning any rights for the Guantanamo detainees," Ratner later said. "The mood in the country was such that CCR could not even find a cooperating attorney in D.C. to help file the papers—even progressives were afraid of the case."[11] Ratner's pessimism about his chances were confirmed five months later when a respected federal judge, Colleen Kollar-Kotelly, dismissed the case. The writ of habeas corpus does not extend to "the military base at Guantanamo Bay, Cuba," she reasoned, because it was "outside the sovereign territory of the United States."[12] The following year, respected judges on the court of appeals unanimously agreed. The legal precedents, looked at dispassionately, did not permit Ratner's clients to go to court.

On June 28, 2004, however, the Supreme Court set off on a very different course. It reversed the lower courts and ruled that despite the *Eisentrager* decision, Ratner's client and every other detainee at GTMO could challenge in court "the legality of the Executive's potentially indefinite detention." Justice Antonin Scalia predicted in his dissent that the decision would bring "the cumbersome machinery of our domestic courts into military affairs." Scalia had no idea. After the 2004 decision, the CCR would coordinate with other organizations and lead hundreds of elite private lawyers—the group was known half-jokingly as the "Guantanamo Bay Bar Association"—in flooding the courts with habeas corpus petitions and related lawsuits. The lawsuits were backed in important ways by a technology-infused social movement consisting of activist groups and journalists from around the globe, foreign governments and courts, and even military officials within the U.S. government. By 2011, these forces had convinced the Supreme Court to issue two other landmark decisions that limited presidential power, conferred novel legal rights on enemy soldiers, influenced military operations abroad, and provoked the usually passive Congress to enact historic legislation that cut into traditional presidential prerogatives. A decade after the GTMO detention facility began its life as a creature of presidential unilateralism, it and the political and legal decisions it spawned stand as a testament to the power of modern wartime checks and balances. But Ratner's achievements came with a large price. Paradoxically, and to Ratner's regret, his victories in court and elsewhere helped Barack Obama to legitimate counterterrorism policies that Ratner sought to end.

CONVINCING THE COURT

"If you had said to people on September 12, 2001, 'The United States is not going to be able to get away with whatever it wants to do in response to this attack,' people would have said, 'Well, what do you mean, who's going to stop it?' " notes Georgetown Law professor and CCR board member David Cole. " 'We just got attacked in one of the most heinous atrocities that we've seen in the modern world by a group that has no powerful supporters and we're the most powerful country in the world. Who's going to stop us?' "[13] Certainly not the Supreme Court, most people thought. And yet the Court did push back against the President—slowly, methodically, but with increasing fortitude over the years, ultimately proving to be one of the most important agents for making the Constitution's checks and balances work in the last decade. It did not stand up to the President through a detached application of the law. What the law required was uncertain at best in 2002, and if anything, it favored the government. Rather, it was moved by broader imperatives and concerns, and it self-consciously crafted its decisions to make constitutional checks and balances work as it thought best. There is no simple or definitive explanation for why the Court did this, but rather a cluster of mutually supportive explanations.

Despite Ratner's pessimism, in wars during the century before 9/11 the Supreme Court had shown small but increasing indications that it would scrutinize the President during war. Since the Civil War it had issued a few decisions invalidating presidential wartime actions after the war, when the costs of opposing the Commander in Chief had faded.[14] During the same period—in World Wars I and II especially—it had reviewed executive branch action during wartime more often and more searchingly than in the past. In a few famous wartime cases that involved matters extraneous to core presidential war powers, the Court had ruled against the President.[15] And while it almost always sided with the executive branch in cases involving his military powers during war, it also subtly ratcheted up its scrutiny of these actions, especially when the Commander in Chief curtailed civil liberties. In the *Quirin* case that upheld Roosevelt's military commission, for example, the Supreme Court charted new ground by making the executive branch come to the Court to explain and defend the legality of its military commission actions in the middle of the war—something that was controversial at the time. These subtle changes led Chief Justice William Rehnquist, in a book on wartime civil liberties published three years before 9/11, to predict that in future wars it is "likely that more careful attention will be paid by the courts to the basis for the government's claims of necessity as a basis for curtailing civil liberty."[16]

Rehnquist built his prescient judgment on an analysis of Supreme Court trends through World War II. Changes in American constitutional law after that war would also prod the Court toward greater engagement after 9/11. The Court led a three-decade civil liberties revolution that dramatically enhanced constitutional protections, for citizens and aliens alike, concerning due process, criminal procedure, free speech, habeas corpus, and much more. By 2001, the Court and the nation had very different expectations about these issues, and about judicial independence. The post–World War II period also saw a large drop in trust of the presidency, especially after Vietnam and Watergate. In July 1942, *New York Times* reporter Arthur Krock defended the elaborate secrecy of Roosevelt's military commission trial by noting that the "FBI vouches for the need of secrecy and the administration's lawyers support the legality of the procedure," adding that "unless these lead to clear abuses, neither is likely to be called into broad question."[17] A passage of this sort appearing in the *Times* after 9/11 was unimaginable, and in fact the *Times* led the charge in criticizing Bush's more open military commission system. In large part as a result of the disclosures about presidential abuses and excesses in the 1960s and 1970s, executive branch officers have received diminished levels of trust—in politics, and by the courts—when there has been a plausible claim that civil liberties are at risk, even, and indeed especially, during war.

When it came to counterterrorism policies, the Bush administration in its early years was oblivious to these trust concerns. Each of the two main legal arguments supporting its GTMO policies—that enemy soldiers caught out of uniform lacked Geneva Convention rights, and that enemy soldiers outside the United States could not challenge their detention in court—was backed by old legal precedents. But the application of these old precedents in a novel and seemingly endless war meant something new and, in modern times, troubling: hundreds of alleged terrorists captured out of uniform would be subject to indefinite detention by the executive branch in a place ungoverned by any law or any court. Regardless of the merits of the legal arguments, this was a scary proposition in a war in which enemy soldiers are hard to distinguish from civilians. The Bush administration made it scarier because of the way it presented its counterterrorism powers to the public. Its commitment to expanding presidential power led it to craft its GTMO and related counterterrorism policies broadly and to announce them unilaterally. The main effect of this public stance was to cause the public, the press, the Congress, and the courts to view Bush's wartime practices in a suspicious light, especially as the 9/11 threat faded from view.

This was the background against which the Center for Constitutional Rights and lawyers in a companion case from the law firm of Shearman & Sterling approached the first Supreme Court case over GTMO detainees. The CCR/Shearman team made a self-conscious decision to try to change the narrative that had dominated the consideration of judicial review in the lower courts. "The posture of the cases in the lower courts was 'the terrorists versus the government,' " notes Douglass Cassel, a human rights law expert then at Northwestern Law School who helped the Shearman/CCR team craft its Supreme Court strategy. "In the Supreme Court we tried to change the narrative to 'the rule of law v. the government.' " The problem was that the GTMO detainees, alleged terrorists, could not effectively make this pitch. "And so we decided to reach out to a broad-based group of credible people who had no sympathy for terrorism but who did have a commitment to the rule of law," notes Cassel, who coordinated the strategy.[18] The Supreme Court permits any "amicus curiae," or "friend of the court," to file a legal brief that "brings to the attention of the Court relevant matter not already brought to its attention by the parties."[19] Cassel organized a slew of *amicus* briefs by establishment figures from many different quarters to help bolster the rule-of-law focus of the case. In the end, seventeen *amicus* briefs were filed in Rasul's support (and only four were filed in support of the government). It is impossible to know how much of an impact the legal arguments in these briefs had on the Court's decision. But the participants in the briefs, and the rule-of-law arguments they made, provide a window on the social, cultural, and informational influences on the Court.

One *amicus* brief was filed by Fred Korematsu, an American citizen of Japanese descent who as a young man resisted Franklin D. Roosevelt's exclusion of him and thousands of other persons of Japanese ancestry from the West Coast of the United States during World War II. None of the Japanese-Americans were individually suspected of wrongdoing. When the government convicted Korematsu for resisting FDR's order, he appealed to the Supreme Court, which, in a famous case that bears his name, rejected his plea out of deference to the Commander in Chief. Justice Frank Murphy charged in his dissent that the Roosevelt order "goes over 'the very brink of constitutional power,' and falls into the ugly abyss of racism."[20] This is how Roosevelt's order, and the Supreme Court decision upholding it, came to be seen in the decades after World War II.[21] The political and legal establishment would condemn the decision for indulging the Commander in Chief's panicked and unnecessary curtailment of civil liberties based on a racial stereotype. Gerald Ford issued a presidential proclamation in 1976 stating that the exclusion was "wrong" and calling on the American people to "resolve that this kind of action shall never again be repeated."[22] A few years later, the commission on the Japanese exclusion and internment recommended that the nation formally apologize for the episode. Congress took this advice in 1988 by "apologiz[ing] on behalf of the nation" and paying reparations. The year before, a federal court formally vacated Korematsu's conviction. In 1998, Korematsu, who had devoted his life to the preservation of civil liberties, received the Presidential Medal of Freedom, the nation's highest civilian honor.

The Supreme Court justices did not need Fred Korematsu to tell them in 2004 that the *Korematsu* decision had "harmed" the Supreme Court and brought it "longlasting shame," as Justice Stephen Breyer noted in his 2010 book about the Court.[23] The justices were well aware that in the *Korematsu* case and at other times in American history, the Court had allowed the executive branch to curtail civil liberties in the name of national security only to see the nation later regret such incursions into core liberties. And yet an *amicus* brief about the ghost of the *Korematsu* case, brought to the Court's attention by Fred Korematsu himself, must have had special salience. "To avoid repeating the mistakes of the past, this Court should . . . affirm that the United States respects fundamental constitutional and human rights—even in time of war," Korematsu argued. "Let us not now set the foundation for later apologies," he added. "Let us instead underscore the role of the courts in assuring the indispensable safeguards by which we are, and should be, measured as a just society."[24] Justice Breyer would later say that *Rasul* and related cases "presented the Court with a challenge similar to that presented in *Korematsu*," a challenge he characterized as finding a way to protect civil liberties during wartime without "taking from the president discretionary powers that war might require him to exercise."[25]

Like Korematsu, other *amici*, including scores of former U.S. judges, diplomats, and other government officials, would file briefs emphasizing the domestic rule-of-law stakes of the GTMO cases. Another major theme in the briefs was that the international rule of law hung in the balance. Since World War II, and motivated by the Holocaust, nations had agreed in treaties to outlaw genocide and torture, and to provide extensive protections for civil and political rights for persons under their control. These and related international law instruments grew in prominence after the Berlin Wall fell, when a consensus on the importance and legitimacy of Western-style rights seemed to emerge. Nongovernmental organizations (NGOs)—some of which, like Amnesty International, had been around for a while, but many of which were born after the Cold War—led the charge to enhance the impact of international human rights law and the norms they embodied. They collected facts about human rights abuses, packaged them in splashy reports, and used the information strategically, backed by the rhetoric of human rights law, to pressure governments to improve their treatment of individuals.[26] They also developed expertise on the content of international human rights law and advocated for their vision of international law in domestic and international courts. In their reports and advocacy efforts, the NGOs established themselves as influential counterpoints to governments as interpreters of international norms. The digital revolution that began when the Cold War ended amplified this influence by making it much easier for NGOs to work with like-minded individuals—across borders and institutions—in gathering and processing information, and in advocating for favored norms. During the same period, journalists, many of whom shared the general aims of the NGOs, began to treat NGO reports as news events, and increasingly included the commentary of NGO officials in their stories.

As the influence of international human rights law and associated NGOs grew, they began to influence U.S. law and institutions. After the Cold War the number of courses in international human rights law exploded in American law schools. So too did human rights scholarship. Dozens of law professors, many with human rights NGO affiliations, wrote article after article about how international human rights law should influence U.S. law. Human rights clinics sprang up, giving law students a way to work directly with the NGOs on cases and reports, and argue for the relevance of international human rights law in the domestic U.S. legal system. Michael Ratner's Center for Constitutional Rights was at the core of this movement. In 1980, the CCR, working with legal academics, convinced a New York federal court to recognize a "universal jurisdiction" lawsuit by a Paraguayan man suing Paraguayan officials for violating international human rights law in Paraguay, a watershed decision that set off decades of ever-more-imaginative international human rights lawsuits and judicial decisions against foreign officials and corporations.[27] A decade later, just after the Cold War ended, Ratner joined with human rights advocate and Yale Law School professor (and later Obama's top State Department lawyer) Harold Koh to establish an influential human rights advocacy clinic at Yale that worked with NGOs and law professors in lawsuits arguing, often successfully, that international human rights law should influence how judges interpret domestic U.S. law.[28]

A generation of law professors, law students, and lower federal courts advocating for the increased relevance of international human rights law, combined with the growing public awareness of human rights law and language, ultimately had an impact on the Supreme Court. Both before and after 9/11, the Court recognized various ways that international human rights law could inform domestic legal principles in contexts like the death penalty, discrimination against homosexuals, and human rights lawsuits against foreign officials.[29] The Court's growing reliance on international law (and, relatedly, foreign law) as a tool for interpreting domestic law was part of a larger cosmopolitan turn by some of the justices on the Court, most notably swing justice Anthony Kennedy.[30] After communism's collapse, American constitutional law experts, including Supreme Court justices, were in enormous demand to help new democracies design their constitutions. These experiences were bolstered by a globalization-enabled increase in meetings and interchanges between judges from different countries. In these "informal exchanges," noted Justice Kennedy, "[y]ou can't help but be influenced by what you see and what you hear." American lawyers, including justices, became much more aware of the profound influence of the U.S. Supreme Court and U.S. constitutional traditions—especially its tradition of judicial review—on other nations. Some of the justices also drew the lesson that the United States could learn from other constitutional and international traditions. "If we are asking the rest of the world to adopt our idea of freedom," said Kennedy, speaking of the influence of the U.S. Supreme Court abroad, "it does seem to me that there may be some mutuality there, that other nations and other peoples can define and interpret freedom in a way that's at least instructive to us."[31]

This was the context in which the *amici* in the *Rasul* case made their international rule-of-law pitch. "The exercise of executive power without the possibility of judicial review jeopardizes the keystone of our existence as nations—namely, the rule of law—

as well as the effective protection for human rights as a matter of international obligation," said one brief. "This Court should preserve the judiciary's vital role to insure that executive actions violate neither the Constitution of the United States of America nor the international rule of law and human rights." The *amici* also argued that a failure to review the GTMO detentions would undermine U.S. diplomatic efforts abroad, including its rule-of-law efforts in developing countries. "The perception of this case abroad—that the power of the United States can be exercised outside the law and even, it is presumed, in conflict with the law—will diminish our stature and repute in the wider world," argued another brief. What is remarkable about these passages, and many similar ones, is that they were not written by lawyers for human rights NGOs. They were instead written by pillars of the establishment, which by 2001 was chock-full of sympathizers to the international human rights law movement. The first excerpt was from an unprecedented brief filed by 175 members of the British Parliament and the House of Lords.[32] And the second was written on behalf of twenty-three prominent former American diplomats.[33] Similar points were made in briefs filed by respected former judges and other former government officials.

Human rights NGOs made similar *amicus* pitches to the Supreme Court about the domestic and international rule-of-law stakes in the case. But these arguments were less important than the effective work the NGOs had done in establishing these points in the public debate long before the case reached the Supreme Court. These organizations represent a source of accountability that has grown very important in American politics in the last decade: well-networked, well-resourced groups of experts devoted to criticizing the government's war and security policies in the name of individual rights. These groups had worked with detainee lawyers and journalists around the world to develop—in the media and in their own reports—a broad narrative that many of the GTMO detainees were innocent or being abused or both. The ecology of transparency described in Chapter 3—including firsthand investigative reporting by journalists, and documents released in FOIA suits by the ACLU and others—gave these reports credibility. Also feeding the credibility of the rule-of-law concerns was the harsh and highly publicized judgment of other foreign establishment figures and international law institutions. A member of the British House of Lords made global headlines with a lecture entitled "Guantanamo Bay: The Legal Black Hole."[34] The International Committee of the Red Cross had charged that the United States had placed the GTMO detainees "beyond the law."[35] The Special Rapporteur for the United Nations Commission on Human Rights charged that the detention without trial at GTMO "offends the first principle of the rule of law."[36] And the Inter-American Commission on Human Rights, in a suit brought by the CCR, ruled that "no person under the authority and control of a state, regardless of his or her circumstances, is devoid of legal protection for his or her fundamental and non-derogable human rights."[37]

Of all of the establishment *amicus* briefs condemning the Bush administration and defending the rule of law before the Supreme Court, however, perhaps none were as significant as the ones filed by military officers who purported to represent the views of soldiers fighting in the war on terrorism.[38] Former U.S. military officers and military lawyers filed briefs that emphasized the importance to the military of the post–World War II Geneva Conventions, and especially their procedural protections for prisoner rights that, they charged, the Bush administration was flouting. The United States had long taken the lead in extending and enforcing these rights, they maintained, and American soldiers would suffer most from the Bush administration's disregard of them. "If American detention of the Guantanamo prisoners—indefinite confinement without any type of review by a court or tribunal—is regarded as precedent for similar actions by countries with which we are at peace, it is obvious that it may be similarly regarded by enemies who capture American soldiers in an existing or future conflict," argued the retired military officers. Even more remarkable was the *amicus* brief filed by *current* military lawyers representing alleged terrorist detainees in military commissions. There lawyers, in a public rebuke to the Commander in Chief they served, described the administration's claims about GTMO as a "monarchical regime."[39]

As with Korematsu and the civilian government officials, the military briefs were not telling the justices much that they had not learned in the newspapers in the previous two years. Since 2001 the judge advocates general (JAGs) in the Pentagon had been pushing back hard against what they viewed as the Bush administration's disregard of military law and traditions. Two legal commitments by the military were especially important. One was the 1950 Uniform Code of Military Justice (UCMJ), which replaced a command-dominated justice system with a system of courts-martial that eventually looked much like the civilian counterpart in its commitment to independence and due process. Another was the Geneva Conventions and related customary international laws of war. By 2001 both the UCMJ and the laws of war had become pillars of U.S. military discipline and central to the military's self-understanding as honorable warriors.

The JAGs were the guardians of these laws, with a deserved reputation for interpreting and enforcing them in ways that both protected the integrity of the military and reflected the realistic needs of battlefield discipline. For decades the U.S. military had built its doctrine, training, and policies around the JAG understandings of the UCMJ and the laws of war. And for decades their vision of law-governed military operations led them to have professional and even ideological points of contact and agreement with human rights groups and especially with the International Committee of the Red Cross. Of course, the military lawyers did not agree on all points with these NGOs. But as Harvard Law School professor David Kennedy notes, "They all know one another, hang out at the same places, read the same things, and have their own parallel problems with more exuberant people in their own 'camps.' "[40] They shared a general outlook, especially about the relevance of certain international laws, and it was an outlook not shared by the Bush administration.

The Bush administration's post-9/11 counterterrorism policies were a direct affront to the JAG view of the world and the Defense Department institutions that had built up around it. Vice Presidential Counsel David Addington and Defense Department General Counsel Jim Haynes had a principled commitment to reducing JAG independence based on notions of civilian control of the military. They also had principled views about the non-applicability of the UCMJ and the Geneva Conventions to certain aspects of the war on terrorism, and about vindicating these views—which were, after all, the views of the President—throughout the military. The JAGs fought hard against these policies inside the Pentagon, in public testimony, and in leaks to the press. The first clash came in November 2001 when the Bush administration announced its military commissions with little input from the JAGs. The JAGs viewed the commissions' departures from the UCMJ as both illegal under domestic and international law and a challenge to the authority they had built up around the UCMJ as the standard-bearers of military justice. The next clash came over the Bush administration's decision in January 2002 to proclaim that the Geneva Conventions had no application in the war on terrorism, a proclamation that the JAGs argued was illegal and dangerous for U.S. soldiers who might one day need Geneva protections. The third clash, which began in the fall of 2002, concerned the Bush administration's aggressive interrogation techniques, which the JAGs once again vehemently opposed on legal and policy grounds.

Never before had military lawyers so thoroughly disagreed with civilian officials during war over legal matters. The JAGs in the post-9/11 world were—like inspectors general, and like lawyers in other agencies, but with more power—yet another fount of independent scrutiny, law enforcement, and pushback inside the executive branch. The JAG counterattack on legal issues was remarkable because it was directed toward the Commander in Chief, who is supposed to be the chief law interpreter for the executive branch and whose power is supposed to be at its height during war. It was all the more remarkable because for assistance in their fights, the JAGs turned to human rights organizations with which, on these issues, they had a greater commonality of interests than with the President.[41] The ecology of transparency ensured that the clashes between military and civilian lawyers spilled into the public realm, and was churned by commentators, by the time the Supreme Court considered the GTMO cases in the spring of 2004. In a testament to the JAGs' reputation and independence, and to the mistrust of the Bush administration by this point, the stories about the law fights inside the Pentagon were not generally treated as military subordination or affronts to civilian control. They were, rather, treated as JAGs standing up to the law-defying Bush administration in the name of the rule of law.

The presidency was untrustworthy, out of control, and defying the rule of law and military traditions. That was the message the *amici* in Rasul's case sent to the Court—a message the Court had heard long before it read the briefs. Two months before the Court issued its final decision in the case on habeas corpus rights for GTMO detainees, the message received devastating public confirmation. On April 28, 2004, Justice Ruth Bader Ginsburg asked Deputy Solicitor General Paul Clement a seemingly innocuous set of questions in a case about the government's power to detain a U.S. citizen in the United States with little judicial scrutiny. "So what is it that would be a check against torture?" she asked. "What's constraining? . . . Is it just up to the good will of the executive?" Clement answered that the possibility of executive abuse in war "is not a good and sufficient reason for judicial micromanagement and overseeing of that authority." He added, "You have to recognize that in situations where there is a war—where the Government is on a war footing, that you have to trust the executive to make the kind of quintessential military judgments that are involved in things like that."[42] Seven hours later, the CBS program *60 Minutes* published the first photographs of U.S. soldiers abusing detainees at Abu Ghraib. The vile and shameful photos visualized years of worries and stories and charges about the dangers of unchecked executive power. They became the face of what it meant to trust the executive branch in war.

On June 18, 2004, the Supreme Court ruled that Ratner's client and almost six hundred other GTMO detainees could file petitions for habeas corpus in federal court to seek their release. The decision marked the first time in American history that enemy soldiers held outside the United States during wartime could force the executive branch to explain and defend their detention before a court. The Court did not mention Abu Ghraib or any of the *amicus* briefs. But it tied its decision to the tradition, dating back to before the Magna Carta, of judges employing the writ of habeas corpus to review "oppressive and lawless" executive detentions. And in a related war-on-terror case decided the same day, Justice Sandra Day O'Connor noted that "history and common sense teach us that an unchecked system of detention carries the potential to become a means for oppression and abuse of others."[43] The Court explained its decision on a narrow ground: that Congress had intended for courts' habeas corpus power to extend to places like GTMO that were under U.S. control. This was an implausible rationale that defied *Eisentrager*, which the Court did cartwheels to distinguish. But it had the virtue of making the Court's momentous step a relatively small one, for it left open the possibility that Congress could retract habeas corpus power from GTMO, and it said practically nothing about what legal rights, if any, these detainees possessed. As Justice Breyer would later say, the Court in *Rasul* "found a way to hold the president accountable to [the] limited extent" of allowing GTMO detainees to challenge their detention "while leaving much to be worked out later."[44]

There was indeed much to be worked out, but the *Rasul* decision still had an immediate impact. The administration had already released eighty detainees from GTMO in reaction to the Court's grant of review the previous November.[45] In response to the decision, it set up Combatant Status Review Tribunals (CRSTs) composed of military officers to review the legality of detentions for each person held at GTMO. CSRTs were based on Army regulations for detaining prisoners of war, and gave detainees the right to hear evidence against them, the right to challenge the detention by testifying and introducing evidence and calling witnesses, and the right to a personal representative to assist. Also in response to *Rasul*, the Bush administration established Administrative Review Boards (ARBs) to help ensure going forward that only detainees who remain dangerous were detained. The CSRTs determined that thirty-eight detainees could not be held as enemy combatants, and by 2006 the ARBs had determined that an additional 188 detainees could be released or transferred from GTMO.[46] All in all, the threat and reality of judicial review in *Rasul* caused the executive branch to tighten its detention standards and contributed to the discharge of 308 detainees from GTMO.

In 2006 the Supreme Court issued an even more significant decision in a case that asked whether Salim Ahmed Hamdan, Osama Bin Laden's bodyguard and driver, could be tried in the military commission system that President Bush announced in November 2001. On the surface, once again, the executive branch's legal arguments looked sound, since President Bush's order establishing the commissions had relied on the same language that FDR had used for his commissions in World War II and that the Supreme Court had approved in *Quirin*. But that 1942 precedent seemed like a relic in light of the massive intervening changes in military justice, criminal procedure, and the laws of war. And the rule-of-law concerns had grown in the intervening two years with the leak of the so-called torture memos; the floodgates opening on news reports of abuse in GTMO, Iraq, Afghanistan, and in secret prisons; and the *New York Times*' revelation of the warrantless wiretapping program known as the "Terrorist Surveillance Program" and other secret surveillance initiatives. Hamdan's lawyers, which included his military lawyer assigned to the case, argued that Bush's commissions violated the Constitution, congressional commands, and the international laws of war. Once again, *amici* swarmed the Court, this time with a 37–5 balance against the government's position, and with a yet broader array of U.S. and foreign government officials and former officials weighing in on domestic and international rule-of-law concerns.[47]

On June 29, 2006, the Supreme Court invalidated the Bush

military commissions, reasoning that they did not comply with conditions previously imposed by Congress. This ruling left the President free to go to Congress to seek approval for commissions. "The Court simply limited the President's authority to act as he had *on his own*, without legislative authority," Justice Breyer later explained. "Insofar as the Court rested its holding on statutes, it did not limit the President's ability, or that of the military, to act in time of hostilities."[48] But this is a drastically incomplete statement of what the decision accomplished, for the Court also ruled that Common Article 3 of the Geneva Conventions governed the "conflict with al Qaeda." This was a far-reaching ruling that altered the entire character of the President's legal authorities in the "war on terrorism." The non-application of the Geneva Conventions was the foundation for the Bush administration's post-9/11 counterterrorism program. It allowed the administration to avoid the Conventions' trial requirements and prohibitions on torture and cruel and inhuman treatment; it also allowed the administration to avoid the criminal prohibitions of the congressional War Crimes Act that were tied to the application of the Geneva Conventions. The Court's ruling on Common Article 3 thus brought a sudden rush of law and international precedent—backed with the threat of criminal sanctions—into GTMO's legal black hole, and to military operations around the globe. It also called into question the legality of the CIA's interrogation program. As we saw in Chapter 4, the Bush administration had, six months before the *Hamdan* decision, suspended the CIA interrogation program temporarily following a congressional ban on cruel, inhuman, and degrading treatment. But the December 2005 ban was not a criminal prohibition. The Court's Article 3 ruling brought into play a criminal law that was more restrictive than the earlier non-criminal congressional ban.

The *Hamdan* decision had an immediate impact. One week after the decision Deputy Secretary of Defense Gordon England issued a memorandum to the entire U.S. military. It noted the Court's Common Article 3 ruling and ordered the entire military establishment to "ensure that all DoD personnel adhere to these standards." It further ordered a review, to be completed within three weeks, of "all relevant directives, regulations, policies, practices, and procedures . . . to ensure that they comply with the standards of Common Article 3."[49] The decision also had a big effect on the CIA, which became more fearful than ever of criminal recriminations for its interrogation program. Just over two months after the *Hamdan* decision, President Bush, at the urging of CIA Director Michael Hayden, disclosed the secret CIA program that by that point everyone knew about, and announced that Khalid Sheikh Mohammed, the 9/11 mastermind, and thirteen other senior terrorists were being transferred to GTMO. The President also acknowledged that the terrorists who had no legal rights in the secret prisons just a few months earlier would now, at GTMO, receive the protections of Article 3; meet with the International Committee of the Red Cross; have access to the same food, clothing, medical care, and opportunities for worship as other detainees; and be subject to questioning only pursuant to the relatively mild U.S. Army Field Manual. Such were the beginnings of the fruits of the Supreme Court's international law decision in *Hamdan*.

CONGRESS GETS INVOLVED

The framers of the U.S. Constitution would have been very surprised to see the U.S. Supreme Court interpreting law and precedent so creatively to push back against the Commander in Chief during war. They would have expected Congress, not the courts, to be the primary check on presidential war powers. In the Constitution they conferred on Congress the power to "declare War" and control over all military (and other) appropriations. They also empowered Congress to "make rules for the government and regulation of the land and naval forces," and to make laws "necessary and proper for carrying into execution" these powers. Conventional wisdom says that for more than two centuries Congress has mostly given these powers away to the President through delegation and acquiescence. Rather than guiding and checking the President's war powers, the story goes, Congress prefers to sit on the sidelines, let the President decide when and how to go to war, see how things turn out, and then join in the celebration if the military operations go well or criticize the President harshly if they don't. Moreover, the story continues, even if Congress wants to check the presidency, it faces enormous collective action problems in generating bicameral consensus and in overriding a presidential veto.

This conventional wisdom has a large element of truth with respect to the President's power over the initiation of war. The men who wrote the Constitution thought the President would need congressional approval before using military force abroad, if for no other reason than that the nation had a tiny standing army and without congressional approval to fund troops, ships, and materiel, the President had no military to deploy. As U.S. global interests and defense needs grew, Congress approved a larger and larger standing military force. And as the military expanded, Presidents used it with greater frequency without congressional authorization—well over a hundred times, in wars large and small, over the course of American history. Every modern President has claimed the power, under Article II of the Constitution, to use military force abroad without congressional authorization. Congress has done little in response to presidential war unilateralism other than to continue to feed the beast by funding a larger and larger military force without setting conditions on how it can be used. Congress's one attempt to check the presidency in war—the War Powers Resolution—is effectively a carte blanche for presidential war-making for sixty days, and is chock-full of loopholes for operations after that. Political scientists have shown that Presidents hesitate to use military force, especially on a large scale, based on the expected political reaction of Congress.[50] But, as President Obama's 2011 military intervention in Libya without congressional approval makes plain, legal checks on unilateral uses of military force are weak at best, especially with regard to low-level uses of force that do not involve ground troops.[51]

Congress's effective capitulation of legal control on the initiation of military force is not germane to our story about checks and balances in the long war on terrorism. It is not germane because Congress on September 18, 2001, expressly authorized the President to use "all necessary and appropriate force against those nations, organizations, or persons he determines" were responsible for 9/11.[52] This authorization would have far-reaching consequences in both empowering and constraining the President. President Bush had asked Congress for much more. He had asked for the authority to use military force not only against those responsible for 9/11, but also against unrelated terrorist threats and any nation planning aggression against the United States.[53] Even in the terrifying days after 9/11, Congress would not go this far. In a surprisingly informed congressional debate, members of Congress, many of them invoking the example of the Gulf of Tonkin Resolution for the Vietnam War, agreed with Democratic Representative Peter DeFazio that "the earlier drafts [of the congressional authorization] ceded too much authority to the executive branch."[54]

Congress's conferral of narrower authority to use military action against just those responsible for 9/11 would prove vital legal support for two Presidents to detain without trial, and target to kill, enemy forces. But its requirement of a nexus to 9/11 would prove to be a vital constraint on presidential power as well, a constraint enforced against the executive branch by courts and executive branch lawyers. Even the controversial provisions of the PATRIOT Act, enacted in October 2001, contained an unusual restraint.[55] The original law had a sunset clause that terminated the law's most controversial provisions after a few years, thus requiring the President to remake the case to Congress that the provisions were still justified, and requiring Congress to consider new evidence before authorizing it again if Congress deemed appropriate.

Congress would constrain the President in more robust ways during the war on terrorism. We have already seen some examples in operation. In pre-9/11 treaties and laws such as the Geneva Conventions, the War Crimes Act, the Torture Convention and torture law, and the Foreign Intelligence Surveillance Act, the Senate (in the treaties) and Congress (in the laws) significantly constrained what the President could do in war. The Bush administration tried to skirt some of these laws, and met resistance in doing so both by lawyers inside the executive branch and by activists and journalists outside the executive branch who used the laws as a basis for harsh criticism. Other laws delegated Congress's oversight responsibilities very effectively to actors inside and outside the executive branch. John Helgerson's extraordinary investigations inside the CIA, and the similar post-9/11 efforts of other inspectors general, would not have been possible if Congress had not created an independent office of inspector general in the national security agencies. Similarly, congressional actions in the 1960s and 1970s made possible the aggressive use of the Freedom of Information Act by the ACLU and many others to extract secrets from U.S. military and intelligence agencies.

More unusual, and in many ways unprecedented, were Congress's efforts to push back against the President's core military powers with new laws after 9/11.[56] In 2005–2006, while controlled by the President's party, Congress rejected the President's understanding of his core unilateral military powers to detain the enemy, to interrogate him, and to try him in military commissions; and it replaced them with a different, congressional regime. The man most responsible for these actions was Republican Senator Lindsey Graham of South Carolina. Graham had unusual qualities that made him an effective broker on counterterrorism issues. He had credibility with many Republicans because he was a counterterrorism hawk; he believed that aggressive tactics were necessary in the war on terrorism; and he strongly disagreed with the Supreme Court's *Rasul* decision extending habeas corpus rights to GTMO detainees. Graham was also, however, committed to the idea that law-governed behavior was vital to success in the war on terrorism. "What I wanted to do was to find a way to create a hybrid system that recognizes that we are at war but that also understands that we are in a different kind of war, an endless war, that requires much more law and process," he said. Graham also believed that the nation needed counterterrorism policies "that live within our values, because that is the way you beat this enemy in an ideological struggle."[57]

In identifying the values the United States should pursue, Graham looked to the U.S. military and especially to its lawyers. He looked in that direction because he served as a judge advocate general for four years after law school and has remained one for three decades, up to the present, as a reserve military lawyer or judge. "Becoming a judge advocate was probably the highlight of my life," says Graham, recounting how he cut his teeth as a young lawyer trying and defending soldiers in courts-martial all over Europe in the 1970s. "I love being a senator," he said in a 2011 interview, "but even better is wearing the Nation's uniform and getting to practice law . . . in the military."[58] Graham identified with military lawyers and their values, and he would use his intimate relationship with them strategically and effectively to push back against the policy aims of their Commander in Chief.

Graham's first effort at reining in the Commander in Chief came in the Detainee Treatment Act of 2005. This was the law that included the John McCain–inspired ban on "cruel, inhuman, and degrading" treatment, which effectively ended the original CIA interrogation program and also limited U.S. military interrogation techniques to those found in the Army Field Manual. On top of these novel interrogation constraints, Graham marshaled other new statutory protections for alleged enemy combatants. He did so as part of a compromise for eliminating what Graham viewed as the undisciplined habeas corpus review process for GTMO detainees established by the Supreme Court in its 2004 *Rasul* decision. Reversing *Rasul* is something the Bush administration very much wanted in order to stop the rush of GTMO habeas corpus petitions that the Center for Constitutional Rights was coordinating in federal court.

But Graham replaced habeas corpus with something the administration did not want at all: judicial review of the military's CSRT determinations for GTMO detainees, combined with additional procedural rights for detainees in CSRTs, on top of the ones already recognized by the military. The Graham Amendment, as it was known, also required the courts to ensure that the Defense Department's status decisions complied with that department's rules, and to examine whether those rules were consistent with the Constitution. Compared to the more robust protections that courts would impose a few years later, these were relatively modest constraints on the executive branch. But compared to the previous 216 years of American history, these were bold protections that far exceeded the requirements of the Geneva Conventions. The Detainee Treatment Act represented Congress's taking ownership of detention matters traditionally left to the President.

Graham's next effort in presidential control came in the fall of 2006 when the Supreme Court decision in *Hamdan* forced President Bush to seek Congress's authorization for military commissions. The Bush administration originally sought a simple one-line approval for the old commissions, akin to the discretionary power that Commanders in Chief from George Washington to Franklin D. Roosevelt had exercised. But Graham immediately deemed that move "a mistake," adding that "we have a chance to start over."[59] He and Republican Senators John Warner and John McCain—both, like Graham, veterans with close ties to the military—stood up to their Republican colleagues in the Congress and to the President in insisting on more robust legal protections in commissions. The Democrats in the minority mostly acquiesced in this effort, delighted to not be in the lead in enhancing detainee rights.

A key issue for Graham was ensuring that commission defendants had a right to know all of the evidence used against them. Another key issue concerned the Geneva Conventions. Graham disagreed with the Supreme Court ruling that Common Article 3 of the Conventions applied to the war on terrorism, but once it came down, he resisted the Bush administration's efforts to water down Article 3's requirements. Graham took his cues on these issues from military lawyers in the Pentagon and skillfully exploited his connections with them. "How did I use the JAGs? I called them up and I ran things by them."[60] He would also seek their personal views, in letters or testimony, to elicit their disagreement with the White House on legal interpretation and on legal policy. This strategy drove the White House and civilian leaders in the Pentagon crazy. There can be no greater affront to the Bush theory of unitary control over the executive branch than military lawyers, at the behest of a member of Congress who himself is a reserve military lawyer, publicly disagreeing with the Commander in Chief's legal views in time of war. But that is precisely what happened, and it gave Graham significant public leverage in pushing back against the White House.

Most commentators characterized the Military Commissions Act of 2006 that emerged from these negotiations as a victory for President Bush, for the new law gave the President many things he wanted, all supported by Senator Graham. It reaffirmed Congress's reversal of the Supreme Court's *Rasul* decision and once again eliminated statutory habeas corpus review for GTMO detainees. It gave the CIA wiggle room on a scaled-down interrogation program and relief from criminal investigation for its past actions. And it reconstituted military commissions, which the Supreme Court had invalidated a few months earlier. But in the longer view, the 2006 law was a defeat for the presidency and a victory for Congress. The President had never before gone begging to Congress for permission to convene military commissions. Congress had in the past put down a few basic legal markers on commissions (as the Court ruled in *Hamdan*). But in the 2006 law, Congress prescribed in detail the contours and procedures for military commissions. And the rules it prescribed were more protective to defendants than the President's commission scheme.[61] As with Graham's detention reforms in 2005, the military commission reforms in 2006 would be strengthened further a few years later. But the effort Graham led in 2006, against the background of what had gone on in wars for two centuries before, represented a shift in the allocation of war power from the presidency to Congress.

So too did the efforts by Senator Graham and many others in Congress to make it hard for President Obama to transfer GTMO detainees to third countries, and make it even harder—practically impossible—to bring GTMO detainees to the United States for detention or trial. These efforts, already described in Chapter 2, were yet another affront to traditional executive authority. "Never before has the Congress sought to so limit and micromanage the military and other elements of our national security community in matters as basic as a detainee transfer," complained an Obama White House memorandum in response to a new round of proposed congressional restrictions in June 2011.[62]

JUDICIAL SUPREMACY

While Congress put its stamp on presidential tactics more than is generally appreciated after 9/11, the courts would remain supreme. When the Supreme Court's *Rasul* decision in 2004 eliminated the taboo within the legal community on representing alleged terrorists, the antiestablishment activists at the Center for Constitutional Rights suddenly found themselves bombarded by hundreds of attorneys, including many from America's most elite law firms, seeking to help with the habeas corpus petitions that the GTMO detainees could now file in federal court. These lawyers offered their services pro bono, in effect contributing hundreds of millions of dollars of free legal services to ensure that the alleged terrorists at GTMO got their full day in court. Like many legal aspects of the war on terrorism, nothing like this participation by establishment lawyers on the side of alleged enemy combatants had ever happened before. The CCR vetted these lawyers, trained them, and assigned them clients. And they quickly flooded federal courts with habeas corpus petitions from detainees seeking release from GTMO.

At this point some in the CCR predicted that GTMO would be closed in a year. But Congress quickly squelched this enthusiasm. In both the 2005 Detainee Treatment Act and again in the 2006 Military Commissions Act, Congress extinguished the statutory habeas corpus right that the Supreme Court had recognized in *Rasul*. So while the *Rasul* decision and related pressures had led the government to release hundreds of detainees before 2008, five hundred or so detainees remained in the island detention facility without habeas corpus review. The detainees did have the military and judicial review that Lindsey Graham had helped to establish. But Michael Ratner and his colleagues were habeas corpus purists who believed the alternate procedures were "kangaroo courts." And so he and the CCR went back to court to argue, once again, for habeas corpus rights for detainees.

This time the legal hurdles would appear even higher than they had in 2004. The focus through 2007 had been on whether Congress wanted habeas corpus to extend to GTMO. Now that Congress had made it crystal clear that it did not, the focus shifted to the U.S. Constitution, which provided that the writ of habeas corpus shall not be suspended "except when in cases of rebellion or invasion the public safety may require it." The CCR argument in the Supreme Court was that Congress had acted illegally in suspending the writ of habeas corpus outside of the Constitution's strictures. The Bush administration, in response, argued that "the founders expected that the Congress and President, together, would determine the appropriate process for individuals detained overseas during military operations—just as those political branches together share in important respects responsibility for the national defense and the constitutionally conferred war powers."[63]

Just as in *Rasul* in 2004, the court of appeals had bought the administration's argument, which reflected the best reading of the precedents, strictly construed. But just as in *Rasul*, the Supreme Court, motivated by larger concerns, ruled for Ratner's client. "We hold that petitioners may invoke the fundamental procedural protections of habeas corpus," noted Justice Kennedy in his opinion for the Court in the *Boumediene* case. "The laws and Constitution are designed to survive, and remain in force, in extraordinary times."[64] This was yet another landmark Supreme Court decision. Also for the first time in American history, the Court invalidated a wartime measure—a statute that stripped habeas corpus in lieu of detention review by a military tribunal and a federal court—that had the support of both Congress and the President. Also for the first time in American history, enemy forces held outside the United States had a constitutional right to go to federal court to seek release. Because the Court had ruled by interpreting the Constitution, there was nothing this time that Congress or the courts could do in response except to comply.

The GTMO Bar quickly began to file new habeas corpus petitions in the summer and fall of 2008 in order to make the government prove that it had a factual and legal basis for detention. "We think it's unlikely in most of the cases the government will be able to do that," said a gleeful Ratner.[65] Ratner grew happier, and more confident, after Barack Obama was elected President five months later. He and sixty-nine other members of the GTMO Bar had signed a letter in 2008 supporting Senator Obama for President.[66] And Ratner was elated when Obama issued his first-week executive orders that seemed to reverse the Bush-era policies. "We are finally seeing the beginning of a reversal of some of the nastiest inhuman practices of the Bush administration," Ratner said at the time.[67] CCR-coordinated defense lawyers at GTMO had celebrated a few nights earlier, after inauguration night, when the new President ordered military prosecutors to suspend military commission proceedings. "Rule of law, baby!" they shouted.[68]

We now know that things would not turn out as the GTMO Bar hoped. In March 2009, two months after the inauguration, the Obama administration filed its first brief in a constitutional habeas corpus case from GTMO. To Ratner's and his colleagues' astonishment, the brief made arguments for a broad power of indefinite detention over GTMO detainees that were almost identical to ones the Bush administration had made. The Obama administration added insult to injury when it cited as support for military detention some of the lower court decisions that CCR had litigated and lost years earlier.[69] "We really thought that

Obama wouldn't fight us in court on the rights of the detainees, that he would get the detainees either to another country or he would charge and try them," Ratner later said.[70]

But the Obama crew did fight them. It made its initial arguments for indefinite detention as part of a holding pattern so that the President's Guantanamo Review Task Force could determine what to do with the 241 detainees who were at GTMO when Obama assumed office. By the late spring, the task force had determined that very few of the detainees (fewer than forty) could be brought to trial and that many of the rest remained very dangerous.[71] Faced with the reality of dangerous terrorists at GTMO who could not be tried, and cognizant of the powerful legal authorities established over the decade after 9/11, including the Military Commissions Act of 2006 and new judicial precedents handed down in 2009, the administration concluded that it had no choice but to continue military detention without trial at GTMO and defend the practice in court. This general pattern would replicate itself on other issues such as military commissions, habeas corpus, state secrets, and more. The terror threat and the management of war proved much more challenging than the Obama administration officials had realized before they took office, and the legal support from Congress and the courts for aggressive action to meet these challenges—legal support that had emerged from bruising separation-of-powers battles during the Bush administration— was robust. The new Commander in Chief could not responsibly walk away from asserting these authorities that had been blessed by the other branches of government. And so he did not.

The Obama administration continued Bush-era arguments for military detention, but the fate of the arguments now rested with the lower federal courts. The problem these courts faced was that the Supreme Court decision that established constitutional habeas corpus review said practically nothing about what procedures they should use or what rights the detainees possessed. "The majority," charged Chief Justice John Roberts in his dissent in *Boumediene*, "merely replaces a review system designed by the people's representatives with a set of shapeless procedures to be defined by federal courts at some future date."[72] As a result, the lower courts were forced to devise a system of detention authority and review essentially from scratch. This was not a task they welcomed. "It is unfortunate that the Legislative Branch of our government and the Executive Branch have not moved more strongly to provide uniform, clear rules and laws for handling these cases," complained Judge Thomas Hogan, who was charged with coordinating the GTMO habeas cases.[73] But the lower courts plunged ahead, deciding many dozens of habeas cases over the next few years, and establishing several important legal principles in the process.

The most important principle was that the President could, as the Bush and Obama administrations claimed, detain members of al Qaeda and the Taliban, including those captured outside Afghanistan, "until hostilities cease."[74] In acknowledging this principle, the courts also placed a number of procedural and evidentiary requirements on how the government must prove to the courts its detention authority. Most of these requirements are nontrivial, and some are burdensome. All amount to unprecedented (that term, again) demands on the Commander in Chief's traditional detention authority and unprecedented demands of evidence collection by soldiers in the field. They also establish a new role for the courts. In "pass[ing] judgment on the admissibility of evidence collected on the battlefield, and thus on the propriety of the methods used for such collection," the courts "monitor, and to a degree supervise, the battlefield conduct of the U.S. military," noted Judge Stephen Williams, in one of the habeas cases. "That is a consequence of *Boumediene*, in which the federal judiciary assumed an entirely new role in the nation's military operations," he added.[75]

Some have doubted that these decisions had much of an effect on the President's discretion because the lower courts have rejected most of the habeas petitions from GTMO on the merits.[76] The issue is hard to judge because the executive branch, under various legal and political pressures over the years, had released four hundred or so detainees by 2009, and so most of the ones remaining at GTMO at that point were truly "the worst of the worst," as Donald Rumsfeld had quipped in 2002.[77] Even taking this fact into account, the courts in 2009–2011 granted habeas relief to detainees in fourteen cases that the government ultimately did not subsequently challenge, a number that amounts to almost a quarter of the habeas cases brought by GTMO detainees.[78] The government also released others because they believed they could not meet detention standards announced by the courts.[79] But the courts' impact on presidential discretion went far beyond these cases, and included unusual influences on the battlefield beyond the evidence gathering and the distractions that resulted from the habeas cases themselves.

One influence was on the executive branch's targeting practices. Courts in the habeas cases ruling on who could and could not be detained in effect defined the scope of the conflict with al Qaeda under the 2001 congressional authorization of force. When Obama administration lawyers determine how far they can go in targeting terrorist threats—especially threats off the traditional battlefield in places like Yemen and Somalia—they are guided by some of the analysis and basic restrictions recognized in these cases.[80] The habeas cases also affect detention operations in places like Afghanistan. The definition of "the enemy" used by the Obama administration in the GTMO habeas cases is the same one employed in Afghanistan, and no one is detained there who does not meet this definition. This definition is, as one senior lawyer in Afghanistan says, "a direct response to Supreme Court decisions in *Rasul, Hamdi, Hamdan,* and *Boumediene.*"[81] Subsequently the federal appellate court in the District of Columbia has ruled that habeas jurisdiction does not extend to Afghanistan. But that does not mean that the courts did not influence detention standards there. On the contrary, the hope of reaching this result is one reason the Obama administration decided to raise detention standards in Afghanistan in the summer of 2009.[82] And senior lawyers in Afghanistan still live with the concern that the Supreme Court will overturn this habeas decision. "I warn capturing units that [law-of-war detention] must adhere the highest legal standards to avoid habeas litigation," said one such lawyer. "This creates a huge burden on [law-of-war detention] in that we must perform customary military legal operations in a combat zone with an eye toward defensive litigation [and] must be concerned how a civilian court will view our legal actions and decisions."[83]

In these and other ways, the GTMO habeas corpus cases have had a constraining impact on the President, his senior national security advisers, and soldiers in the field. But these constraints have also empowered the presidency and the military, directly and indirectly, in important ways. "Our opinion does not undermine the Executive's powers as Commander in Chief," asserted Justice Kennedy in his *Boumediene* opinion for the Supreme Court. "On the contrary, the exercise of those powers is vindicated, not eroded, when confirmed by the Judicial Branch."[84] The unusual burdens imposed by the *Boumediene* decision and the other landmark Supreme Court decisions in the last decade have been accompanied by judicial and legislative approval for some extraordinary presidential powers in the long war against terrorists. It is a remarkable fact that in the eleventh year of the "war on terrorism," the administration of Barack Obama is detaining over 170 terrorist soldiers in GTMO without charge or trial, is planning to try some of these detainees in a military commission on the island, and is detaining almost two thousand more in Afghanistan. These practices remain controversial in some quarters, and are not what the Obama administration set out to do. But as a result of judicial and legislative interventions over the last decade, there is no doubt now that these practices are lawful and legitimate within the American constitutional system. The presidency was empowered to exercise these and other military prerogatives in this unusual war because the other branches of the government considered the matter and, with caveats, told the President he could.

The legitimation and continuance of these unusual executive powers are enormous disappointments to Michael Ratner and his colleagues. The lawsuits and activist campaigns by these men and women accomplished much in the decade after 9/11, much more than they anticipated at the beginning. They built up a global social movement of activists, lawyers, foreign governments, and the media, to bring habeas corpus rights to GTMO and to pressure the government to release all but the most dangerous prisoners there. "Obviously, getting six or seven hundred people out of Guantanamo out of the nine hundred was a huge accomplishment," notes Ratner. Working in the ecology of transparency, Ratner and his colleagues, as Ratner himself said, "have also taken on what I consider the most egregious aspects of what I call the national security state since 9/11, and made them public debating issues." By making the issues matters of public debate, they ensured that the courts and Congress and the American people had to engage in the issues, and to address them.

But the bitter reality for Ratner and his colleagues in the GTMO Bar is that the courts, Congress, and the American people do not share their outlook, and the United States is in a place at the end of 2011 where Ratner desperately did not want it to be. The GTMO Bar won landmark Supreme Court decisions on due process for detainees, on habeas corpus, and on the limits of presidential power over military commissions. And yet stepping back from these battles, Ratner believes that he and his colleagues lost the war. "We lost on the enemy combatant issue, and the definition. We lost on the preventive detention issue, more or less. We lost on the military commission issue, more or less." They lost on these issues because while the courts and Congress imposed significant constraints on these traditional practices by the Commander in Chief, they also affirmed the legitimacy of the practices in the round. The efforts of the other branches of the government placed these practices on a much firmer foundation than they were during the early unilateralist era of George W. Bush. The foundation became firmer yet because it was embraced, albeit grudgingly, by the administration of Barack Obama. "My problem is that when you have a Democrat doing it as well as a Republican, . . . both the good and the bad becomes embedded in the rule of law," says Ratner. This is a problem for Ratner because he thinks that military detention, military commissions, and many other wartime prerogatives of the Commander in Chief are unnecessary, immoral, or illegal. But for those who disagree with Ratner on these points—for those who believe that the terrorist threat remains real and scary, and that the nation needs a Commander in Chief empowered to meet the threat in unusual ways—embedding these presidential prerogatives in the rule of law is an enormous blessing. It is a blessing, ironically, for which the nation has Michael Ratner and his colleagues to thank.

THE NEXT GTMO

Parallel to the intense litigation over the legality of detention at GTMO was a rash of lawsuits by a new breed of lawyers—in NGOs, law firms, and the academy—who were associated with or spawned by the GTMO Bar, and who specialized in questioning wartime presidential authority. These lawsuits challenged the legality of every element of the government's counterterrorism tactics, including detention, rendition, interrogation, surveillance, and targeted killing, and many of them sought compensation from current and former government officials as a result of their involvement in these activities. Most of these lawsuits have been dismissed by judges on technical grounds. Critics charge that these dismissals show that courts are ineffectual tools of presidential accountability in these contexts. But as a failed lawsuit over targeted killing shows, the focus on courts alone is too narrow, and the truth is more complex.

The U.S. government has for years been increasingly reliant on unmanned aerial vehicles, or drones, to find, target, and kill high-value terrorists in Afghanistan, Pakistan, Yemen, and other countries. Relentless drone attacks have helped to decimate al Qaeda's top leadership, and the government's reliance on drones for counterterrorism operations will only grow as the United States steps up its troop withdrawal from Afghanistan. In some senses drones represent humanitarian progress because they enable military action without introducing traditional military forces, and they are extraordinarily precise in their fire. But they are also controversial—especially when deployed outside of traditional battlefields like Afghanistan—because of their antiseptic technological wizardry, their stealth, the safety they bring their operators (who are often located thousands of miles away), and the perceived unfair advantage they give the United States.

In 2010, the Center for Constitutional Rights and the ACLU joined forces to challenge the use of drones off the traditional battlefield. They did so in a carefully chosen lawsuit against the Obama administration over its plans to target and kill Anwar al-Aulaqi, the U.S.-Yemeni citizen living in Yemen whom the government alleged played a role in terrorist attacks like the attempted Christmas 2009 bombing of a Detroit-bound airliner. The human rights organizations argued that the government was asserting a "sweeping authority to impose extrajudicial death sentences" over U.S. citizens who had not been charged, tried, or convicted by a court.[85] It asked the court to enjoin the President from killing al-Aulaqi until he presents an imminent threat and then only as a last resort. Such an injunction, the government responded, would "improperly inject the courts into decisions of the President and his advisors about how to protect the American people from the threat of armed attacks, including imminent threats, posed by a foreign organization against which the political branches have authorized the use of necessary and appropriate force."[86] Federal District Court Judge John Bates agreed with the government and dismissed the lawsuit, reasoning that in wartime the Constitution left it to the President and Congress, not the courts, to decide military targeting issues. Jameel Jaffer of the ACLU was not pleased. The President now has "unreviewable authority to carry out the targeted killing of any American, anywhere, whom the president deems to be a threat to the nation," he said, on behalf of his organization and the CCR. "It is a profound mistake to allow this unparalleled power to be exercised free from the checks and balances that apply in every other context."[87]

But the President's military targeting practices were not operating free of checks and balances. Lawyers inside the government placed limits on when the president could use force against U.S. citizens. The President was forced to appear before a federal court in an unprecedented situation to explain and defend his targeting authorities. And while the court handed the President a victory, it also issued small but important judicial pronouncements—such as its suggestion that the Constitution's Fourth Amendment prohibition on unreasonable "seizures" imposes limits on the President's ability to target enemy forces outside the United States—that will influence executive branch lawyers and shape U.S. government targeting decisions going forward.[88] In addition, and pursuant to the "grand bargain" described in Chapter 4, any significant CIA intelligence and paramilitary involvement in drone strikes in Yemen and elsewhere would have been reported to and scrutinized by the congressional intelligence committees. And while the U.S. military's involvement in the strikes is not reported as robustly to Congress, it is heavily scrutinized, as described in Chapter 5, by layers of lawyers, and others, inside and outside the Pentagon.

These sorts of institutional ripples were what the ACLU and the CCR were aiming at more broadly. These organizations did not bring the al-Aulaqi lawsuit only (or even mainly) to win in court. They also sued to promote media attention to the issue, to get the government to disclose more information about its practices, and to pressure the government to adopt tighter internal controls. On these scores the lawsuit was something of a victory. The public already knew a bit about the supposedly secret operations in Yemen against al-Aulaqi. But the lawsuit caused new details to spill out and brought greater attention to the targeted killing issue. In response to an ACLU Freedom of Information request, the government released documents that explained its targeting decision-making practice.[89] Beyond that, information about the care with which terrorists are placed on high-value target lists, about the National Security Council's oversight of the program, about the legal analysis supporting the targeting, and about the actual operations in Yemen and elsewhere leaked to the press through the ecology of transparency, both before and, in much greater detail, after al-Aulaqi was killed in October 2011. In addition, the controversy sparked by the lawsuit was the predicate for State Department Legal Advisor Harold Koh's speech, discussed in Chapter 1, which explained and defended the legality of the practice. It was also the predicate for a similar speech, providing new legal details, by President Obama's chief counterterrorism adviser, John Brennan, in September 2011.[90] All of this information allows Congress and the American people (who are the ultimate checks on the presidency) to analyze what the government is doing in their name in secret and push back if they deem the operations unwarranted. Thus far—and in contrast to, say, Bush-era interrogation practices—they have largely sided with the government, even when it killed an American citizen.

For the GTMO Bar and its cousin NGOs and activists, however, the al-Aulaqi lawsuit, like other lawsuits on different issues, was merely an early battle in a long war over the legitimacy of U.S. targeting practices—a war that will take place not just in the United States, but in other countries as well. When the CCR failed to achieve what it viewed as adequate accountability for Bush administration officials in the United States in connection with interrogation and detention practices, it started pursuing, and continues to pursue, lawsuits and prosecutions against U.S. officials in Spain, Germany, and other European countries. "You look for every niche you can when you can take on the issues that you think are important," said Michael Ratner, explaining the CCR's strategy for pursuing lawsuits in Europe.

Clive Stafford Smith, a former CCR attorney who was instrumental in its early GTMO victories and who now leads the British advocacy organization Reprieve, is using this strategy in the targeted killing context. "There are endless ways in which the courts in Britain, the courts in America, the international courts and

Pakistani courts can get involved" in scrutinizing U.S. targeting killing practices, he argues. "It's going to be the next 'Guantanamo Bay' issue."[91] Working in a global network of NGO activists, Stafford Smith has begun a process in Pakistan to seek the arrest of former CIA lawyer John Rizzo in connection with drone strikes in Pakistan, and he is planning more lawsuits in the United States and elsewhere against drone operators.[92] "The crucial court here is the court of public opinion," he said, explaining why the lawsuits are important even if he loses. His efforts are backed by a growing web of proclamations in the United Nations, foreign capitals, the press, and the academy that U.S. drone practices are unlawful. What American University law professor Ken Anderson has described as the "international legal-media-academic-NGO-international organization-global opinion complex" is hard at work to stigmatize drones and those who support and operate them.[93]

This strategy is having an impact. The slew of lawsuits in the United States and threatened prosecutions in Europe against Bush administration officials imposes reputational, emotional, and financial costs on them that help to promote the human rights groups' ideological goals, even if courts never actually rule against the officials. By design, these suits also give pause to current officials who are considering controversial actions for fear that the same thing might later happen to them. This effect is starting to be felt with drones. Several Obama administration officials have told me that they worry targeted killings will be seen in the future (as Stafford Smith predicts) as their administration's GTMO. The attempted judicial action against Rizzo, the earlier lawsuits against top CIA officials in Pakistan and elsewhere, and the louder and louder proclamations of illegality around the world—all of which have gained momentum after al-Aulaqi's killing—are also having an impact. These actions are rallying cries for protest and political pushback in the countries where the drone strikes take place. And they lead CIA operators to worry about legal exposure before becoming involved in the Agency's drone program.[94] We don't know yet whether these forces have affected actual targeting practices and related tactics. But they induce the officials involved to take more caution. And it is only a matter of time, if it has not happened already, before they lead the U.S. government to forgo lawful targeted killing actions otherwise deemed to be in the interest of U.S. national security.

Part Three

ASSESSMENT

Chapter Seven

THE PRESIDENTIAL
SYNOPTICON

DAVID BRIN is a science-fiction writer who in 1998 turned his imagination to a nonfiction book about privacy called *The Transparent Society*. Brin argued that individual privacy was on a path to extinction because government surveillance tools—tinier and tinier cameras and recorders, more robust electronic snooping, and bigger and bigger databases—were growing irreversibly more powerful. His solution to this attack on personal space was not to erect privacy walls, which he thought were futile, but rather to induce responsible government action by turning the surveillance devices on the government itself. A government that citizens can watch, Brin argued, is one subject to criticism and reprisals for its errors and abuses, and one that is more careful and responsible in the first place for fear of this backlash. A transparent government, in short, is an accountable one. "If neo-western civilization has one great trick in its repertoire, a technique more responsible than any other for its success, that trick is accountability," Brin argues, "[e]specially the knack—which no other culture ever mastered—of making accountability apply to the mighty."[1]

Brin's notion of reciprocal transparency is in some ways the inverse of the penological design known as a "panopticon," made famous by the eighteenth-century English utilitarian philosopher

Jeremy Bentham. Bentham's brother Samuel had designed a prison in Paris that allowed an "inspector" to monitor all of the inmates from a central location without the prisoners knowing whether or when they were being watched (and thus when they might be sanctioned for bad behavior). Bentham described the panopticon prison as a "new mode of obtaining power of mind over mind" because it allowed a single guard to control many prisoners merely by conveying that he might be watching.[2] The idea that a "watcher" could gain enormous social control over the "watched" through constant surveillance backed with threats of punishment has proved influential. Michel Foucault invoked Bentham's panopticon as a model for how modern societies and governments watch people in order to control them.[3] George Orwell invoked a similar idea three decades earlier with the panoptical telescreen in his novel *1984*. More recently, Yale Law School professor Jack Balkin used the panopticon as a metaphor for what he calls the "National Surveillance State," in which governments "use surveillance, data collection, and data mining technologies not only to keep Americans safe from terrorist attacks but also to prevent ordinary crime and deliver social services."[4]

The direction of the panopticon can be reversed, however, creating a "synopticon" in which many can watch one, including the government.[5] The television is a synopticon that enables millions to watch the same governmental speech or hearing, though it is not a terribly robust one because the government can control the broadcast. Digital technology and the Internet combine to make a more powerful synopticon that allows many individuals to record and watch an official event or document in sometimes surprising ways. Video recorders placed in police stations and police cars, cell-phone video cameras, and similar tools increase citizens' ability to watch and record government activity. This new media content can be broadcast on the Internet and through other channels to give citizens synoptical power over the government—a power that some describe as "sousveillance" (watching from below).[6] These and related forms of watching can have a disciplining effect on government akin to Brin's reciprocal transparency.

The various forms of watching and checking the presidency described in this book constitute a vibrant presidential synopticon. Empowered by legal reform and technological change, the "many"—in the form of courts, members of Congress and their staff, human rights activists, journalists and their collaborators, and lawyers and watchdogs inside and outside the executive branch—constantly gaze on the "one," the presidency. Acting alone and in mutually reinforcing networks that crossed organizational boundaries, these institutions extracted and revealed information about the executive branch's conduct in war—sometimes to adversarial actors inside the government, and sometimes to the public. The revelations, in turn, forced the executive branch to account for its actions and enabled many institutions to influence its operations. The presidential synopticon also promoted responsible executive action merely through its broadening gaze. One consequence of a panopticon, in Foucault's words, is "to induce in the inmate a state of conscious and permanent visibility that assures the automatic functioning of power."[7] The same thing has happened in reverse but to similar effect within the executive branch, where officials are much more careful merely by virture of being watched.

The presidential synopticon is in some respects not new. Victor Davis Hanson has argued that "war amid audit, scrutiny, and self-critique" has been a defining feature of the Western tradition for 2,500 years.[8] From the founding of the nation, American war presidents have been subject to intense scrutiny and criticism in the unusually open society that has characterized the United States. And many of the accountability mechanisms described in this book have been growing since the 1970s in step with the modern presidency. What is new, however, is the scope and depth of these modern mechanisms, their intense legalization, and their robust operation during wartime. In previous major wars the President determined when, how, and where to surveil, target, detain, transfer, and interrogate enemy soldiers, often without public knowledge, and almost entirely without unwanted legal interference from within the executive branch itself or from the other branches

of government.[9] Today these decisions are known inside and outside the government to an unprecedented degree and are heavily
regulated by laws and judicial decisions that are enforced daily by
lawyers and critics inside and outside the presidency. Never before
have Congress, the courts, and lawyers had such a say in day-to-
day military activities; never before has the Commander in Chief
been so influenced, and constrained, by law.

This regime has many historical antecedents, but it came
together and hit the Commander in Chief hard for the first time
in the last decade. It did so because of extensive concerns about
excessive presidential power in an indefinite and unusually secretive war fought among civilians, not just abroad but at home as
well. These concerns were exacerbated and given credibility by
the rhetoric and reality of the Bush administration's executive
unilateralism—a strategy that was designed to free it from the
web of military and intelligence laws but that instead galvanized
forces of reaction to presidential power and deepened the laws'
impact. Added to this mix were enormous changes in communication and collaboration technologies that grew to maturity in the
decade after 9/11. These changes helped render executive branch
secrets harder to keep, and had a flattening effect on the executive
branch just as it had on other hierarchical institutions, making
connections between (and thus accountability to) actors inside and
outside the presidency much more extensive.

These checks on the Commander in Chief have vindicated the
system of government control established by the Constitution.
The framers did not think of constraints on the presidency primarily in terms of fixed limits on its size and authorities. The
Constitution was not designed to prevent the President from
taking steps needed to keep the nation secure, including novel
steps as the challenges facing the nation evolved. "The Founding Fathers were intensely practical men determined to charter
a republic that would work and last in a dangerous world," noted
Arthur Schlesinger Jr.[10] They knew that the world would change
and that the responsibilities and powers of the institutions it created would change as well. "In framing a system which we wish to

last for the ages, we [should] not lose sight of the changes the ages will produce," Madison said in his notes on the Constitutional Convention.[11]

Instead of placing fixed limits on presidential power, the framers sought to check presidential excesses by giving Congress and the courts, aided by a constitutionally protected press, the motives and tools to keep the presidency within contextualized limits measured by the national security challenge before the nation. This structure has grown more decentralized and today involves many actors beyond Congress, the courts, the traditional press, and voters. But the modern presidential synopticon translates in a rough way the framers' original design of making presidential action accountable, both to the wishes of the people as expressed in Congress and the press and elections, and to the law as enforced by congressional sanction and judicial action.[12] Though many of the players in the modern accountability system are new, they combine with older ones to help ensure that the other institutions of government know about the President's actions, can require him to account for them, and can punish him if they think he is engaged in the wrong policy or acting unlawfully.

The test of such presidential accountability in wartime is what Arthur Schlesinger Jr. described as "the vital mechanism of self-correction"—the ability of our institutions to redirect presidential wartime initiatives that do not garner the approval of the other institutions of government and of the people.[13] Self-correction is an apt description for the events of the last decade. Immediately after 9/11, the government and the nation were uncertain about the nature of the terrorist threat and how it should be met. The Bush administration, acting on public demand, initiated a number of aggressive counterterrorism programs. Most of those that were known, and some of the secret ones about which there were only hints, had the general support of the nation for the first two years. Over time, as the public and the government came to better understand the extent of these actions and their downsides, and as the terror threat faded from public view, the nation began to have doubts. Beginning in 2004, Congress and the courts altered some programs significantly and others modestly; actors inside the government initiated reforms even earlier.

By the time Barack Obama became President, these forces had operated for many years, and a general consensus had emerged about what tools the President could use in fighting the threat, including military detention pursuant to Congress's 2001 authorization and subject to judicial review, refined military commissions, aggressive surveillance with accountability strings attached, habeas corpus for GTMO but not beyond, narrowed interrogation policies, aggressive targeted killing, and the like. Of course, the nation still debates how these powers should be deployed and whether they should be expanded or contracted at the margins—especially in the context of military detention. But among politicians, judges, and most of the American people, there is agreement on the legitimacy of and basic constraints on these powers, especially compared to the 2001–2004 baseline. This equilibrium—and the legal and political settlement that undergirds it—is the main reason Obama continued so many Bush counterterrorism policies as they stood in 2009. The same legal and political pressures that influenced the evolution of Bush's policies continued to influence the development of Obama's policies, though in different ways.

To say that the presidential synopticon helped generate a consensus about the counterterrorism policies the President can legitimately use does not, unfortunately, mean that it generated the right policies—the ones best designed to prevent terrorist attacks while at the same time preserving other values as much as possible. Assessing the propriety of the current resting place of U.S. counterterrorism policies and associated accountability mechanisms, the aim of this chapter, is much harder than this book's primary aim of showing how these novel accountability mechanisms worked to generate a consensus in support of these policies.

This assessment is harder because a decade after 9/11, neither the American people nor its government have enough relevant information. Even after Bin Laden's death, we do not know precisely how serious the Islamist terrorist threat is, or the likelihood of an attack, or its likely location or scale, or how much investment in what types of policies would best prevent attacks. Nor do we know the degree to which the accountability mechanisms for counterterrorism policies prevent mistakes or chill government officials from taking useful actions. The government knows more about these things than the public, but it still engages in guesswork. It must additionally guess how much risk and what kinds of security precautions, and how many and what types of mistakes, the nation is willing to absorb in exchange for safety from attacks (though it knows for sure that public attitudes toward this issue differ dramatically before and after an attack).

On top of these factual uncertainties are legal uncertainties. We want the President to abide by the law except in truly exigent circumstances of national danger. But in many contexts the law is unsettled or flexible and thus subject to multiple interpretations. How far the government is permitted to go under the law depends to a great extent on context and the timing of judgment and the happenstance of who the interpreter is. And even if all of the factual and legal questions were resolved, the assessment of proper counterterrorism policies and accountability mechanisms would still be guided by moral intuitions that are more diverse than we like to admit. Many find waterboarding, military commissions, and detention without trial repulsive; many others do not.

Despite these uncertainties, some tentative assessments about the presidential synopticon in its first decade of operation after 9/11 are possible, especially concerning its three defining features: transparency, legalization, and accountability.

TRANSPARENCY

David Brin's key insight is that the essence of accountability is transparency. The post-9/11 accountability system for the presidency was, at bottom, a system of transparency. The system reveals some details about "secret" government operations to the public. And while most aspects of most secret operations do not leak, the system makes these operations transparent to adversarial actors within the executive branch, to Congress and, sometimes, to the courts.

Many forces made the government transparent in these ways. Journalists and WikiLeaks and other content collectors and producers around the globe discovered and published deep secrets without government authorization and in the face of government protests. FOIA requesters used the courts to pry from the government previously classified or very sensitive documents. Similar information spilled out, on purpose and inadvertently, in habeas litigation and other lawsuits. On the inside, inspectors general had legally guaranteed access to secret information throughout the national security bureaucracy, and gathered and packaged it for Congress, prosecutors, and, eventually, the public. Congress additionally required the intelligence community and the military to spend endless hours each year collecting, organizing, and reporting information about what they are doing. Courts reviewed government representations out of public view in areas involving FOIA, state secrets, and foreign intelligence surveillance. And executive branch lawyers asked question after question before signing off on military and intelligence operations.

The presidential synopticon's production of this information enabled the questioning, criticism, and pushback that produced the counterterrorism adjustments of the last decade. That is the happy side of informational transparency. But there are large downsides to transparency as well. Many authorized disclosures of government war operations—through FOIA, congressional reporting and hearings, habeas litigation, and more—contained information that was in some respects harmful to U.S. counterterrorism efforts. A prominent example is the FOIA release of CIA and Justice Department documents concerning the interrogation and detention regime. CIA Director Leon Panetta and four previous CIA Directors opposed the release of the FOIA documents, and argued for more redactions in those that were released, on the grounds that their disclosure would describe to our enemies the outer limits to which America was willing to go in interrogation, would chill future CIA actions in reliance on Justice Department legal opinions, and would erode the trust of U.S. foreign intelligence services that cooperated with the United States based on promises of secrecy.[14] President Obama did not deny these costs in deciding to release classified documents. But he made a judgment that the costs were outweighed by the benefits from releasing them.

When secret information comes out pursuant to authorized disclosures in this way, the Congress in drafting the disclosure laws, the courts in enforcing them, and the executive branch in implementing them exercise an official judgment that weighs the costs of disclosure against the benefits. When secret information becomes public via the American news media—as it has so often in the past decade—it is media editors, and not the government, who weigh the costs and benefits of disclosure. We have seen that these editors sometimes decide against publication, as when the *Washington Post*'s Leonard Downie Jr. chose not to disclose the location of the European prisons. This type of media self-censorship about U.S. national security operations happens more than is generally realized, and much more than with foreign media (like Al Jazeera or *The Guardian*) or WikiLeaks. Nonetheless, American journalists do not always exercise this responsibility intelligently or well, and their publications sometimes cause significant national security harm.

Most editors and journalists say they will not publish a secret that "puts lives at concrete and immediate risk," as *Time* magazine's Barton Gellman puts it.[15] This usually means they won't publish troop movements, the identities of secret agents, and other "operational intelligence." The norms against publication of this information have broken down over the last decade as elite media outlets have told us more than before about secret identities and operations, and as many new media outlets have chucked the norms altogether. Classified disclosures of this sort can literally destroy human intelligence assets. Intelligence officials rarely talk publicly about these matters for fear that they will make matters worse by revealing relationships and operations they would rather keep secret. But then-CIA Director Michael Hayden revealed a bit in a speech in Wye River, Maryland, in 2006. "When a covert CIA presence in a denied area was revealed in the media, two assets in the area were detained and executed," Hayden said, in a purposefully roundabout way so as not to make the problem worse. A similar "spate of stories cost five promising counterterrorism and counter proliferation assets, who feared we couldn't guarantee their security," he added.[16]

Even when journalists decline to publish secrets they think will cause immediate harm, they still publish secrets that cause diffuse but no less real harms. Leonard Downie Jr. credited the White House argument that disclosing the prison locations would harm ongoing intelligence operations but not its claim that publishing the secret prisons story on the whole would harm future intelligence operations with foreign liaison services. "I focus on the main impact of the story, not speculative effects," Downie explains. "Lots of things go wrong in the intelligence business, and it is hard to say that something bad that happens following one of our stories was in fact caused by one of our stories, because it might have happened anyway."[17] This is a self-serving rationale. It is obvious that the publication of national security secrets has future effects on intelligence operations with foreign intelligence officers, human sources, and private firms, all of whom are—quite rationally—less likely to cooperate with a U.S. government that cannot credibly claim to keep its operations secret.[18] These harms are no less real because they are hard to discern at the time of publication. The media's resistance to this point is ironic. Reporters fiercely protect their sources because they know that revelation of a source destroys the reporter's future credibility for keeping promises and discourages new sources from coming forward. But they reject this logic when the government makes the same argument.

There is perhaps no area where journalists underestimate the harms of publication more than government surveillance. The best example is the U.S. program of monitoring terrorist-related financial transfers in a global banking consortium known as the "Society for Worldwide Interbank Financial Telecommunication," or SWIFT. The classified SWIFT program was executed pursuant to an administrative subpoena, it violated no American privacy laws, and it was a straightforward exercise of powers that Congress had given the President. Nonetheless, the *New York Times* (and two other papers) disclosed it in June 2006, over the strong objections of Secretary of the Treasury John Snow. The *Times* did so after concluding that the harms from publication were "oblique at best," in the words of Eric Lichtblau, one of the story's authors.[19] The SWIFT story bore "no resemblance to security breaches, like disclosures of troop locations, that would clearly compromise the immediate safety of specific individuals," claimed a *Times* editorial.[20]

Such discounting of the indirect harms from publication drives national security officials crazy. "My God," responded Michael Hayden. "Like it would be permissible to compromise the long-term safety of the masses, which is exactly what the SWIFT story did!"[21] The *Times*' invocation of the troop movement analogy—the inevitable example journalists invoke—is outdated. "Most of us grew up in the Cold War when the enemy was big and powerful; he wasn't hard to find, he was just hard to stop," says Hayden. In the war against terrorists in networks, however, "the enemy frankly is easy to kill; he's just very hard to find." Hayden says that it "misses the point" to view troop movements as the real secrets to be protected. "The real secrets now are things like the SWIFT program that allowed us to track terrorist financing and locate terrorists," he notes, adding that undercutting the government's ability to track terrorists in programs like SWIFT "will just as surely lead to the deaths of Americans."[22]

Another reason the *Times* published the SWIFT story, says former editor Bill Keller, is that "we weren't really telling the terrorists anything they didn't know" because "terrorists assume that governments do everything in their power to spy on them and thwart their intents."[23] This explanation betrays an inadequate understanding of the intelligence world. Money is the lifeblood of terrorism, and following it allows the government to discover plots and to take steps to thwart them. Terrorists might assume government is tracking their finances, but they do not know for sure where or how they are doing so. The *Times* itself reported that the SWIFT program led to the capture of the al Qaeda architect of the 2002 Bali bombings. This success is harder to replicate after the *Times* told everyone about it. Just as a target who learns that his phone is being tapped can hang up, a terrorist who learns that his bank transfers are being monitored can switch financing methods. This, in general, is why surveillance secrets are so fragile. If plans for a new missile system leak, the enemy still must expend resources to figure out how to defend against it. But when a surveillance method leaks, the harm is complete because the target can simply cease the communication method.

Journalists misjudge the national security harms of publishing classified secrets not only because they lack expertise but also because they are motivated in part by fame and money. A national security scoop like the secret prisons story or the Terrorist Surveillance Program story often leads to a Pulitzer or other prizes and higher circulation or ratings. These factors inevitably influence journalists and editors to place a thumb on the scale in favor of publication. Other questionable considerations do as well. The *New York Times* rushed the SWIFT story to publication because it feared being scooped by other newspapers; it published the original Terrorist Surveillance Program story because it feared being scooped by its own reporter, James Risen.[24] Neither reason has any connection to the security-publication trade-off. Another reason that apparently led the *Times* to publish the SWIFT story was that it was, in the words of one of its coauthors, "an interesting yarn about the administration's extraordinary efforts since 9/11 to stop another attack."[25] The aesthetic merits of a story might be relevant to newspaper sales, but they are hardly relevant to the careful exercise of judgment about whether public accountability warrants a compromise of national security.

The extensive disclosure of national security secrets by the traditional U.S. news media since 9/11 has had an undoubtedly detrimental impact on U.S. national security—an impact exacerbated by foreign and newer media reporting, and organizations like WikiLeaks. Unauthorized disclosures of classified information "have become one of the biggest threats to the survival of U.S. intelligence," said former CIA Director George Tenet.[26] Tenet made this remark in October 2000, at the twilight of the Clinton administration, before 9/11 and the gush of revelations of the last decade. After 9/11, but before the WikiLeaks disclosures, the CIA reported that "al Qaeda planners have learned much about our counterterrorist intelligence capabilities from U.S. and foreign media," and that the cumulative effect of these disclosures "has jeopardized highly fragile and very sensitive intelligence capabilities."[27] A bipartisan intelligence study reported in 2005—before the run of surveillance disclosures that began later that year—that "several leaks . . . have collectively cost the American people hundreds of millions of dollars, and have done grave harm."[28] These costs of disclosures are more devastating, and the stakes higher, than these conclusory sentences indicate. Journalists, however, tend to sneer at such claims. "Prove it," they insist, even though they know well that to do so the government would have to release details that make the problem worse. Journalists could discover the truth if they were to pursue and examine these claims with the same vigor they use to pursue other secrets. One looks in vain, however, for national security reporting of this sort, which would complicate journalists' heroic self-conception of their role in American democracy.

The many costs of media and related disclosures of national security secrets cannot be ignored in an assessment of the presidential synopticon. But it does not follow that the media's pursuit of government secrets is bad for American society, or even for national security, all things considered. The reason is that there are serious harms—including harms to national security—from excessive government secrecy. "Wartime heightens the case for secrecy because the value of security is at its peak," notes Barton Gellman. "But secrecy is never more damaging to self-government than in wartime, because making war is the very paradigm of political choice," and the "life-and-death stakes give equal urgency to the project of holding our leaders accountable for their use of power."[29] When the executive branch acts in the secret world it defines for itself, it makes more mistakes than usual, and the mistakes are harder to correct because the normal checking functions of the government cannot operate. The media and other vehicles of unauthorized information disclosure are a corrective to the necessary but unfortunate secrecy of war and intelligence operations. Many of the sensational media disclosures of the past decade revealed mistakes or abuses that led Congress and the courts and executive insiders to change government war policy. These accountability mechanisms would not have worked nearly as well if the press had not been in the shadows reporting how the government was fighting the war. And even when the press didn't uncover secrets, fear of leaks caused national security officials to think twice about what they do, and deterred them from doing things they shouldn't.

And so we have a system in which the executive branch, in the secret aspects of its wars and intelligence operations, sometimes makes mistakes that can harm national security, and in which the press and others seeking to hold the executive branch accountable sometimes publish information that can harm national security. There are costs and benefits to national security from both secrecy and disclosure, but we do not have great tools to measure or compare them. The beginning of wisdom in sorting out this conundrum is to recognize that, while the press sometimes acts irresponsibly in publishing national security secrets, the government is the primary source of the problem and the only institution that can possibly cure it.

"The responsibility must be where the power is," Justice Potter Stewart said in the Pentagon Papers case. "If the Constitution gives the Executive a large degree of unshared power in the conduct of foreign affairs and the maintenance of our national defense, then under the Constitution the Executive must have the largely unshared duty to determine and preserve the degree of internal security necessary to exercise that power successfully."[30] The executive branch does an atrocious job of protecting its secrets. Part of the problem lies in technological changes that make secrecy-keeping harder, and that the government can do little to alter. Many leaks in the last decade were connected to perceptions of illegality or illegitimacy inside the government that the government can take (and has taken) steps to fix. The government has also taken steps to make its secrecy systems more secure. There is no reason why Army Private Bradley Manning, along with five hundred thousand others, should have had access to the classified SIPRNet, in which rested the midlevel secrets of the Defense and State Departments.[31]

The government has done little, by contrast, to fix the rampant problem of classifying way too much information. Nor has it done much to stop the opportunistic and hypocritical manipulation of the secrecy system by top officials, which inures the media to leaks and makes it disrespectful of security classifications and governmental claims of harm when deciding whether to publish. One reason the *New York Times* ran the SWIFT terrorist financing story was the diminished credibility of Treasury Secretary Snow, who had frequently "discussed many sensitive details" of the Treasury Department's monitoring efforts in the hopes that the press would write about "the administration's relentlessness against the terrorist threat," according to Bill Keller. "One man's security breach is another man's P.R. campaign—and sometimes they are the same man."[32] Or so it seems to a media made cynical by decades of opportunistic executive branch manipulation of the secrecy stamp.

The executive branch's overdeployment and manipulation of the secrecy stamp is an important justification for an aggressive press to find and publish these secrets. But, says Michael Hayden, "the public has already decided through its elected officials what it wants to know and what it doesn't want to know." The responsibility for "weighing the merits of release against the risks of relief, is one that the public through its representatives has reposed to the President," he adds. "Nobody's elected Bill Keller of the NYT to perform that duty."[33] Hayden is right that no one (other than the publisher of the New York Times Company) elected Keller to do this job. But he is not right to say that the public and Congress, or the Constitution, have given the task of weighing the merits of releasing classified information to the President alone. To the contrary, our legal and political system tolerates and has effectively countenanced press reporting of classified national security secrets. Not only does the executive branch, where most leaks originate, do little to fix the broken secrecy system. Despite steady leaks of sensitive and classified information throughout our nation's history, and despite the rash of leaks in the last decade, the government as a whole has taken few steps to punish those responsible for leaking and publishing.

"Leakers are rarely seen to suffer consequences for leaking classified information," bemoaned a recent congressional report.[34] One reason is that leakers are hard to find. Another is that a lot of them are former government employees against whom many of the executive branch's punishment tools—revoking security clearances, suspension, or termination—have little consequence. And the executive branch rarely uses its most extreme option, prosecution. We can count on two hands the number of leak prosecutions against government officials in American history: nine. This number has risen in the past decade of unprecedented leaks—three attempted prosecutions in the 220 years before 9/11, and six since 9/11.[35] The Obama administration's aggressive pursuit of government leakers—five of those six were charged during its first two years in office—underscores how serious a problem leaks have become for the executive branch. These prosecutions, however, have not been terribly successful to date.[36] And the number of prosecutions has been very small, as has the overall effort, compared to the overall number of leaks. The prosecution-to-leak ratio is tiny because prosecutions in this context are politically controversial, they threaten to reveal yet more classified information, and the relevant laws are old and vague, making prosecution difficult. Despite many complaints, especially after WikiLeaks released reams of classified documents, Congress has not updated these outdated laws. It might do so in the future because of a pattern of leaks that many think has reached a crisis point. But it is doubtful that legally and politically acceptable changes in the law would have a big impact on the massive leaking from the government.

The U.S. government is even more hands-off with the press. It has never prosecuted a member of the media for publishing secret government information. This restraint is not, as many journalists believe, required by the First Amendment. The Pentagon Papers case rejected only a prior restraint on the press. At the same time, three Supreme Court justices stated that the First Amendment was not a bar to post-publication prosecutions, and at least two others implied as much. Here even more so than with leakers, the government is held back by politics, poor laws, and the threat of more classified information revelations. They are also held back by courts that give special scrutiny to government punishment of the press. "It is a curiously American phenomenon," notes Leonard Downie's successor at the *Washington Post*, Marcus Brauchli, "that the most powerful officials in the world's most powerful nation have virtually no power to do anything but ask an editor to weigh the national interest against the impulse to publish— and then leave the editor to make his decision."[37] The philosophy underlying this curious phenomenon has been apparent during the WikiLeaks saga. The Department of Justice has openly struggled to find a theory to permit the prosecution of Julian Assange for extracting and publishing classified information while at the same time making clear to the public that it will not pursue the American media, which does exactly the same thing every day.

The executive branch could sanction the press in other ways besides prosecution. It could, for example, be more aggressive in asking journalists to identify sources for their stories containing classified information. This has happened more than usual in the last decade, but only a bit more. In the leak trial of former CIA officer Jeffrey Sterling, for example, the Obama administration tried to force *New York Times* reporter James Risen to disclose details about how he learned the information he had reported, on penalty (if he refused) of jail. The trial judge rejected the government's attempt.[38] If this exercise of government power were to succeed, it could affect the balance between secrecy and disclosure. But what is remarkable about the last decade is not the slight increase in attempts to use subpoenas against journalists but rather the relatively sparse use of subpoenas given the number and type of leaks. Even more significant is the fact that the Justice Department has done nothing to change its self-imposed rules that create a heavy burden before even seeking information from the press.[39]

The U.S. government, in short, complains and complains about national security leaks and the undoubted harms they cause. But the too-secretive and too-leaky government, not the press that reports these leaked secrets, is the main source of the problem. And the government has been remarkably restrained in reacting to the problem even after a decade of harmful wartime disclosures. Courts have been skeptical about government crackdowns on leakers and the media establishments to which they leak. Congress has done little to make it easier for the executive branch to pursue leakers. And the executive branch, despite some novel actions against leakers, has proceeded slowly, cautiously, and (compared to the size of the problem) selectively.

Underlying this persistent restraint is a recognition—based in part on politics and in part on a powerful constitutional tradition—that press coverage of secret executive branch action serves a vital function in American democracy, even though the press often miscalculates the harm of publishing secrets and thus often harms national security. "Some degree of abuse is inseparable from the proper use of every thing; and in no instance is this more true than in that of the press," said Madison. "It has accordingly been decided . . . that it is better to leave a few of its noxious branches to their luxuriant growth, than, by pruning them away, to injure the vigor of those yielding the proper fruits."[40] Madison did not have publication of national security secrets in mind, but his reasoning applies to the issue. It is no accident that, as Brauchli notes, the nation with the largest and most powerful military and intelligence services in the world is also the nation that, by a large margin, gives its media the freest reins in discovering and publishing classified secrets. There is in theory room to tighten these reins. But the United States has basically decided that a self-serving and institutionally biased media which pursues and publishes government secrets that sometimes harm national security achieves important account-ability benefits that on balance outweigh the harms to national security.

LAWFARE

Perfidy is the war crime of inviting an enemy soldier's confidence by feigning the protection of the laws of war. Raising a white flag in order to lower the enemy's guard before attacking him is a classic act of perfidy. Perfidy is the terrorist's "general principle of operation," as General Mark Martins puts it, because the terror-ist wears no uniform or insignia when blending into the civilian population, thereby exploiting the trust of those around him in order to ensure his attack is more deadly.[41] He also exploits the laws of war by hiding out in hospitals, mosques, homes, and other presumptively protected places, and regularly uses innocent civil-ians as human shields. By taking advantage of U.S. compliance with the laws of war and by violating the law's insistence that they distinguish themselves from civilians, terrorists force the United States to choose between not attacking the enemy or risking con-troversial civilian casualties.

Perfidy is a despicable practice that has come to be seen as a form of "lawfare," a term that now retired Air Force General Charles Dunlap defined as the "use of law as a weapon of war" in an influential essay presented at Harvard's Kennedy School of Government a few months after 9/11.[42] A variant of lawfare can be found in the al Qaeda handbook discovered in a Manchester, England, safe house. Chapter 18 of the manual has a list of rules, the first of which is that "brothers must insist on proving that torture was inflicted" and the second of which is "to complain [in court] of mistreatment while in prison."[43] Al Qaeda members and other terrorists are trained to make false accusations against

U.S. officials, and more generally to exploit the U.S. legal system to their advantage when possible. These tactics constitute what Dunlap described as "a cynical manipulation of the rule of law and the humanitarian values it represents" that is designed to make the United States seem like a lawbreaker and thereby to undermine support for its counterterrorism actions at home and abroad. By making the United States hesitate and by undermining its support, enemy soldiers use law as an asymmetrical weapon of warfare to increase their relative power in the face of the United States' overwhelming traditional military capabilities.

In the past decade, the term "lawfare" has left its academic origins and entered mainstream discussions of the war on terrorism. Along the way the term retained its negative connotation. But it broadened from its association with the aims and actions of enemy terrorists to include the aims and actions of the lawyers who represented them in court, other advocates who challenge the legality of U.S. counterterrorism policies, and even U.S. officials—such as judges, inspectors general, or court-martial prosecutors—who apply accountability mechanisms against other U.S. officials during wartime.[44] The essence of the lawfare critique is that these actors are abusing law and legal systems to further their strategic or political aims, including the aim of thwarting U.S. efforts to defeat Islamist terrorists.[45]

In some senses, the use of law as a weapon in war, like informational transparency in war, is not new. Military adversaries and critics of presidential wartime action have long used domestic and international law strategically to achieve their ends. What is new is the extraordinary significance of law in war.[46] War has become hyper-legalized, and legality has become the global currency of legitimacy for military and intelligence action. As law in war has grown, the Commander in Chief has lost the relative control he used to have over its interpretation and enforcement. Courts in the United States have shed their traditional skittishness about enforcing law against the Commander in Chief during war. Courts abroad have grown bold in questioning U.S. military and intelligence actions in court. Lawyers inside the executive branch are constantly influencing the President's options. Activist groups outside the executive branch have huge professional staffs devoted to criticizing the President's actions in the language of law, and to bringing lawsuits in the United States and abroad to challenge his actions. And the media more than ever uses the language of law to judge the President's action. All of the watchers in the presidential synopticon, in short, use law as a measure of critique and a tool of sanction. And many of them, no doubt, do so strategically to suit their ends.

So too, though, does the executive branch. The President's legitimate power in war to surveil, to prosecute, to detain, and to kill flows from domestic and international law. To justify these actions, the President every day invokes his constitutional, statutory, and international law authorities, and his lawyers are in constant battle—with European allies, the media, NGOs such as the International Committee of the Red Cross, and terrorists in federal court—for their favored understandings of the law. In these contexts, the President and his lawyers interpret and employ law strategically to further their aims. The Obama administration, for example, invoked the 2001 congressional authorization to use force, his discretion as Commander in Chief, the right of self-defense under the UN Charter, and the right to target and kill combatants under the international laws of war, as a basis to invade Pakistan and kill Osama Bin Laden.[47] Its arguments were sound, but they were also contested, and required justification and explanation. The United States also employs law strategically when it seizes terrorist assets, buys commercial satellite imagery, hires private security forces, threatens sanctions, and engages in thousands of other war-related acts every day.[48] Counterinsurgency strategy is also a form of using law strategically as a weapon in war. As we saw in Chapter 5, in Afghanistan today U.S. soldiers fight to establish criminal justice institutions with the aim of promoting the legitimacy of the Afghan government and defeating the insurgency. "Lawfare in this sense," as Martins notes, "is in many respects the opposite of the manipulative original connotation of the term."[49]

There is no escaping the strategic use of law in war because law defines and touches on every aspect of modern war. This is why the essence of the lawfare critique is not that law is employed strategically, but rather that it is abused. Abuse, however, is often in the eye of the beholder. Former prosecutor Andrew McCarthy argues that the Center for Constitutional Rights is "a hard Left redoubt" whose "general purpose [is] to defeat the U.S. war effort" and whose "specific goal is to frustrate our capacity to collect the other most valuable species of intelligence: the fruits of interrogation, information from actual operatives about ongoing terror plots."[50] CCR is a frequent target of the lawfare charge, and McCarthy might be right about its motives. Michael Ratner, CCR's antiwar activist leader, acknowledges that the habeas litigation is "brutal" for the U.S. government, and "makes it much harder to do what they're doing" at GTMO, including interrogation.[51]

It does not follow, though, that CCR acted illegitimately or abused the law or the legal system. The precedents did not favor the organization when it brought its first habeas corpus lawsuits in 2002. But the significance of precedents changes with context, and litigants in our legal system are allowed to challenge or reinterpret precedents as long as their arguments are not frivolous. Far from being frivolous or abusive, the CCR lawsuits resulted in victory in landmark cases before the Supreme Court. There are certainly abuses of law in war. But in a world in which legal norms touching on war are contested and the interpreters of these norms are many and varied, it is often hard to say, except in cases of dishonesty, that law is used abusively.

While lawfare critics talk about the abuse of the legal system, their real beef is that the legalization of warfare harms U.S. counterterrorism efforts. "However well our troops do on the battlefield, a reality of modern times is that the U.S. can still lose the war on terror in the courtroom," laments the *Wall Street Journal's* editors.[52] This focus on the costs of lawfare is a more fruitful line of criticism.[53]

One cost of lawfare is generated by the people and institutions enforcing the law against the presidency. These people and institutions have their own interests and biases, they are not necessarily expert on the matters they review, and they sometimes, like the executive branch officials they watch, commit mistakes or abuses. In the early years after 9/11, lawyers in the Justice Department and elsewhere sometimes misinterpreted the law or did not enforce it properly against the executive branch. The Justice Department's Office of Professional Responsibility made errors in its aggressive ethics review of some of the resulting legal opinions.[54] More broadly, government lawyers charged with holding the President accountable to law make mistakes, sometimes saying "no" to a proposed operation when they should say "yes" (or vice versa). There is no reason to think that courts charged with novel responsibilities in the post-9/11 world always make the right decision either. The landmark rulings in the war on terrorism sharply split the Supreme Court, and many rules crafted by lower courts are (as some of the judges on these courts acknowledge) based on national security intuitions beyond their expertise. These courts quite likely have both enabled dangerous terrorists to be released and erroneously denied habeas corpus to detainees who should be released. Some of John Helgerson's aggressive inspector general investigations were widely viewed within the CIA as factually inaccurate and tendentious. The human rights organizations that have been so influential in holding the government to account in the last decade have frequently engaged in exaggerated, partisan, and often vicious attacks on government officials. And they sometimes file lawsuits "to win public support to harass American officials—military and civilian—and to score ideological victories," as Donald Rumsfeld put it in his memoirs.[55]

These examples, which could be multiplied, raise the ancient question of who guards the guardians. The guardians are subject to various sorts of checks, some stronger than others. We saw how a career official in the Deputy Attorney General's Office, David Margolis, overruled the Justice Department ethics report on Jay Bybee and John Yoo because of its many errors.[56] In 2007, CIA Director Michael Hayden ordered a "management review" of John Helgerson's inspector general shop and convinced him—in the face of great controversy—to create, among other reforms, a "quality control officer" to ensure the factual accuracy of his reports and an ombudsman to field and channel complaints about the inspector general's work.[57] The decisions of the Supreme Court, so consequential in the war on terrorism, are hard to overturn. The court is influenced to some degree by public criticism and debate in the United States. But these forms of influence have no real analogue among the growing cast of foreign courts that seek to subject U.S. officials to judicial accountability. Although the human rights groups and other organizations that file lawsuits against U.S. officials are disciplined by courts that review and rule on their claims, the mistaken or tendentious legal charges they often make in reports and campaigns are restrained only by public sentiment in the marketplace of ideas. There is no Archimedean point here. Just as the press cannot be trusted to define the line of secrecy, the watchers who enforce law against the presidency cannot be trusted to review and sanction without bias or error. They have real power, but it is hard to know if they are adequately watched, or how they could be watched more, consistent with other values.

Another cost of lawfare is the fragmentation of authority within the executive branch during war. The Commander in Chief traditionally had unified hierarchical command over the executive branch that empowered him to act quickly and that promoted accountability to the public by identifying him as the person responsible for all executive action. This understanding has broken down in the last decade. We have seen how consequential independent inspectors general are in checking the presidency's national security goals. Lawyers too have gained more independence and power that the President cannot effectively control, especially in the military, but in other pockets of the executive branch as well. These lawyers enforce the law (when they interpret it correctly), but they also attenuate the unity of accountability and command. The increasing involvement of courts and other outside actors in military and intelligence decisions does not violate the theory of the unitary executive, but it has a similar effect on the executive branch. As we have seen, judicial review of wartime tactics has all sorts of hard-to-see constraining consequences on presidential decision-making.

The decentralized legal enforcers that have risen in power in the last decade splinter the Commander in Chief's executive unity like nothing in American wartime history. Benjamin Wittes closes his book *Detention and Denial* by speculating what would happen if a prisoner released from GTMO is later found in an al Qaeda leadership position. "We have no accountability when our system fails," he says, before asking, "Were these releases the fault of courts (whose threats of review spurred them), the Bush administration (which carried them out), . . . or the left and the international community (which ruthlessly pushed for them)?"[58] The problem is deeper and wider than Wittes describes. It is deeper because he does not mention the independent players inside the executive branch who shape and constrain presidential action through investigation and legal interpretation. And it is broader because it applies far beyond the detention context to surveillance, targeting, and every element of the war on terrorism. Moreover, the opposite of Wittes's speculation is also possible, indeed likely: the President will be blamed when something goes wrong even if, because of the splintering of executive authority, he lacked the effective power to do what in retrospect should have been done. Distributed accountability can bring many benefits, but its undoubted costs are the difficulty of identifying the locus of accountability when something goes wrong, and the possibility that the leader of the flattened organization will be blamed even though he lacked effective control.

A related cost of lawfare is the weakening of wartime presidential initiative and dispatch. When more eyes have to review an operation in advance, it takes longer. Covert operations have many layers of review and approval beginning with many in the CIA and moving up through other bureaucracies to the President. Decisions on the targets in this war often go through a similarly extensive review process for targets off the traditional battlefield, and less extensive but still elaborate reviews for targets on a traditional battlefield. In general, all military and intelligence actions of any significance have elaborate and law-heavy preclearance processes. These up-front reviews delay action and can be so burdensome to negotiate that they result in otherwise useful and appropriate actions not being taken at all.

Another factor slowing down and sometimes precluding executive action is the anticipated personal and professional costs of accountability. The rise of powerful, networked, and harshly critical NGOs has meant that not only top government officials, but midlevel ones as well, are subject to vivid, reputation-harming charges published globally on the Internet, as well as the possibility of lawsuits in the United States and abroad. The "mere threat of lawsuits and legal charges effectively bullies American decision makers, alters their actions, intimidates our security forces, and limits our country's ability to gather intelligence," says Donald Rumsfeld, lamenting lawfare's effect.[59]

Stripped of its negative connotations, Rumsfeld's judgment—which in less colorful terms applies to every accountability constraint described in this book—should not be controversial. "Bullying" and "intimidating" are forms of influencing, and influencing government behavior to make it more prudent and lawful is the point of the legalized accountability mechanisms. "I think people should think twice; I think that's a good thing," says the ACLU's Jameel Jaffer upon learning about the effect of legal scrutiny and criticism on government officials. "I don't want people to think twice about doing things that are both in the national interest and consistent with the law but if by think twice you mean think twice before sticking a man in a box with a bug, then absolutely, think twice," he adds, referring to one of the Bush administration's most controversial interrogation techniques.[60]

There is no doubt that lawfare significantly influences and constrains officials, not only by direct prohibitions but also, and more significantly, by getting them to "think twice" about what they are doing. The hard question is whether this influence goes too far. The bug-in-the-box is now prohibited by law, partly as a result of Jaffer's efforts, but in many cases what is in the national interest and what is lawful are not black and white, but rather various shades of gray. Government officials every day have to decide how far to push into this gray area. The accountability mechanisms give them pause and lead them not to push as far into the darker shades. Whether that leads them to a place in the gray area where they should be or short of where they should be depends on facts about the future that no one has, as well as one's view of the relevant law, which is not always clear. As a result of the last decade executive officials up and down the chain of command are much more sensitive to law and accountability, and many worry that this sensitivity leads to excessive caution. It is hard to know if they are right, but Jaffer's opposite and easy-sounding injunction—follow the law and act in the national security interest—is far too simple.

A full assessment of the legalization of warfare, in sum, must acknowledge that the synoptical enforcers sometimes act tendentiously, make mistakes for which they are unevenly accountable, splinter presidential decision-making, and slow or chill executive action. But to paraphrase Madison, abuses and errors are inseparable from the proper use of everything. The vices in the exercise of legal constraints are inextricably tied to their virtues. Most of the vices emerge from the independence of the enforcers, which is what makes them effective. John Helgerson's inspector general review of the CIA was an affront to the unitary executive and may well have been biased and full of mistakes, as his critics charge. But it set in motion a series of events that ended with the Congress self-consciously rejecting much of the program, and it led to other forms of accountability as well. Critics charge that the Supreme Court's habeas corpus rulings rested on mistaken interpretations of law that harmed national security. But these rulings also pressured Congress and the executive branch to significantly improve the detention review process; a decade after 9/11 nearly two hundred dangerous terrorists remain at GTMO, legitimately and with relatively little controversy, in military detention without trial—an extraordinary accomplishment. Military lawyers sometimes prevent targeters from killing bad guys. But they also sometimes prevent them from mistakenly killing innocent civilians. COIN-inspired detention operations require release of some terrorists but also make it possible to detain more terrorists on the whole. In these and many other ways, the strategic use of law during wartime resulted in better planning, better policies, self-corrections, and legitimated and empowered presidential action.

There are surely ways to maintain the adequate independence of the watchers while lowering the costs of their watching. But knowing which discrete reforms make sense turns, again, not just on contested normative assumptions but also on contested facts. How significant is the chilling effect on government actors caused by lawfare? What operations were delayed or aborted as a result of this chilling effect or of mistaken vetoes by government lawyers? How might those operations, discounted by the possibility of mistaken execution or unanticipated blowback, have improved U.S. security? How much intelligence is the United States losing as a result of its killing rather than detaining and interrogating high-value terrorists? How do we measure this lost intelligence against the political and legal costs of capturing and interrogating these detainees? Many of the most difficult issues of counterterrorism policy turn on unanswerable questions like these, which are easy to multiply.

While it is difficult to make firm conclusions about optimal counterterrorism policies and their associated accountability mechanisms, the experiences of the last decade provide a second-order solace. The presidential synopticon incessantly generates new information about the terror threat and the appropriateness and efficacy of counterterrorism measures to meet this threat, and our flexible political and legal institutions respond relatively quickly to this information. The dizzying and often painful swirl of investigations, lawsuits, reviews, reports, and accusations that characterize the presidential synopticon forces the government to recalibrate its counterterrorism policies and accountability mechanisms constantly based on ever-changing information and ever-changing legal and political constraints. This is the essence of Schlesinger's insight about the self-correcting effects of robust checks and balances.

ACCOUNTABILITY

"In releasing these memos, it is our intention to assure those who carried out their duties relying in good faith upon legal advice from the Department of Justice that they will not be subject to prosecution," said President Obama on April 16, 2009, in conjunction with one of his controversial releases of CIA and Justice Department documents in response to the ACLU's FOIA litigation.[61] A few days later his Chief of Staff, Rahm Emanuel, said the administration also would not pursue criminal investigations of those in the CIA, Justice Department, and White House who devised the program. The administration did not reach either of these decisions—to release the documents and not to open a broad investigation of the program they represented—lightly.[62] The lawyer-President carefully read John Helgerson's inspector general report and the Office of Legal Counsel memos, and deliberated for a month with his top political, legal, and national security advisers. He decided to reject a broad, backward-looking inquiry because he had already banned the practice and because investigating it further would inflame the country and distract it from his new administration's many goals (most notably, at the time, health care reform). "What we don't need now is to become a sort of feeding frenzy where we go back and re-litigate all this," said one senior adviser, explaining the President's decision.[63]

President Obama did relitigate Bush-era interrogation practices to some degree, however, first with his decision to repudiate the CIA program and then with his decision to release the documents. The judge in the ACLU case, Alvin Hellerstein, had not ordered the administration to disclose the Office of Legal Counsel memoranda in the form that they were released in April 2009, but rather simply to process them quickly, consistent with FOIA's command. The administration could have fought for exemptions and redactions beyond those it ultimately imposed. It probably could have won some additional exemptions and redactions (though not nearly all, given Hellerstein's pressure and prior rulings); it certainly could have dragged out the process. But rejecting the CIA interrogation program was the administration's main break from the Bush era and the one the President felt most strongly about. Fighting for FOIA exemptions for documents the general contents of which were well known would have seemed hypocritical and would have opened the administration to the criticism, pressed by the ACLU at the time, that it was protecting information about human rights abuses. When Obama said in his statement that the documents' release was "required by the rule of law," most thought he was referring to the ACLU's FOIA litigation. But his statement was ambiguous in light of Hellerstein's order, and may have referred to the rule of law that he believed he was upholding by exposing what he thought were the wrongs of the previous administration. The release was a form of "accounting [for] the past," the President said.[64]

But it was not nearly enough of an accounting for the human rights NGO community. Two days after former Vice President Cheney blasted the Obama administration for endangering national security by releasing the documents, Jameel Jaffer and his ACLU colleague Ben Wizner blasted the administration for "sanctioning impunity for government officials who authorized torture" by announcing it would not investigate the program the documents supported. The abuses and deaths uncovered in the FOIA pointed to "grave criminality" that warranted full investigation and then prosecution, they argued. "Accountability is needed for Bush-era torture."[65] This would become a frequent refrain from the left, which viewed many of the Bush administration's early practices—especially its interrogation practices—with horror and derision, and bristled at the fact that no top American civilian or military official has been charged with a crime for these actions.[66]

This critique—the polar opposite of the lawfare charge—rests on an impoverished understanding of accountability. At its core (and as used throughout this book), "accountability" means to be subject to an account, which in turn means to disclose one's activities, explain and answer for them, and subject oneself to the consequences of the institution to which one is accounting. Criminal trials are but one form of accountability. Others include lawyer scrutiny, reporting requirements, inspector general and congressional investigations, Accountability Board proceedings, prosecutorial and ethics investigations, civil trials, FOIA processing and disclosures, public criticism and calumny, and elections, all of which impose various forms of psychological, professional, reputational, financial, and political costs on those held accountable. There was little accountability for the CIA in Allen Dulles's era because very few, inside or outside the government, knew what the CIA was doing. The crux of modern accountability in the national security bureaucracy is that secrecy of this sort is significantly diminished. The people and institutions inside and outside the government that constitute the presidential synopticon know what the intelligence and military agencies are up to and can take steps to punish or influence their actions if they disapprove. That is exactly what happened to the now repudiated CIA program and to many other early Bush-era programs.

Whether too much or too little accountability was imposed for the CIA program is, like the related question about the proper strategic uses of law, a harder question. But many factors suggest that an insistence on criminal trials is misplaced. The officials who devised the CIA program have been subject to investigations and brutal public criticism that brought many of them—especially the lawyers and psychologists—reputational, professional, and financial harm. Accountability is also reflected in the congressional pushback on the program, Obama's repudiation of it, the release of the CIA program documents, and the attendant public scrutiny and criticism. Critics insist on prosecutions beyond these measures, but they should be careful what they wish for. A criminal prosecution would divide the country and show that a broad swath of the American people supports the CIA program. The evidence in the trial would further churn the debate about the intelligence value of the CIA program. And the trial itself would almost certainly result in acquittal. The legality of the original CIA interrogation techniques under the purposefully loophole-ridden torture law was always a closer question than critics have publicly acknowledged (though some admit it in private).[67] Some of the early Department of Justice opinions were withdrawn because they made flawed and unnecessary arguments far beyond what was needed to support the techniques in question.[68] But many outstanding lawyers of unquestioned integrity subsequently concluded that the techniques themselves, if exercised with care, and however morally repugnant they seem to some, were lawful under the then prevailing law.[69] In this light, a prosecution of top officials for hard decisions made at one of the scariest times in American history would almost certainly not succeed. It would thus bring neither the punishment nor the lucid renunciation of the CIA program that many critics want. If anything, the trial might weaken the relative opprobrium that currently attaches to the program.

The case for criminal investigation is stronger for CIA officers who acted beyond their authorizations. That is precisely why the officers have been thoroughly investigated by the inspector general, two different career prosecutors, and many Accountability Boards. After a second round of criminal investigations, prosecutor John Durham determined that two incidents warranted further criminal investigation but that many dozens of others did not. Some argue that the CIA Accountability Boards for those not prosecuted did not impose steep enough sanctions.[70] We don't know the full extent of their sanctions. But the aim of the boards is not to punish every mistake, including (as harsh as it sounds) every death or mistaken identity that results in an erroneous rendition. Analogous mistakes occur in the fog of war in military targeting, and their complete elimination in every instance would require a degree of caution inconsistent with protecting national security. The question for the CIA discipliners is not whether officers made a mistake, but whether they acted reasonably under the circumstances. In answering this question, and in doling out sanctions, the discipliners face a "built-in tension between supporting officers who make difficult decisions and holding them responsible when those decisions are incorrect," in the words of former CIA Director James Woolsey.[71] In resolving the tension, the Accountability Board must look not just at individual culpability but also at the effect of sanctions on the Agency's overall mission. The board must consider what sanctions are needed to deter future imprudent behavior but must also worry that excessive sanctions might dull the initiative and risk-taking of those officers. It must also consider the costs to the CIA and the nation from harshly sanctioning officers who made mistakes but who have years of valuable training, operational experience, and language skills.

The larger point here—one that applies to all accountability mechanisms—is that accountability includes much more than criminal punishment and does not turn only on individual mistakes or wrongdoing. Accountability includes a whole array of sanctions, and an assessment of the proper sanction includes an assessment of the costs of various forms of accountability on the community or the nation. Prosecutors deciding whether and how to enforce the criminal law take into account the broader consequences of prosecution and sometimes reach a plea deal or decline prosecution in a strong case because of these considerations. That judgment is at the core of prosecutorial discretion. The state secrets doctrine reflects a judgment—made and enforced by courts—that in some cases, protecting national security is more important than a plaintiff's right to seek justice through his day in court. President Obama's decision against a broad investigation or truth commission for Bush-era actions reflected a judgment about the adequacy of prior accountability sanctions and the costs to the nation of imposing more. It is hard to conclude that he was wrong in this judgment, but in any event, in our system this judgment is clearly his to exercise.

While critics of the accountability meted out in the last decade insist on backward-looking criminal punishment, the real concern is about the future. A failure to prosecute top officials would "invite abuses by future administrations," Jaffer and Wizner think, because "nothing would prevent any lawyer for any President from telling any interrogator that he could do anything to any prisoner."[72] This is a frequent refrain from human rights activists, and one that seemed to garner credibility when some Republican presidential candidates endorsed waterboarding in 2011, but it is almost certainly wrong. There are many things—some attributable to the work of the human rights organizations—that would prevent a lawyer or President from doing this.

The first is the law, which changed quite a lot in the last decade. Most notably, Congress and the Supreme Court in 2005 and 2006 narrowed the lawful scope of interrogation in ways that (as many Bush attorneys believed at the time) rule out a return to most of the controversial early techniques. The many other changes in the law since 9/11 outlined in this book would in the future rule out a return to other early post-9/11 practices.

The second thing that would prevent a return to the early post-9/11 interrogation practices is the presidential synopticon, which is more robust now than in 2001. Today many more people and institutions, inside and outside the government, have more power and greater opportunity to watch what our intelligence and military services do, and to threaten sanctions. Cutting legal corners in secret now is significantly harder than in 2001.

The third thing that would prevent a return to the early interrogation practices is that every lawyer in the government now knows about the brutal recriminations that Jay Bybee, John Yoo, and other lawyers suffered as a result of legal opinions written at a time of scary threats and public demand for aggressive action. Government national security lawyers today ask themselves not only whether an operation is effective and lawful, and not only how it will "look and feel" if it is made public down the road, but also what its effects might be for their careers and their families when the political winds change. "It gets you right where you live," says John Rizzo.[73] And when the lawyers hesitate, so too do the people who rely on their advice.

The final reason we almost certainly won't return to the early interrogation and other early post-9/11 counterterrorism practices is that the intelligence community today draws less comfort from the grand bargain that was supposed to give it the cover and legitimacy to do its controversial work. The CIA sought all of the right assurances up front for its detention and interrogation mission; it dutifully reported its subsequent mistakes; and it cooperated with the many resulting investigations. From the CIA's perspective, the other parties to the grand bargain did not reciprocate. The Justice Department withdrew legal opinions that the CIA relied on for dangerous missions, and it reopened criminal investigations it said were closed. Congressional intelligence committee leaders to whom the CIA often reported nodded in quiet approval in dangerous times but then turned on the Agency when the program became public and controversial. The President, in response to FOIA requests, disclosed highly classified documents that the CIA assumed would remain secret. CIA whistle-blowers leaked information to the press rather than follow internal whistle-blower procedures. Many CIA officials who complied with the rules they were given in carrying out a controversial mission they did not seek were criticized in public as craven torturers or worse, often in misleading reports to which they could not respond because doing so would violate professional norms and secrecy rules.

The CIA has a fatalistic attitude toward all of this. "Suck it up and do your job" is its philosophy. And yet it and the rest of the national security bureaucracy have changed as a result of the accountability measures of the last decade. Everyone in the CIA, and every national security lawyer in the government, knows that the threshold of sin has lowered. They assume that controversial secret operations will one day leak, probably sooner than expected. And they know that if the operation is too controversial, especially morally controversial, all of the grand-bargain cover in the world will not save those involved from personal censure. "The Agency has a can-do culture, and will do what the President asks it to do if it is lawful," says Rizzo. "But the experiences of the last decade, which were one hundred times more wrenching than Iran-Contra, have changed the Agency forever, and made its lawyers and operators much more cautious and less inclined to take initiative." One indication of this skittishness came just after the inauguration of Barack Obama in January 2009. For reasons of policy and optics, the new administration ditched altogether the already narrowed Bush interrogation program. At that point, however, an official in the Obama interrogation working group informally urged the CIA to be creative in coming up with a different list of lawful interrogation techniques that were more aggressive than those found in the Army Field Manual. The Agency demurred. "After seven years of being pummeled and investigated and accused," recalls John Rizzo, "the unanimous collective view of the career cadre at CIA" was that any interrogations beyond the Army Field Manual, even if lawful, were a "no man's land" for the Agency.[74]

Such skittishness now cannot guarantee that a future government won't return to the interrogation practices of 2002–2005 if the threat environment becomes severe enough. Nor, for that matter, would criminal prosecution of Bush administration officials. We can't ever completely rule out a return to the past. But if the past is any guide, such a return is very unlikely. A persistent theme in American history is that when Presidents act aggressively to curtail civil liberties at the dawn of a war or an emergency in a way that is later regretted, those regrets are remembered in the next war or emergency and are not repeated. No President has replicated Lincoln's indiscriminate suspension of the writ of habeas corpus or his military trials for civilians in the United States. We have never again seen loyalty prosecutions as in World War I, or anything like the World War II exclusion of Japanese-Americans. The public criticism, regret, and ostracism that followed these practices stigmatized them and prevented their repetition. The same is likely true for officially sanctioned waterboarding. This does not mean that in the face of a new security threat, future Presidents won't take different aggressive actions that the nation will regret at a later, calmer time. They likely will, as they almost always have in the past. It simply means that when the new security emergency arises, the perceived abuses of the past will be baselines of opprobrium in determining which civil liberties restrictions are appropriate.[75]

There is a paradox in the human rights community's belief that waterboarding is still on the table, despite the unprecedented accountability and pushback of the past decade. That accountability and pushback resulted because human rights organizations, like many others throughout the presidential synopticon, believed that there was inadequate accountability and pushback and fought hard to achieve more. Many in the presidential synopticon, especially in the human rights community, remain alarmed by what they see as endless and undefined war, excessive presidential secrecy, insufficient judicial review of the President's actions, too much surveillance, inadequate congressional involvement, and many other evils of the post-9/11 presidency. They continue to push hard against the government with lawsuits, FOIA requests, accountability campaigns, and strident charges against public officials. This is all very healthy for the presidency and for national security. The continued efficacy of the presidential synopticon depends on just this type of skeptical attitude about the synopticon's efficacy.

This paradox points to larger truths. In writing this book I spoke with dozens of people who represented every perspective in the presidential synopticon, including Bush and Obama administration officials, military and intelligence officers, federal judges, members of Congress and their staffs, journalists and their editors, bloggers and other new media representatives, inspectors general, lawyers throughout the national security bureaucracy, and leaders of prominent human rights organizations. They all shared three traits. First, they were serious, knowledgeable, and principled in their approach to quite different jobs. Second, they saw the topics of transparency, law, and accountability in the war on terrorism from the perspective of the institutions for which they worked. Put less charitably, they all had biases—mostly hidden to themselves—in their approach to counterterrorism issues. (So too did I, as much as I tried to transcend them.) And finally, they all believed that they were on the losing end of the stick in trying to influence U.S. counterterrorism policies and their associated accountability mechanisms.

This last trait is perhaps the most important. President Obama and his Attorney General believe the executive branch leaks like a sieve, that the *New York Times*' publication of these secrets harms national security, and that the executive branch should crack down more on journalists and their sources. Editors and journalists at the *Times* believe the executive branch hoards too many secrets, manipulates the secrecy system, and unduly harasses journalists. The CIA believes it spends way too much time reporting to and responding to investigations by politicized congressional intelligence committees that don't understand what they are doing. The intelligence committees believe the CIA underreports its activities and cannot be trusted. The Defense Department too complains about its committees' burdensome reporting requirements, as well as their micromanagement of military affairs. The armed services committees believe the same of the military as the intelligence committees do of the CIA. Many in the executive branch believe inspectors general are biased and in Congress's pocket; Congress believes they are under-resourced and need more authorities. National security lawyers think they are besieged bastions of independence holding the executive branch in check; activist and media critics believe the lawyers are apologists for executive power. Conservatives believe Michael Ratner's Center for Constitutional Rights sympathizes with terrorists and achieved illegitimate victories in the Supreme Court that have hamstrung the President and emboldened terrorists. Michael Ratner believes he won a few battles but lost the war because Barack Obama, building on judicial and congressional efforts, institutionalized military detention and military commissions and extended the war paradigm to more countries than George W. Bush did. Many lower court judges are unhappy that the Supreme Court dumped on them the duty to make terrorist detention policy from whole cloth in habeas corpus cases, and are frustrated that Congress has not stepped in to fill the void. Some critics charge that these judges have released way too many GTMO detainees; others charge that they have released too few. Congress believes Barack Obama would endanger national security by trying GTMO terrorists in civilian trials in the United States; Barack Obama believes that

Congress endangers national security by barring these trials. And so on, and so on.

In 1788, in the fifty-first Federalist Paper, James Madison famously announced that the U.S. Constitution embodied the "important idea" that a well-structured government is one in which "its several constituent parts may, by their mutual relations, be the means of keeping each other in their proper places."[76] Madison believed that a properly designed government "would check interest with interest, class with class, faction with faction, and one branch of government with another in a harmonious system of mutual frustration," as Columbia historian Richard Hofstadter put it in his classic 1948 book, *The American Political Tradition.*[77] If Madison were alive today, he would be astonished and probably appalled to see the gargantuan presidency exercising so much power, much of it in secret, in an endless global war against non-state actor terrorists. He would also be surprised by the reticulate presidential synopticon that has grown up to watch, check, and legitimate the presidency in war. But after adjusting to the modern world and studying the vitriolic clashes of the last decade between the presidency and its synopticon, Madison would discover a harmonious system of mutual frustration undergirding a surprising national consensus—a consensus always fruitfully under pressure from various quarters—about the proper scope of the President's counterterrorism authorities. And then the father of the Constitution would smile.

Afterword

AFTER THE NEXT
ATTACK

"WE'RE NOT GOING TO STOP every attack," Michael Leiter told National Public Radio a few days before Umar Farouk Abdulmutallab tried to blow himself up on a plane near Detroit on December 25, 2009. "Americans have to very much understand that it is impossible to stop every terrorist event."[1]

Leiter is a former Navy flight officer and Harvard-trained federal prosecutor who ran the little-known National Counterterrorism Center (NCTC) from 2007–2011. The NCTC Director's job—one of the hardest and most important counterterrorism jobs in the government—is to "connect the dots" from fragmented pieces of intelligence information in order to prevent terrorist attacks like the one that Abdulmutallab attempted. The main criticism of the U.S. government after the 9/11 attacks was that it had information about the plot in its databases but failed to piece it together because intelligence and law enforcement agencies did not share, analyze, and coordinate the information properly. The NCTC was the main solution to this problem. Housed in a futuristic computer-stuffed building near the CIA, the NCTC is supposed to receive all terrorism-related information available to the U.S. government. Each day the U.S. intelligence community receives terabytes and sometimes petabytes

of data containing eight to ten thousand new pieces of terrorism intelligence and more than ten thousand names of people
with suspicion of ties to terrorists.[2] The NCTC draws on this
information to enter terrorist names into a database of known
and suspected terrorists called the "Terrorist Identities Datamart
Environment," or TIDE. Hundreds of analysts from dozens of
government organizations, "co-located" at the NCTC, scour the
TIDE and other sources of intelligence information around the
clock, and piece the data together into an endless stream of threat
reports and other assessments. These reports and assessments, in
turn, are integrated into the President's Daily Brief of national
security threats as well as numerous intelligence assessments distributed to federal, state, and local officials who are trying to
discover and thwart terrorist attacks.

The NCTC is designed to be "a one stop shop for mapping
out the terrorism threat and designing a plan for the U.S. Government to counter it—whether it is immediate, emerging, or
long-term," Leiter said in 2008.[3] It has done an extraordinary job
of sorting through the fog of data to connect the dots, and has
contributed to the prevention of several terrorist plots, many of
them unknown to the public. But as the near attack over Detroit
made clear, the NCTC is not perfect. In the NCTC databases on
December 25 was recent information that Abdulmutallab's father
had told the U.S. embassy in Nigeria that his son held "extreme
religious views" and might be in Yemen. The NCTC also had sep-
arate intelligence indicating that Yemeni militants had recruited a
Nigerian to carry out a terrorist attack on the United States. The
NCTC and its intelligence partners failed to put this information
together, in part because additional information on Abdulmutallab from the State Department and the National Security Agency
was not fully shared, in part because the NCTC was focused at
the time primarily on Pakistan and Afghanistan and underplayed
the threat from Yemen, and in part because partial names and
different spellings obscured the linkage.[4] Abdulmutallab himself was one of the 550,000 names in the TIDE. But he was not
on the 400,000-person watch list of suspected terrorists or the

4,000-person no-fly list of people barred from boarding airplanes headed for the United States. He was not on these lists not only because information about him was not linked, but also because the Bush administration in 2008 had tightened the criteria for getting on the lists in response to complaints from civil liberties organizations, members of Congress, and some in the media that the criteria for inclusion on them were too lax. "The pressure on the no-fly list was to make them smaller," Director of National Intelligence Dennis Blair told the Senate Committee on Homeland Security. "Shame on us for giving in to that pressure."[5]

These are a few of what a May 2010 report from the Senate Select Committee on Intelligence would describe as "fourteen specific points of failure—a series of human errors, technical problems, systemic obstacles, analytical misjudgments, and competing priorities—which resulted in Abdulmutallab being able to travel to the United States on December 25, 2009." Before detailing these failures, the report paused for a one-paragraph "Note on Historical Hindsight." Several intelligence officials had told the committee that the information about the plot discovered in their databases was one "among thousands of other intelligence reports," and that "other terrorist threats were assessed to be more pressing at the time." The committee acknowledged "the benefit of '20-20 hindsight' " in its investigation. But the report quickly discarded this qualification and with the crystalline clarity of hindsight picked out from the giant haystack of information in government databases the few needles of information about the plot that the executive branch could have put together to prevent it. The committee concluded that the intelligence community "failed to connect and appropriately analyze the information in its possession," and "should have taken steps to prevent Abdulmutallab" from boarding the flight to Detroit.[6] The Obama administration acknowledged these and similar criticisms. Michael Leiter led the implementation of new reforms, including modified watch list criteria, new systems to enhance the integration of terrorist information and to reduce redundancies and biases in NCTC analyses, and "Pursuit Groups" within the NCTC to follow up on early terrorist leads and pursue non-obvious terrorist relationships.

"All of these efforts are being pursued vehemently," Leiter testified before the House Committee on Homeland Security in February 2011. "But," he added, in a necessary nod to modern presidential accountability, "they also require careful consideration of complex legal, policy, and technical issues as well as the implementation of appropriate privacy, civil liberty, and security protections."[7] The NCTC has four lawyers, a civil liberties protection officer, technical auditors, and an inspector general in the Office of the Director of National Intelligence, of which NCTC is a component. These officials enforce—with in-time review and after-the-fact audits—elaborate statutory and regulatory restrictions on how the information the NCTC receives from other intelligence agencies can be stored, viewed, analyzed, and shared, and how its products can be distributed. (The NCTC enforces these restrictions on top of analogous restrictions that contributing agencies like the National Security Agency, CIA, and FBI implement before they share data with the NCTC.) In addition to these internal watchers, some of whom report directly to Congress, the NCTC has many other reporting duties to numerous congressional committees, and Leiter himself regularly conferred, formally and informally, with the members of a dozen congressional committees, many of whom are skeptical or critical of the NCTC's work. The NCTC is also closely watched by the ACLU, the Electronic Frontier Foundation, and the Electronic Privacy Information Center. "We look at everything we do through a civil liberties lens," Leiter said in 2011.[8] It is no accident that Leiter's replacement as the director of the NCTC, Matt Olsen, is also a lawyer.

When he was the director of the NCTC, Leiter would frequently emphasize that despite the NCTC's best efforts, despite extraordinary improvements in the government's intelligence collection and sharing, despite its significantly better global military capabilities, despite better defenses at home, despite a reduction in the likelihood of the most catastrophic chemical, nuclear, and

biological attacks, and despite very few and relatively small terrorist attacks as a result of these changes, there *will* be another
Islamist terrorist attack, possibly catastrophic, on the homeland.[9]
Even after Bin Laden's death, al Qaeda still possesses the aims and
means to do the nation real harm. So too do al Qaeda's regional
affiliates, the many Islamist terrorist movements and organizations around the globe with only loose (if any) ties to al Qaeda,
and homegrown radicals inside the United States. These latter
groups and individuals are proliferating with independence from
the relatively hierarchical al Qaeda leadership, and they increasingly focus their efforts on smaller-scale attacks that require less
coordination and thus are harder to detect.[10] In this environment,
no amount of sophisticated intelligence, modern weaponry, and
defensive walls can forever prevent every attack. "The aggressor
has to find only one crucial weakness; the defender has to find all
of them, and in advance," wrote Herman Kahn in 1960 in his
famous book *On Thermonuclear War.*[11] Under the Kahn principle,
some terrorists will succeed. "We aim for perfection, but perfection will not be achieved," says Leiter.[12]

In this book I have told a relatively sanguine story about how
modern constitutional checks operated in a novel war against
Islamist terrorists to help the institutions of our government
learn about, alter, and legitimate presidential power. This system
of accountability evolved hand in hand with the evolution of
counterterrorism policies over the last decade—policies that, as
I write these words in the fall of 2011, have sufficed to prevent
another major attack on the homeland. But our great fortune in
not having anything like a repeat of 9/11—a fortune few would
have thought possible a decade ago—will not persist. There will
be another terrorist attack at home, perhaps one as catastrophic
as 9/11. When this happens, the presidential synopticon and its
accountability regime, depending on the size of the attack, will
come under intense pressure. But it will survive the attack. And
like the presidency it watches, the synopticon will likely grow in
importance.

The nation's reaction to the 2009 Christmas Day bombing

attempt is a microcosmic preview of what will happen after the next catastrophic attack—at least if it is a visible kinetic attack that causes many deaths (as opposed to a slow-developing biological or cyber-attack, the source of which is hard to attribute). After a few days the recriminations against the President will begin, regardless of the precautions he and his advisers took or other extenuating circumstances. Congress, the media, and the next National Commission on Terrorist Attacks will unwind the clock to see what the executive branch did wrong. They will all acknowledge that hindsight is 20-20. But they will forget the acknowledgment each time they make it. And from the perspective of hindsight, they will discover disparate pieces of information that the intelligence community could have pieced together but missed. They will also discover that some degree of human errors, technical problems, systemic obstacles, analytical misjudgments, and competing priorities prevented the presidency from connecting the dots. Many of them will denounce the President and his counterterrorism officials in righteous tones for not keeping the country safe.

After the recriminations against the presidency will come the recriminations against the accountability system for the presidency. The Congress and the next National Commission will hear testimony about how intelligence officials had been pressured by human rights groups, Congress, and the media into balancing the security-liberty trade-off too far in favor of civil liberties. Some officials will lament giving in to that pressure. They will also lament how distracted they were from their task of keeping the nation safe by endless inspector general investigations, lawsuits, FOIA requests, congressional reporting requirements, and media leaks. Some will claim that these accountability constraints chilled them from taking risks that in hindsight they should have taken. Lawyers will get whacked for similar reasons. Some of the lawyers who said "no" to operations will be criticized when it seems in hindsight that they should have said "yes." But the main complaint likely will not be that the lawyers declined to approve an action, but rather that they were so demanding and nit-picky, and so scary in their admonitions to not cross certain lines, that officials decided not even to ask for permission to take steps that might have stopped the attack. Top-secret e-mails and memoranda will be produced to support these claims, through either official channels or leaks. Some of the memoranda will contain legal analysis but no author, because lawyers themselves were afraid to put their names on legal documents as a result of recriminations against their predecessors. Courts too may come in for criticism, especially if someone involved in the attack was released from GTMO, but also, more generally, if it becomes clear that the novel habeas corpus regime the courts imposed after 9/11 chilled the government from detaining or interrogating someone connected to the attack.

The third thing that will happen after the next attack is that the next National Commission on Terrorist Attacks will recommend reforms to strengthen the President's hand in fighting terrorists. The executive branch as well will produce a laundry list of new legal authorities that it thought it needed to meet the terrorist threat but that it declined to seek before the attack for fear that Congress and the public would not support them. Congress will give the presidency the new authorities that it seeks because the public demands security and because the presidency is the only institution in our government with the expertise, organization, resources, initiative, and sense of responsibility needed to take on the extraordinarily complex task of protecting the nation from the terrorist threat. Congress will be especially generous in giving the President new authorities related to intelligence collection, for intelligence failures will likely be seen as the main cause of the next attack and intelligence collection improvements the best hope of preventing another one. It will also likely give the President broader powers to capture, interrogate, detain, and kill terrorists. Congress will be careful, however, not to authorize stigmatized activities like waterboarding and the bug-in-the-box.

The fourth thing that will happen is that the much-criticized accountability mechanisms, which had already grown in strength during the first decade after 9/11, will grow in strength yet more. The media, motivated by new forms of executive branch secrecy, will redouble its efforts to report from the shadows. Congress, bucked up by the media and an alarmist human rights community, will worry about the unprecedented new authorities it is conferring on the presidency. Many of the authorities will involve granting the President discretion to do things in secret that, if abused, would seriously harm civil liberties. And so in granting these powers—especially the ones concerning electronic surveillance and other novel forms of intelligence collection—Congress will require that a secret court review the President's general plans in advance to make sure they are constitutional, and will require the inspector general in many agencies to constantly review the President's actions and to report the many mistakes and errors it finds to Congress. The new authorities will also be conditioned on executive branch officials compiling burdensome compliance reports for Congress, which in turn will require hordes of executive branch lawyers to monitor and guarantee compliance. Congress may cut back on the Freedom of Information Act a bit and may not confer new causes of action against the government. But clever, motivated, well-financed human rights organizations will find ways to bring novel claims against the novel forms of presidential power they deem scary. And independent courts, having mastered their fear of wartime judicial review in the decade after 9/11, will, despite criticisms after the next attack, and especially after the passage of a few years, grant some of these novel claims. This revived presidential synopticon will discover that some of the new authorities exercised by the presidency in secret at the outset of the new crisis led to mistakes and abuses that the nation will regret, especially as the threat appears to recede over time.

And so the cycle will begin again. It might seem that we should just get the balance of presidential authorities and presidential accountability right in the first place, before the next attack arrives, in order to prevent it. But we are prisoners of informational uncertainty and psychological biases, and government is an imperfect science. We do not know in advance exactly what must be done to keep us safe, and our concerns about the threat recede as the indicia of the threat recede from public view. Like the framers of the Constitution, we worry about a too-powerful government, and especially a too-powerful presidency, almost as much as we do about national security. And we know that every new expansion of presidential power brings the possibility of mistake, abuse, or unnecessary restriction of liberty. We nonetheless expand the President's powers over time, especially at the dawn of a crisis, as national security threats grow more menacing and labyrinthine. A bigger and bigger presidency is necessary, and has necessary drawbacks. The same is true of the presidential synopticon. It has grown, and will continue to grow, in step with the presidency it watches. And it generates many problems of its own. But it also belies the many apocalyptic claims that we are living in an era of unrestrained presidential power.

Acknowledgments

I interviewed over sixty current and former government officials in all three branches of the government about how national security checks and balances have worked in the last decade. Some of these men and women agreed to be quoted on the record or to have their interviews cited. Most, understandably, did not. I will not list these officials here, but they know who they are, and I hope they also know how grateful I am for their time, their valuable insights, and their service to the nation.

I interviewed many journalists and editors for this book, including Spencer Ackerman, Philip Bennett, Marcus Brauchli, Leonard Downie Jr., Barton Gellman, Tim Golden, Nicholas Lemann, Seymour Hersh, Bill Keller, Dafna Linzer, Jane Mayer, Dana Priest, and Scott Shane. These men and women taught me a lot about "accountability journalism" and about many other things as well. I also learned a great deal from the leaders in the human rights community who spoke with me: Douglass Cassel, David Cole, Karen Greenburg, Jameel Jaffer, Elisa Massimino, Michael Ratner, and Anthony Romero. Steven Aftergood of the Federation of American Scientists and Ken Anderson of American University's Washington College of Law also sat for very helpful interviews.

Several people read the whole manuscript and provided truly

great comments: Ken Anderson, David Barron, Gabby Blum, Curtis Bradley, Robert Chesney, Charles Fried, Ben Kleinerman, Marty Lederman, Daryl Levinson, John Manning, Rick Pildes, Dan Meltzer, Martha Minow, Eric Posner, Sam Rascoff, Alan Rozenshtein, Charlie Savage, Gabe Schoenfeld, Paul Stephan, Matthew Waxman, and Ted White. Others provided very helpful feedback on individual chapters: Steve Aftergood, Fred Borch, Jeff Bovarnick, Phil Carter, Noah Feldman, Renn Gade, David Kennedy, Liz Magill, John Radsan, Lindsay Rodman, Dale Stephens, Adrian Vermeule, Andru Wall, and Amy Zegart. As with my last book, Ben Wittes and Andrew Woods provided incisive comments on the entire manuscript and indispensable advice on matters small and large. None of these people agree with everything I wrote, and some of them disagree with much of it, but they all helped me to improve the book enormously.

I also thank my colleagues in the Hoover Task Force on National Security and Law who provided terrific feedback and criticism on the themes in this book over several years. In particular I thank Peter Berkowitz, the Task Force's chair, for his wise counsel on the arguments in the book and on other matters as well. I also thank Stanford Law School's Constitutional Law Center, and its director, Michael McConnell, for inviting me to present some of the ideas in the book in a lecture on Constitution Day 2010. I am grateful as well to *The New Republic*, and especially Leon Wieseltier, for allowing me to try out some of the ideas of the book in essays and books reviews; to Blakey Vermeule for bringing the synopticon idea to my attention; to Roger Hurwitz for helping me to see that modern checks and balances might fruitfully be viewed as a distributed network; to John and Martha Evans for their generous hospitality during my many trips to Washington; and to Franny Annese for his early morning friendship.

There cannot be a better place to write a book than Harvard Law School. The outstanding members of the FRIDA staff responded to hundreds of research queries with extraordinary speed; I cannot thank them enough. My friends in the IT department kept my computers running in difficult circumstances. Many extraordinary Harvard law students helped me with research, including Matthew Bobby, Sarah Crandall, David Denton, Ivana Deyrup, Maureen Mathis, and Jonathan Murray. My assistant, Jan Qashat, kept me organized, on time, and moving forward; the book would have been much harder to write without her help. And my dean, Martha Minow, gave me untiring support during the writing of the book in addition to great comments on the manuscript.

I thank Andrew Wylie, my agent, for all that he does. I also thank Starling Lawrence, Mary Babcock, Melody Conroy, and the many other people at W. W. Norton who worked hard to see the book through to publication.

Finally, I thank my family. My joyous boys, Jack and Will, were upbeat and encouraging during the long hours it took to write the book. My wife, Leslie, was, as ever, patient and supportive. She also spotted many errors in the manuscript and made dozens of great suggestions; I could not have written the book without her. My 101-year-old grandfather, Jack Sr., has been an inspiration my whole life. So too has my mother, Brenda Lou, to whom I dedicate the book with much love.

Notes

INTRODUCTION

1. President George W. Bush, Remarks to Employees at the Pentagon and an Exchange with Reporters in Arlington, Virginia (Sept. 17, 2001), *in* 2 Pub. Papers 1117, 1120.
2. President George W. Bush, Address before a Joint Session of the Congress on the United States Response to the Terrorist Attacks of September 11 (Sept. 20, 2001), *in* 2 Pub. Papers 1140, 1142.
3. Declaration of National Emergency by Reason of Certain Terrorist Attacks, 2 Pub. Papers 1109 (Sept. 14, 2001).
4. Message from the President to Congress Regarding the Continuation of the National Emergency with Respect to Certain Terrorist Attacks, Sept. 9, 2011, http://www.whitehouse.gov/the-press-office/2011/09/09/message-president-regarding-continuation-national-emergency-respect-cert; Letter to Congressional Leaders on Continuation of the National Emergency with Respect to Certain Terrorist Attacks, 2010 Daily Comp. Pres. Doc. 741 (Sept. 10, 2010); Notice on Continuation of the National Emergency with Respect to Certain Terrorist Attacks, 2009 Daily Comp. Pres. Doc. 697 (Sept. 10, 2009).
5. George W. Bush, Decision Points 182 (2010).
6. *See* Jonathan Mahler, *After the Imperial Presidency*, N.Y. Times, Nov. 7, 2008.
7. President Barack Hussein Obama, Inaugural Address (Jan. 21, 2009), http://www.whitehouse.gov/blog/inaugural-address/.
8. Julian E. Zelizer, Posting to *When It Comes to Expansive Presidential Authority, Is Obama Much Different Than Bush? If So, How Do You Like It?* Arena, Oct. 6, 2009, http://www.politico.com/arena/archive/executive-power-obama-v-bush.html.

9. JAMES MADISON POLITICAL OBSERVATIONS (Apr. 20, 1975), *reprinted in* 4 LET-
   TERS AND OTHER WRITINGS OF JAMES MADISON 491 (1865).
10. GARRY WILLS, BOMB POWER: THE MODERN PRESIDENCY AND THE
    NATIONAL SECURITY STATE (2010); BRUCE ACKERMAN, THE DECLINE AND
    FALL OF THE AMERICAN REPUBLIC (2010); PETER M. SHANE, MADISON'S
    NIGHTMARE: HOW EXECUTIVE POWER THREATENS AMERICAN DEMOCRACY
    (2009); ERIC A. POSNER & ADRIAN VERMEULE, THE EXECUTIVE UNBOUND:
    AFTER THE MADISONIAN REPUBLIC (2011). Posner's and Vermeule's thesis
    about the legally unconstrained executive branch extends beyond the mili-
    tary and national security context, but that context is one of their main
    focuses.
11. POSNER & VERMEULE, *supra* note 10, at 4.
12. For my reflections on my time in government, see JACK GOLDSMITH, THE
    TERROR PRESIDENCY: LAW AND JUDGMENT INSIDE THE BUSH ADMINISTRA-
    TION (2007).
13. ARTHUR M. SCHLESINGER JR., THE IMPERIAL PRESIDENCY xxviii (1974).
14. *Id.*

CHAPTER ONE: THE NEW NORMAL

1. Restoring the Rule of Law, Hearing before the Senate Subcommittee on
   the Constitution of the Senate Committee on the Judiciary, 110th Cong. 14
   (Sept. 16, 2008) (Statement of Harold Hongju Koh, Dean and Gerard C. &
   Bernice Latrobe Smith Professor of International Law, Yale Law School),
   http://judiciary.senate.gov/hearings/testimony.cfm?id=e655f9e2809e5476
   862f735da1406a46&wit_id=e655f9e2809e5476862f735da1406a46-1-3.
2. *Id.* at 16.
3. Senator Barack Obama, Candidate, Democratic U.S. Presidential Nominee, Address at the Woodrow Wilson International Center (Aug. 1, 2007),
   http://www.cfr.org/publication/13974/obamas_speech_at_woodrow_
   wilson_center.html.
4. President Barack Hussein Obama, Inaugural Address (Jan. 21, 2009),
   http://www.whitehouse.gov/blog/inaugural-address/.
5. Exec. Order No. 13493, 74 FED. REG. 4,901 (Jan. 22, 2009).
6. *See* Scott Shane, *Obama Orders Secret Prisons and Detention Camps Closed*, N.Y.
   TIMES, Jan. 22, 2009.
7. Dana Priest, *Bush's "War" on Terror Comes to a Sudden End*, WASH. POST, Jan.
   23, 2009.
8. In April 2008, I wrote, "Don't count on the next president to undo George
   W. Bush's legal policies in the war on terrorism. . . . [M]any controversial
   Bush administration policies have already been revised to satisfy congressional and judicial critics. And after receiving a few harrowing threat briefings
   and absorbing the awesome personal responsibility of keeping Americans
   safe, the new commander in chief won't rush to eliminate the Bush program

as it stands next January." Jack Goldsmith, *The Laws in Wartime*, SLATE, Apr. 2, 2008, http://www.slate.com/id/2187870/.

9. Authorization for Use of Military Force, Pub. L. No. 107-40, § 2(a) 115 Stat. 224, 224 (Sept. 18, 2001).

10. One example is Harold Koh, whose views on these issues are described at the end of this chapter.

11. Respondents' Memorandum Regarding the Government's Detention Authority Relative to Detainees Held at Guantanamo Bay, *In re* Guantanamo Bay Detainee Litigation, Misc. No. 08-0442, Mar. 13, 2009, http://www.justice.gov/opa/documents/memo-re-det-auth.pdf.

12. *Id.* at 7.

13. *Id.* (quoting Khalid v. Bush, 355 F. Supp. 2d 311, 320 (D.D.C. 2005)).

14. *Id.* at 6 n.2 (quoting Lichter v. United States, 334 U.S. 742, 767 n.9 (1948) [citation and internal quotations and alterations omitted]).

15. *See Obama, McCain Continue to Clash on Detainees*, CNN, June 18, 2002, http://articles.cnn.com/2008-06-18/politics/candidates.terror_1_john-mccain-foreign-policy-barack-obama/2?_s=PM:POLITICS (campaign foreign policy adviser and later Obama's UN representative Susan Rice says that the way to deal with captured terrorists "is not to hold somebody in violation of our Constitution, indefinitely in detention and never convict them"). Years earlier, Senator Obama arguably suggested that military detention should be changed but not be eliminated. *See* 152 CONG. REC. S10388–89 (daily ed. Sept. 28, 2006) (Statement of Senator Barack Obama), http://obamaspeeches.com/092-Military-Commission-Legislation-Obama-Speech.htm.

16. Remarks by the President on National Security at the National Archives and Records Administration, 2009 DAILY COMP. PRES. DOC. 388 (May 21, 2009), http://www.whitehouse.gov/the_press_office/Remarks-by-the-President-On-National-Security-5-21-09/.

17. Final Report: Guantanamo Review Task Force, Jan. 22, 2010, http://www.justice.gov/ag/guantanamo-review-final-report.pdf.

18. Executive Order—Periodic Review of Individuals Detained at Guantánamo Bay Naval Station Pursuant to the Authorization for Use of Military Force, Mar. 7, 2011, http://www.whitehouse.gov/the-press-office/2011/03/07/executive-order-periodic-review-individuals-detained-guant-namo-bay-nava; *see generally* Dafna Linzer, *Obama Makes Indefinite Detention and Military Commissions His Own*, PROPUBLICA, Mar. 8, 2011, http://www.propublica.org/article/obama-makes-indefinite-detention-and-military-commissions-his-own.

19. Remarks by the President on National Security, *supra* note 16.

20. Respondents' Memorandum Regarding the Government's Detention Authority Relative to Detainees Held at Guantanamo Bay, *supra* note 11, at 3, 5–6.

21. *Id.* at 2. Obama administration officials would claim that they, unlike the Bush administration, used international law to inform the scope of the 2001 congres-

sional authorization, but this claim is inaccurate, for the Bush administration did the same thing. *See* Jack Goldsmith, *Detention, the AUMF, and the Bush Administration—Correcting the Record*, LAWFARE, Sept. 14, 2010, http://www.lawfareblog .com/2010/09/detention-the-aumf-and-the-bush-administration-correcting-the-record/. They also claimed that they, unlike the Bush administration, did not rely on Article II of the Constitution for detention power. This is true but misleading, for the Obama administration did not reject that argument either, and moreover the Bush administration did not rely on that argument in its second term. *Id.*

22. William Glaberson, *U.S. Won't Label Terror Suspects as "Combatants,"* N.Y. TIMES, Mar. 13, 2009.

23. Gherebi v. Obama, 609 F. Supp. 2d 43, 70 (D.D.C. 2009).

24. Military Order of November 13, 2001, § 4, 66 FED. REG. 57,833 (Nov. 16, 2001), http://www.fas.org/irp/offdocs/eo/mo-111301.htm.

25. Hamdan v. Rumsfeld, 548 U.S. 557, 593–94 (2005).

26. 152 CONG. REC. S103888 (daily ed. Sept. 28, 2006) (Statement of Senator Barack Obama), http://obamaspeeches.com/092-Military-Commission-Leg islation-Obama-Speech.htm.

27. Jake Tapper, *President Obama to Reinstate Revamped Military Tribunals*, POLITI-CAL PUNCH (ABC NEWS), May 14, 2009 (detailing 2006 vote), http://blogs .abcnews.com/politicalpunch/2009/05/president-oba-7.html.

28. Julian E. Barnes, *Obama to Continue Military Tribunals*, L.A. TIMES, May 15, 2009. *See also Q&A: Obama on Foreign Policy*, WASH. POST, Mar. 2, 2008 ("I believe that our civilian courts or our traditional system of military courts-martial can administer justice more quickly while also demonstrating our commitment to the rule of law").

29. Editorial, *First Steps at Guantanamo*, N.Y. TIMES, Jan. 21, 2009.

30. Remarks by the President on National Security, *supra* note 16.

31. Compare 2006 Act, § 948r (permitting use of coerced evidence only if the judge finds the statement reliable and in the interests of justice) with 2009 Act, § 948r (creating an absolute bar on such evidence).

32. Morris Davis, *The Guantanamo Paradox*, HUFFINGTON POST, Aug. 18, 2010, http:// www.huffingtonpost.com/morris-davis/the-guantanamo-paradox_b_687120 .html.

33. David Kris, U.S. Assistant Attorney General, Address at the Brookings Institution (June 11, 2010), http://www.brookings.edu/~/media/Files/events/ 2010/0611_law_enforcement/20100611_law_enforcement_kris.pdf.

34. Press Release, Amnesty International USA, *Obama Breaks Major Campaign Promise as Military Commissions Resume, Says Amnesty International* (May 15, 2009), http://www.commondreams.org/newswire/2009/05/15-2.

35. Benjamin Weiser, *Ruling in Embassy Bombing Case Leads to Mixed Views of Suspect's Fate if He Is Acquitted*, N.Y. TIMES, October 8, 2010, at A21. Obama Defense Department General Counsel Jeh Johnson had earlier argued, "If, for some reason, he's not convicted for a lengthy prison sentence, then, as a matter of legal authority, I think it's our view that we would have the ability

to detain that person." *See* Karen DeYoung, *Indefinite Detentions Are Backed*, WASH. POST, July 8, 2009.

36. *See* Memorandum from Brad Wiegmann and Colonel Mark Martins to the Attorney General and Secretary of Defense, Detention Policy Task Force, Re: Preliminary Report (July 20, 2009), http://www.fas.org/irp/agency/doj/detention072009.pdf.

37. Kris, *supra* note 33.

38. Dick Cheney, Interview with Rush Limbaugh (2008), *quoted in* Andy Barr, *Cheney: Obama "Not Likely to Cede Authority*," POLITICO, Dec. 15, 2008, http://www.politico.com/news/stories/1208/16594.html.

39. Charlie Savage & Andrew Lehren, *U.S. Haggled to Find Takers for Detainees from Guantánamo*, N.Y. TIMES, Nov. 29, 2009.

40. Peter Finn & Anne E. Kornblut, *Guantanamo Bay: Why Obama Hasn't Fulfilled His Promise to Close the Facility*, WASH. POST, Apr. 23, 2011.

41. *Id.*

42. 152 CONG. REC. S10,346–48 (daily ed. Sept. 27, 2006) (Statement of Senator Barack Obama), http://obamaspeeches.com/091-Floor-Statement-on-the-Habeas-Corpus-Amendment-Obama-Speech.htm.

43. *See* Ari Melber, *Obama Targets bin Laden, Defends Constitution and Shames Palin*, WASH. INDEP., Sept. 9, 2008.

44. Boumediene v. Bush, 553 U.S. 723 (2008).

45. *See* Kyle Trygstad, *Obama on SCOTUS Decision*, REAL CLEAR POLITICS BLOG (June 12, 2008), http://realclearpolitics.blogs.time.com/2008/06/12/obama_on_scotus_decision/.

46. Government's Response to This Court's Order of January 22, 2009, at 2, Al Maqaleh v. Gates, 604 F. Supp. 2d 205 (D.D.C. 2009) (No. 06-1669), http://legaltimes.typepad.com/files/dojorder.pdf.

47. Charlie Savage, *Obama Upholds Bush Detainee Policy in Afghanistan*, N.Y. TIMES, Feb. 21, 2009.

48. Charlie Savage, *Detainees Barred from Access to U.S. Courts*, N.Y. TIMES, May 21, 2010.

49. Human Rights First, *Detained and Denied in Afghanistan: How to Make U.S. Detention Comply with the Law* 6 (May 2011), http://www.humanrightsfirst.org/wp-content/uploads/pdf/Detained-Denied-in-Afghanistan.pdf.

50. *Q&A: Obama on Foreign Policy, supra* note 28.

51. Scott Shane, Mark Mazzetti & Robert F. Worth, *Secret Assault on Terrorism Widens on Two Continents*, N.Y. TIMES, Aug. 14, 2010.

52. Leon E. Panetta, Director, Central Intelligence Agency, Director's Remarks at the Pacific Council on International Policy (May 18, 2009), https://www.cia.gov/news-information/speeches-testimony/directors-remarks-at-pacific-council.html.

53. *See, e.g.,* Senator Barack Obama, Remarks of Senator Barack Obama at Labor Day Rally (Sept. 3, 2007), http://www.barackobama.com/2007/09/03/remarks_of_senator_barack_obam_22.php. *Accord* Senator Barack Obama, *Renewing American Leadership*, FOREIGN AFFAIRS (July/August 2007), at 14.

54. Greg Miller, *Obama Preserves Renditions as Counter-Terrorism Tool*, L.A. TIMES, Feb. 1, 2009.

55. Nomination of Leon Panetta to Be Director of the Central Intelligence Agency: Hearing before the Select Committee on Intelligence, United States Senate, 111th Cong. 18 (responses to prehearing questions of Leon E. Panetta, Nominee for Director, Central Intelligence Agency), http://intelligence .senate.gov/090205/answers.pdf.

56. Press Release, Department of Justice, Special Task Force on Interrogations and Transfer Policies Issues Its Recommendations to the President (Aug. 24, 2009), http://www.justice.gov/opa/pr/2009/August/09-ag-835.html.

57. David Johnston, *U.S. Says Rendition to Continue, but with More Oversight*, N.Y. TIMES, Aug. 24, 2009.

58. Eric Schmitt and Mark Mazzetti, *U.S. Relies More on Aid of Allies in Terror Cases*, N.Y. TIMES, May 23, 2009.

59. Mark Mazzetti & William Glaberson, *Obama Issues Directive to Shut Down Guantánamo*, N.Y. TIMES, Jan. 21, 2009.

60. Exec. Order No. 13491, 74 FED. REG. 4,893 (Jan. 22, 2009), http://www .whitehouse.gov/the_press_office/EnsuringLawfulInterrogations/.

61. Alissa J. Rubin, *Afghans Detail Detention in "Black Jail" at U.S. Base*, N.Y. TIMES, Nov. 28, 2009.

62. *See, e.g.*, Marc Ambinder, *Inside the Secret Interrogation Facility at Bagram*, ATLAN-TIC, May 14, 2010.

63. *See* Letter from Joseph I. Lieberman et al. to President Barack Obama (Apr. 8, 2011), *available at* http://hsgac.senate.gov/public/index.cfm?FuseAction=Press .MajorityNews&ContentRecord_id=466A6908-5056-8059-76F5-DB2664 D397D6; Laurie Kellman, *Hill Leaders Agree on Patriot Act*, YAHOO! NEWS, May 19, 2010, http://news.yahoo.com/s/ap/20110519/ap_on_go_co/us_patriot_act.

64. Ellen Nakashima, *NSA Director to Testify at Senate Hearing on Cyber Command Unit*, WASH. POST, Apr. 14, 2010.

65. Press Release, Senator Orin Hatch, Officials Announce Camp Williams as Selection for Cybersecurity Data Center (Oct. 23, 2009); J. Nicholas Hoo-ver, *NSA to Build $1.5 Billion Cybersecurity Data Center*, INFORMATIONWEEK, Oct. 29, 2009, http://www.informationweek.com/news/government/sec urity/showArticle.jhtml?articleID=221100260.

66. *See, e.g.*, Charlie Savage, *U.S. Tries to Make It Easier to Wiretap the Internet*, N.Y. TIMES, Sept. 27, 2010; Ellen Nakashima, *White House Proposal Would Ease FBI Access to Records of Internet Activity*, WASH. POST, July 29, 2010.

67. 187 CONG. REC. S15,027 (daily ed. Dec. 7, 2007) (Statement of Senator Barack Obama); Remarks to White House Senior Staff, 2009 DAILY COMP. PRES. DOC. 12 (Jan. 21, 2009), http://www.gpoaccess.gov/presdocs/2009/ DCPD200900012.htm.

68. *See, e.g.*, Sheryl Gay Stolberg, *On First Day, Obama Quickly Sets a New Tone*, N.Y. TIMES, Jan. 21, 2009. Obama also went further than any President in open-ing up nuclear weapons policy to public scrutiny. *See* U.S. Department of

Defense, Nuclear Posture Review Report (2010), http://www.defense.gov/npr/docs/2010%20Nuclear%20Posture%20Review%20Report.pdf. Steven Aftergood calls this the "single most significant reduction in national security secrecy" under Obama. Steven Aftergood, *First Unclassified Nuclear Posture Review Released,* SECRECY NEWS, Apr. 8, 2010, http://www.fas.org/blog/secrecy/2010/04/unclassified_npr.html.

69. Bill Keller, *Secrecy in Shreds,* N.Y. TIMES MAGAZINE, Apr. 1, 2011. *See also* Citizens for Responsibility and Ethics in Washington, *FOIA at the Mid-term: Obstacles to Transparency Remain* (2010), http://www.rcfp.org/newsitems/docs/20101001_161318_crew_foia_report.pdf; Mike Riggs, *Under Obama, FOIA Reform Relegated to the Back Burner,* DAILY CALLER, Oct. 1, 2010, http://dailycaller.com/2010/10/01/under-obama-foia-reform-relegated-to-the-back-burner/.

70. Office of Management & Budget, Executive Office of the President, Statement of Administration Policy on H.R. 2701—Intelligence Authorization Act for Fiscal Year 2010 (2009), http://www.whitehouse.gov/sites/default/files/omb/legislative/sap/111/saphr2701r_20090708.pdf. President Obama eventually compromised on a scheme in which the President can limit notice of a covert action finding to the Gang of Eight, but must alert other members of the intelligence committees that he has done this, with an explanation why. Intelligence Authorization Act for Fiscal Year 2010, Pub. L. No. 111-259, §331(c) (2010), http://frwebgate.access.gpo.gov/cgi-bin/getdoc.cgi?dbname=111_cong_public_laws&docid=f:publ259.111; 131 CONG. REC. S7558–59 (daily ed. Sept. 27, 2010) (Statement of Senator Kit Bond), http://www.fas.org/irp/congress/2010_cr/sen-fy10auth.html.

71. Josh Gerstein, *Justice Dept. Cracks Down on Leaks,* POLITICO, May 25, 2010, http://www.politico.com/news/stories/0510/37721.html.

72. Memorandum from Eric Holder, Attorney General, to Heads of Executive Departments and Agencies and Heads of Department Components, Policies and Procedures Governing Invocation of the State Secrets Privilege (Sept. 23, 2009), http://www.justice.gov/opa/documents/state-secret-privileges.pdf; Charlie Savage, *Justice Dept. to Limit Use of State Secrets Privilege,* N.Y. TIMES, Sept. 22, 2009.

73. *See* Charlie Savage, *Court Dismisses a Case Asserting Torture by CIA,* N.Y. TIMES, Sept. 8, 2010.

74. *Id.*

75. Opposition to Plaintiff's Motion for Preliminary Injunction and Memorandum in Support of Defendant's Motion to Dismiss at 43 Al-Aulaqi v. Obama, No. 10-cv-1469 (D.D.C. Sept. 25, 2010), http://www.lawfareblog.com/wp-content/uploads/2010/09/usgbrief.pdf.

76. Walter Pincus, *Irony Isn't Lost on Retired CIA General Counsel John Rizzo,* WASH. POST, May 11, 2010.

77. Jeff Mason, *Obama Says Bush-Approved Waterboarding Was Torture,* REUTERS, Apr. 30, 2009, http://www.reuters.com/article/idUSTRE53T16O20090430.

78. AMERICAN CIVIL LIBERTIES UNION, ESTABLISHING A NEW NORMAL: NATIONAL

SECURITY, CIVIL LIBERTIES, AND HUMAN RIGHTS UNDER THE OBAMA ADMINISTRATION 2 (2010), http://www.aclu.org/files/assets/EstablishingNewNormal .pdf.

79. Harold Hongju Koh, "Repairing Our Human Rights Reputation," Speech at the National Immigrant Justice Center (2008), http://www.immigrantjustice .org/midwestlight/midwestlight/kohspeech.html (arguing that "[a]s a nation, we should not accept that indefinite detention without trial . . . other unacceptable practices have now become necessary features of a post-9/11 world."); Koh, Restoring the Rule of Law, *supra* note 1 ("As a nation, we should not accept that indefinite detention without trial . . . and other unacceptable practices have somehow become necessary features of a post-9/11 world").

80. See Harold Hongju Koh, *Restoring America's Human Rights Reputation*, 40 CORNELL INTERNATIONAL L. J. 635, 637 (2007) (describing military commissions in 2007 as "law-free courts"); Harold Hongju Koh, *The Case Against Military Commissions*, 96(2) AM. J. INTERNATIONAL L. 337 (2002) (arguing against the use of military commissions on many grounds, including the one that "[h]owever detailed its rules and procedures may be, a military commission is not an independent court, and its commissioners are not genuinely independent decision makers"). By the time of his 2008 testimony, Koh had softened his stance on commissions a bit. *See* Koh, Restoring the Rule of Law, *supra* note 1 (arguing that the new administration should "repeal the Military Commissions Act, or at a minimum, revise it drastically to repair the inadequacies in that law's procedures identified by the Supreme Court in its 2006 decision in *Hamdan v. Rumsfeld*").

81. Harold Hongju Koh, *Restoring America's Human Rights Reputation*, *supra* note 80, at 65; *see also* Koh, *The Case Against Military Commissions*, *supra* note 81, at 344.

82. Harold Hongju Koh, *National Security, Human Rights, and the Rule of Law*, in CHANGE FOR AMERICA 492 (Mark Green & Michele Jolin eds., 2009) ("Each detainee's case should be individually reviewed to determine whether the detainee falls in to one of four categories: those who have committed crimes against the United States and should be brought to US soil—and imprisoned in supermax facilities, if necessary—for prosecution in regular federal or military courts; those who cannot properly be tried for crimes against the United States and should be extradited for prosecution at home or in a third country; those who have committed no crime against the United States and should be repatriated for home or release; and those who have committed no crime against the United States but must be given asylum").

83. *See* Koh, Restoring the Rule of Law, *supra* note 1.

84. Harold Hongju Koh, *Preserving American Values: The Challenge at Home and Abroad*, in THE AGE OF TERROR 143 (Strobe Talbott & Nayan Chanda eds., 2002).

85. Harold Hongju Koh, Speech before the District of Columbia Bar & American Society of International Law (Feb. 17, 2010), http://www.c-spanvideo .org/program/id/219700.

86. Harold Hongju Koh, "The Obama Administration and International Law,"

Speech before the American Society of International Law (May 25, 2011), http://www.state.gov/s/l/releases/remarks/139119.htm.

87. *Id.*

CHAPTER TWO: FORCES BIGGER THAN THE PRESIDENT

1. PIERRE SALINGER, WITH KENNEDY 114–15 (1966).
2. Interview by William H. Lawrence with President John F. Kennedy (Dec. 17, 1962), http://www.presidency.ucsb.edu/ws/index.php?pid=9060. The video of the interview can be found at http://www.youtube.com/watch?v=xml SbEVXZCs.
3. Peter Baker, *Obama's War over Terror,* N.Y. TIMES MAGAZINE, Jan. 4, 2010.
4. *See* Mark Pazniokas, *Obama Shows Off Drawing Power,* HARTFORD COURANT, Mar. 2, 2008. The video of the speech can be found at http://www.youtube .com/watch?v=eX2nvdTWMRU&feature=related.
5. President Barack Obama, Remarks by the President on National Security (May 21, 2009), http://www.whitehouse.gov/the_press_office/Remarks-by-the-President-On-National-Security-5-21-09/.
6. Baker, *supra* note 3.
7. Interview with senior Obama official, in Washington, D.C. (August 8, 2010)
8. Remarks by the President on National Security, *supra* note 5.
9. Peter Finn, *Obama Set to Revive Military Commissions,* WASH. POST, May 9, 2009.
10. HARRY S. TRUMAN, YEARS OF TRIAL AND HOPE ix (1956).
11. Abraham Lincoln, U.S. President, Special Session Message to Congress (July 4, 1861), http://www.fordham.edu/halsall/mod/1861lincoln-special .html.
12. Remarks by the President on National Security, *supra* note 5.
13. David S. Broder, *Obama in Command,* WASH. POST, May 21, 2009.
14. For an elaboration of this point, see Paul B. Stephan, *The Limits of Change: International Human Rights under the Obama Administration,* FORDHAM J. INTERNATIONAL L. (forthcoming 2012). There are many points of agreement between Stephan's thesis and mine.
15. E-mail communication with John Rizzo (Sept. 27, 2010).
16. Mark Knoller, *White House Not Challenging Rove's Privilege,* CBS NEWS, Feb. 14, 2009, http://www.cbsnews.com/8301-503544_162-4803349-503544.html.
17. Charlie Savage, *Obama's War on Terror May Resemble Bush's in Some Areas,* N.Y. TIMES, Feb. 17, 2009.
18. RICHARD A. CLARKE, AGAINST ALL ENEMIES: INSIDE AMERICA'S WAR ON TERROR 144 (2004).
19. Arthur M. SCHLESINGER JR., THE IMPERIAL PRESIDENCY 286 (First Mariner Books, 2004) (1973).
20. THE FEDERALIST Nos. 48, 51 (James Madison).
21. Abraham Lincoln, State of the Union Address (Dec. 6, 1864), http://www .presidentialrhetoric.com/historicspeeches/lincoln/stateoftheunion1864 .html.

22. Franklin D. Roosevelt, Message to Congress, 88 Cong. Rec. 7042, 7044 (1942).

23. On the information in this paragraph, see generally Aaron L. Friedberg, In the Shadow of the Garrison State (2000).

24. *See* Tim Weiner, Legacy of Ashes: The History of the CIA 29–31 (2007).

25. Assignment of Ground Forces of the United States to Duty in the European Area, Hearings before the Senate Committees on Foreign Relations and Armed Services, 82d Cong., 1st Sess. 92–93 (1951) (Statement of Secretary of State Dean Acheson).

26. J. W. Fulbright, *American Foreign Policy in the 20th Century under an 18th Century Constitution*, 47 Cornell L. Q. 47, 50 (1961).

27. Editorial, *Wider War*, N.Y. Times, Aug. 6, 1964.

28. Schlesinger, *supra* note 19, at 164.

29. Youngstown Sheet & Tube Co. v. Sawyer, 343 U.S. 579 (1952).

30. Andrew Rudalevige, The New Imperial Presidency 101 (2005).

31. James L. Sundquist, The Decline and Resurgence of Congress 7 (1981).

32. Gerald R. Ford, *Imperiled, Not Imperial*, Time, Nov. 10, 1980.

33. *See* 18 USC § 2441 (war crimes); 18 USC § 2340 (torture).

34. See Rudalevige, *supra* note 30, at 240 (noting that "[a]cross the board, the laws passed to reshape executive-legislative relations in the 1970s had failed to channel those relations in the manner foreseen by their framers").

35. Garry Wills, Bomb Power: The Modern Presidency and the National Security State 187 (2010).

36. John Yoo, Crisis and Command 398–409 (2009).

37. Interview by Cokie Roberts with Vice President Dick Cheney, This Week, ABC (Jan. 27, 2002), http://georgewbush-whitehouse.archives.gov/vicepresi dent/news-speeches/speeches/vp20020127.html.

38. *See* David Barron & Martin Lederman, *The Commander-in-Chief at the Lowest Ebb: A Constitutional History*, 121 Harv. L. Rev. 941, 1083–87 (2008); Charlie Savage, Takeover: The Return of the Imperial Presidency and the Subversion of American Democracy (2007).

39. *See* Savage, *supra* note 38; Barton Gellman, Angler: The Cheney Vice Presidency (2008); Jack Goldsmith, The Terror Presidency: Law and Judgment inside the Bush Administration (2007).

40. David Barron & Martin Lederman, *The Commander-in-Chief at the Lowest Ebb*, *supra* note 38, at 715.

41. I recounted my experiences with and views of Bush's unilateral strategy in Goldsmith, *supra* note 39.

42. *See* Protect America Act of 2007, Pub. L. No. 110-55, 121 Stat. 552; Foreign Intelligence Surveillance Act of 1978 Amendments Act of 2008, Pub. L. No. 110-261, 122 Stat. 2436; Military Commissions Act of 2009, Pub. L. No. 111-84; Military Commissions Act of 2006, Pub. L. No. 109-366, 120 Stat. 2600; Detainee Treatment Act, Pub. L. No. 109-148, 119 Stat. 2680 (2005).

43. Hamdan v. Rumsfeld, 548 U.S. 557 (2006).

44. Boumediene v. Bush, 553 U.S. 723 (2008).

45. *Obama's Interview Aboard Air Force One*, N.Y. Times, Mar. 7, 2009.

46. *See generally* GOLDSMITH, *supra* note 39.

47. These lawyers include David Barron, Neal Katyal, and Martin Lederman in the Justice Department and Harold Koh in the State Department.

48. Robert Goodin, *Voting through the Looking Glass*, 77 AM. POL. SCI. REV. 420, 421 (1983).

49. *See* Opposition to Plaintiff's Motion for a Preliminary Injunction, Nasser Al-Aulaqu v. Barack Obama, No. 10-cv-1469 (D.D.C. Sep. 24, 2010), http://www.lawfareblog.com/wp-content/uploads/2010/09/usgbrief.pdf.

50. Mohamed v. Jeppesen, 614 F.3d 1070, 1076 (9th Cir. 2010).

51. Interview by Jim Lehrer with Vice President Dick Cheney, PBS NEWSHOUR, Jan. 14, 2009, http://www.pbs.org/newshour/bb/politics/jan-june09/cheney_01-14.html.

52. John Harris, Mike Allen, & Jim Vandehei, *Cheney Warns of New Attacks*, POLITICO, Feb. 5, 2009, http://www.politico.com/news/stories/0209/18390.html.

53. *See Cheney Says Obama's Policies "Raise the Risk" of US Terror Attack*, CNN, Mar. 15, 2010; Interview by Sean Hannity with Vice President Dick Cheney, HANNITY, FOX NEWS, Apr. 22, 2009, http://www.foxnews.com/story/0,2933,517439,00.html.

54. David Brooks, *Cheney Lost to Bush*, N.Y. TIMES, May 21, 2009.

55. Shailagh Murray, *Senate Demands Plan for Detainees*, WASH. POST, May 20, 2009.

56. Gallup Poll, Jan. 21, 2009 (45% against closing GTMO to 35% for closing it); Gallup Poll, June 3, 2009 (65% against closing to 32% for closing); Gallup Poll, Nov. 2009 (64% against closing to 30% for closing); CNN Poll, Jan. 21, 2009 (47% against closing to 51% for closing); CNN Poll, Mar. 2010 (60% against closing to 39% for closing); Pew Poll, Feb. 2009 (39% against closing to 46% for closing); Pew Poll, Apr. 2009 (38% against closing to 51% for closing); Pew Poll, June 2009 (46% against closing to 45% for closing); Pew Poll, Oct. 2009 (49% against closing to 39% for closing).

57. Massimo Calabresi & Michael Weisskopf, *The Fall of Greg Craig*, TIME, Nov. 19, 2009.

58. In the War of 1812, Congress did authorize the President to detain prisoners of war, but did not constrain his discretion. *See* Brown v. United States, 12 U.S. 110 (1814).

59. The most significant of these many restrictions is 111 P.L. 118, Section 9011.

60. Oversight of the U.S. Department of Justice: Hearing before the Senate Committee on the Judiciary, 111th Cong. (Nov. 18, 2009) (Statement of Eric H. Holder Jr., Attorney General of the United States).

61. Stuart Taylor Jr., *A Course Correction on Terrorism*, NATIONAL JOURNAL, Feb. 6, 2010.

62. *Scott Brown's Victory Speech*, N.Y. TIMES, Jan. 19, 2010, at www.nytimes.com/2010/01/20/us/politics/20text-brown.html.

63. Jane Mayer, *The Trial*, NEW YORKER, Feb. 15, 2010; Josh Gerstein, *Brown a Game Changer on Terrorism*, POLITICO, Jan. 20, 2009, http://www.politico.com/news/stories/0110/31758.html.

64. *See, e.g.,* S. 2977, 111th Cong. (introduced on Feb. 2, 2010, by Senator Lindsey Graham); H.R. 4556, 111th Cong. (introduced on Feb. 2, 2010, by Representative Wolf); H.R. 4542, 111th Cong. (introduced on Jan. 27, 2010, by Representative King); H.R. 4463, 111th Cong. (introduced on Jan. 19, 2010, by Representative Buchanan); S. 3081, 111th Cong. (introduced on Mar. 4, 2010, by Senator McCain).

65. Wil S. Hylton, *Hope. Change. Reality.*, GQ, Dec. 2010.

66. ABRAHAM LINCOLN, 3 THE LINCOLN DOUGLAS DEBATES OF 1858, at 114 (Sparks, ed., 1908); *see also* Adrian Vermeule, *Government by Public Opinion: Bryce's Theory of the Constitution*, Harvard Public Law Working Paper No. 11-13, at http://papers.ssrn.com/sol3/papers.cfm?abstract_id=1809794.

CHAPTER THREE: ACCOUNTABILITY JOURNALISM

1. Interview with Leonard Downie Jr., in Washington, D.C. (Sept. 8, 2010). Unless otherwise indicated, all quotes from Downie come from this interview and a previous one, conducted by telephone, on Aug. 13, 2010.

2. Howard Kurtz, *Bradlee Retiring as Editor of the Post*, WASH. POST, June 21, 1991.

3. Nancy Traver, *Press: Shifting to a Post-Bradlee Post*, TIME, Aug. 13 1990.

4. Exec. Order No. 13,526, 3 C.F.R. 298 (2009).

5. Dana Priest, *CIA Holds Terror Suspects in Secret Prisons*, WASH. POST, Nov. 2, 2005.

6. Dana Priest & Leonard Downie Jr. (moderating), "Accountability Journalism: Walter Reed and Beyond," Schatt Lecture at the Cronkite School of Journalism and Mass Communication at Arizona State University (Mar. 2, 2010), http://cronkite.asu.edu/assets/video/SCHATT_2010_FINAL.mov.

7. BEN BRADLEE, A GOOD LIFE: NEWSPAPERING AND OTHER ADVENTURES 424–26 (1996).

8. Priest & Downie, *supra* note 6.

9. Interview with Stephen Hadley, in Washington, D.C. (Oct. 22, 2010). All quotes from Hadley come from this interview.

10. Interview by Lowell Bergman with Len Downie, Executive Editor, Washington Post, FRONTLINE, PBS, Apr. 19, 2006, http://www.pbs.org/wgbh/pages/frontline/newswar/interviews/downie.html.

11. Priest, *supra* note 5.

12. *See* Detainee Treatment Act of 2005, 42 U.S.C. §2000dd (2006). *See also* Dana Priest & Josh White, *Policies on Terrorism Suspects Come under Fire*, WASH. POST, Nov. 3, 2005.

13. *See, e.g.,* Peter Grier & Gail Russell Chaddock, *Leak about CIA Prisons Overseas Sparks Fury*, CHRISTIAN SCI. MONITOR, Nov. 10, 2005; Tracy Wilkinson, *Europe in Uproar over CIA Operations*, L.A. TIMES, Nov. 26, 2005.

14. *See* Geneva Convention Relative to the Treatment of Prisoners of War, Art. 3, Aug. 12, 1949, 6 U.S.T. 3316, 75 U.N.T.S. 135; Hamdan v. Rumsfeld, 548 U.S. 557, 631 (2006).

15. Leonard Downie Jr. & Robert G. Kaiser, The News about the News: American Journalism in Peril 30–31 (2003).

16. Interview by Tim Russert with Vice President Dick Cheney (Sept. 16, 2001), *quoted in* Dan Froomkin, *Cheney's "Dark Side" Is Showing*, Wash. Post, Nov. 7, 2005.

17. Interview with Philip Bennett, in Washington, D.C. (Sept. 22, 2010).

18. Bob Woodward, *CIA Told to Do "Whatever Necessary" to Kill Bin Laden*, Wash. Post, Oct. 21, 2001.

19. Interview with Bennett, *supra* note 17.

20. Potter Stewart, *"Or of the Press,"* 26 Hastings L. J. 631, 634 (1974).

21. E-mail communication with Jane Mayer (Oct. 12, 2010).

22. Bill Keller, "Editors in Chains: Secrets, Security and the Press," University of Michigan, Davis, Markert, Nickerson Lecture on Academic and Intellectual Freedom (Oct. 16, 2006) (on file with author).

23. *See generally* Gabriel Schoenfeld, Necessary Secrets: National Security, the Media, and the Rule of Law (2010).

24. Exec. Order No. 8985, 3 C.F.R. 323 (Dec. 19, 1941).

25. David Halberstam, The Powers That Be 373–75 (1979).

26. *Id.* at 442–43.

27. *Id.* at 373–75.

28. Philip Taubman, Secret Empire: Eisenhower, the CIA, and the Hidden Story of America's Space Espionage 308–13 (2003).

29. Halberstam, *supra* note 25, at 447–49; Schoenfeld, *supra* note 23, at 162–63.

30. Arthur M. Schlesinger Jr., The Imperial Presidency 343 (First Mariner Books, 2004) (1973).

31. President John F. Kennedy, The President and the Press: Address before the American Newspaper Publishers Association (Apr. 27, 1961), http://www .jfklibrary.org/Research/Ready-Reference/JFK-Speeches/The-President- and-the-Press-Address-before-the-American-Newspaper-Publishers-Associ ation.aspx.

32. New York Times Co. v. United States, 403 U.S. 713, 717 (1971) (Black, J., concurring).

33. Exec. Order No. 10290, 3 C.F.R. 472 (Sept. 27, 1951).

34. Schlesinger, *supra* note 30, at 341.

35. Schoenfeld, *supra* note 23, at 185.

36. Editors, *The Times and Iraq*, N.Y. Times, May 26, 2004.

37. Tim Golden, "Terrorism and Prisoners: Stories That Should be Told," Joe Alex Morris, Jr. Memorial Lecture at the Nieman Foundation for Journalism at Harvard (Feb. 21, 2008), http://www.nieman.harvard.edu/reports/ article/100042/Terrorism-and-Prisoners-Stories-That-Should-Be-Told .aspx.

38. Woodward, *supra* note 18.

39. Rajiv Chandrasekaran & Peter Finn, *U.S. behind Secret Transfer of Terror Suspects*, Wash. Post, Mar. 11, 2002.

40. Dana Priest & Barton Gellman, *U.S. Decries Abuse but Defends Interrogations*, WASH. POST, Dec. 26, 2002.

41. Woodward, *supra* note 18.

42. Chandrasekaran & Finn, *supra* note 39.

43. Priest & Gellman, *supra* note 40.

44. Interview with Dana Priest, in Washington, D.C. (Oct. 11, 2010).

45. NATIONAL COMMISSION ON TERRORIST ATTACKS, THE 9/11 COMMISSION REPORT: FINAL REPORT OF THE NATIONAL COMMISSION ON TERRORIST ATTACKS UPON THE UNITED STATES 93 (2004).

46. Interview with Bill Keller, in New York, New York (Oct. 13, 2010).

47. Priest & Gellman, *supra* note 40.

48. Interview with Keller, *supra* note 46.

49. *Id.*

50. Priest, *supra* note 5.

51. Interview with Bennett, *supra* note 17.

52. Interview with Seymour Hersh, in Washington, D.C. (Oct. 5 2010); Howard Kurtz, *The Post on WMDs: An Inside Story*, WASH. POST, Aug. 12, 2004.

53. *See, e.g.*, Michael Massing, *Now They Tell Us*, N.Y. REV. BOOKS, Jan. 29, 2004; Editors, *The Times and Iraq*, *supra* note 36.

54. The Washington Bureau of Knight-Ridder and Walter Pincus of the Washington Post are typically given the most credit for questioning the government's WMD rationale, but others recounted debate and uncertainty in the government on Iraq's WMD program as well. *See, e.g.*, Dana Milbank, *For Bush, Facts Are Malleable*, WASH. POST, Oct. 22, 2002; Joby Warrick, *Evidence on Iraq Challenged*, WASH. POST, Sept. 19, 2002.

55. Walter Pincus, *U.S. Lacks Specifics on Banned Arms*, WASH. POST, Mar. 16, 2003.

56. Masood Anwar, *Mystery Man Handed Over to US Troops in Karachi*, NEWS INTERNATIONAL, Oct. 25, 2001, http://209.157.64.200/focus/f-news/556778/posts.

57. Dana Priest, *Jet Is an Open Secret in Terror War*, WASH. POST, Dec. 27, 2004.

58. *Id.*; Interview by Lowell Bergman with Dana Priest, FRONTLINE, PBS (Apr. 27, 2006), http://www.pbs.org/wgbh/pages/frontline/newswar/interviews/priest.html; Interview with Priest, *supra* note 44.

59. *See* Priest & Downie, *supra* note 6.

60. *See, e.g.*, Detainee Treatment Act of 2005, 42 U.S.C. §2000dd (2006); Hamdan v. Rumsfeld, 548 U.S. 557, 631 (2006).

61. *See* MARC A. THIESSEN, COURTING DISASTER: HOW THE CIA KEPT AMERICA SAFE AND HOW BARACK OBAMA IS INVITING THE NEXT ATTACK 22, 42–43 (2010).

62. *See* Jack Goldsmith, *Secrecy and Safety*, NEW REPUBLIC, Aug.13, 2008.

63. Interview with General Michael Hayden, in Washington, D.C. (Oct. 6, 2010).

64. Interview with John Rizzo, in Cambridge, Massachusetts (Nov. 8, 2010).

65. Jason Ryan, *President Obama and Intelligence Director Angered over Media Leaks*, ABC

News, Oct. 6, 2010, http://abcnews.go.com/Politics/president-obama-intelli gence-director-angered-media-leaks/story?id=11817252.

66. Advance Questions for Michael Vickers, Nominee for the Position of Under Secretary of Defense for Intelligence, http://www.fas.org/irp/con gress/2011_hr/021511vickers-q.pdf.

67. THE COMMISSION ON THE INTELLIGENCE CAPABILITIES OF THE UNITED STATES REGARDING WEAPONS OF MASS DESTRUCTION, REPORT TO THE PRESIDENT OF THE UNITED STATES 381 (May 31, 2005), http://www.gpoac cess.gov/wmd/pdf/full_wmd_report.pdf; Steven Aftergood, *FBI Found 14 Intel Leak Suspects in Past 5 Years*, SECRECY NEWS, June 21, 2010, http://www .fas.org/blog/secrecy/2010/06/intel_leak.html.

68. Dana Priest & William M. Arkin, *A Hidden World, Growing beyond Control*, WASH. POST, July 19, 2010.

69. *See* Steven Aftergood, *Number of Security Clearances Soars*, SECRECY NEWS, Sept. 20, 2011, http://www.fas.org/blog/secrecy/2011/09/clearances.html.

70. E-mail communication with Steven Aftergood (Oct. 7, 2010).

71. Affidavit of Max Frankel, United States v. N. Y. Times Co., 328 F. Supp. 324 (S.D.N.Y. 1971) (No. 71 Civ. 2662), http://www.pbs.org/wgbh/pages/ frontline/newswar/part1/frankel.html.

72. *See generally* BOB WOODWARD, OBAMA'S WARS (2010).

73. New York Times Co. v. United States, 403 U.S. 713, 729 (1971) (Stewart, J., concurring).

74. Interview with Priest, *supra* note 44; Priest & Downie, *supra* note 6.

75. *See* ERIC LICHTBLAU, BUSH'S LAW: THE REMAKING OF AMERICAN JUSTICE 187–88 (2008).

76. *See, e.g.,* John Barry et al., *The Roots of Torture*, NEWSWEEK, May 24, 2004; Eric Schmitt & Carolyn Marshall, *In Secret Unit's "Black Room": A Grim Portrait of U.S. Abuse*, N.Y. TIMES, Mar. 19, 2006.

77. STEPHEN GREY, GHOST PLANES: THE TRUE STORY OF THE CIA TORTURE PROGRAM 250 (2006).

78. Interview with Hersh, *supra* note 52.

79. RICHARD HELMS, A LOOK OVER MY SHOULDER: A LIFE IN THE CENTRAL INTELLIGENCE AGENCY 184–85 (2003).

80. NATIONAL COMMISSION ON TERRORIST ATTACKS, *supra* note 45, at 417.

81. *Id.*

82. DANIEL ELLSBERG, SECRETS: A MEMOIR OF VIETNAM AND THE PENTAGON PAPERS 300–303, 328–31 (2002).

83. *Id.* at 302.

84. James R. Gosler, *The Digital Dimension*, in TRANSFORMING U.S. INTELLI-GENCE 96 (Jennifer E. Sims & Burton Gerber eds., 2005).

85. Online chat between Adrian Lamo and Private First Class Bradley Manning, *edited transcript available at* Kevin Poulsen & Kim Zetter, *"I Can't Believe What I'm Confessing To You": The Wikileaks Chats*, WIRED, June 10, 2010, http://www.wired.com/threatlevel/2010/06/Wikileaks-chat/.

86. Raffi Khatchadourian, *No Secrets*, NEW YORKER, June 7, 2010.

87. William J. Lynn III, *Defending a New Domain*, FOREIGN AFFAIRS (September/ October 2010).

88. Declan Walsh, *American who sparked diplomatic crisis over Lahore shooting was CIA spy*, THE GUARDIAN, Feb. 20, 2011.

89. Mark Mazzetti et al., *American Held in Pakistan Worked with CIA*, N.Y. TIMES, Feb. 21, 2011.

90. Interview with Hersh, *supra* note 52.

91. Discussion of GABRIEL SCHOENFELD, NECESSARY SECRETS: NATIONAL SECURITY, THE MEDIA, AND THE RULE OF LAW, event at The Hudson Institute, May 25, 2010, http://www.hudson.org/index.cfm?fuseaction =hudson_upcoming_events&id=773.

92. Interview with Priest, *supra* note 44.

93. *See* STEVE HENDRICKS, A KIDNAPPING IN MILAN: THE CIA ON TRIAL (2010); Matthew Cole, *In Italy, CIA Agents Are Undone by Their Cell Phones*, WIRED, June 26, 2007, http://www.wired.com/politics/security/magazine/15-07/ st_cia.

94. GREY, *supra* note 77, at 114–15, 120

95. John Crewdson, *Internet Blows CIA Cover*, CHICAGO TRIB., Mar. 12, 2006.

96. Telephone interview with senior CIA official (Feb. 11, 2011).

97. Barton Gellman, "Security, Secrecy and Self-Government: How I Learn Secrets and Why I Print Them," Address at the Woodrow Wilson School of Public and International Affairs (Oct. 9, 2003) (on file with author).

98. Barton Gellman, *In U.S., Terrorism's Peril Undiminished*, WASH. POST, Dec. 24, 2002; Barton Gellman & Susan Schmidt, *Shadow Government Is at Work in Secret*, WASH. POST, Mar. 1, 2002; E-mail communication with Barton Gellman (Nov. 2, 2010).

99. Milblogs by Country, MILBLOGGING.COM, http://milblogging.com/coun tries.php; Noah Shachtman, *Army Squeezes Soldier Blogs, Maybe to Death*, WIRED, May 2, 2007, http://www.wired.com/politics/onlinerights/news/2007/05/ army_bloggers; Michael Weiss, *Johnny, Close Your Laptop*, SLATE, May 4, 2007, http://www.slate.com/id/2165707/.

100. *See, e.g.*, Martin Lederman, *Understanding the OLC Torture Memos (Parts II & III & coda)*, BALKINIZATION, Jan. 7, 2005, http://balkin.blogspot.com/2005/01/ understanding-olc-torture-memos-part.html.

101. *See* Jack M. Balkin, *Online Legal Scholarship: The Medium and the Message*, Yale Law School Legal Scholarship Repository, Jan. 1, 2006, http://digitalcom mons.law.yale.edu/cgi/viewcontent.cgi?article=1231&context=fss_papers.

102. *See, e.g.*, SHANE HARRIS, THE WATCHERS: THE RISE OF AMERICA'S SURVEIL- LANCE STATE (2010); David E. Pozen, *The Mosaic Theory, National Security, and the Freedom of Information Act*, 115 YALE L. J. 628 (2005); Jack Balkin, *The Constitution and the National Surveillance States*, 93 MINN. L. REV. 1 (2008).

103. E-mail communication with Steven Aftergood (May 9, 2011).

104. DAN GILLMOR, WE THE MEDIA: GRASSROOTS JOURNALISM BY THE PEOPLE, FOR THE PEOPLE 111 (paperback ed., 2004).

105. Adam Goldman & Matt Apuzzo, *At CIA, Mistakes by Officers are Often Overlooked*,

ASSOCIATED PRESS, Feb. 9, 2011, http://www.msnbc.msn.com/id/41484983/ns/us_news-security/t/cia-officers-make-grave-mistakes-get-promoted/.

106. *Quoted in* Ryan M. Check & Afsheen John Radsan, *One Lantern in the Darkest Night: The CIA's Inspector General*, 4 J. NATIONAL SECURITY L. & POLICY 247 (2010).

107. Leonard Downie Jr., "The New News," James Cameron Memorial Lecture at the City University, London (Sept. 22, 2010), http://image.guardian.co.uk/sys-files/Media/documents/2010/09/23/DownieCameron.pdf.

108. Clay Shirky, *Let a Thousand Flowers Bloom to Replace Newspapers; Don't Build a Paywall around a Public Good*, NIEMAN JOURNALISM LAB, Sept. 23, 2009, http://www.niemanlab.org/2009/09/clay-shirky-let-a-thousand-flowers-bloom-to-replace-newspapers-dont-build-a-paywall-around-a-public-good/.

109. Chelsea Ide & Kanupriya Vashisht, *Today's Investigative Reporters Lack Resources*, REPUBLIC, May 28, 2006, http://www.azcentral.com/specials/special01/0528bolles-stateofreporting.html; Clay Shirky, *Newspapers and Thinking the Unthinkable*, CLAY SHIRKY, Mar. 13, 2009, http://www.shirky.com/weblog/2009/03/newspapers-and-thinking-the-unthinkable/; Paul Steiger, *Investigative Reporting in the Web Era*, WHAT MATTERS, Oct. 14, 2009, http://whatmatters.mckinseydigital.com/internet/investigative-reporting-in-the-web-era.

110. Leonard Downie Jr. & Michael Schudson, *The Reconstruction of American Journalism*, COLUM. JOURNALISM REV., Oct. 19, 2009; Downie, *supra* note 107; Shirky, *supra* note 109.

CHAPTER FOUR: SPIES UNDER A GOVERNMENT MICROSCOPE

1. *See* TIM WEINER, LEGACY OF ASHES: THE HISTORY OF THE CIA, Part Two (2007).

2. ALLEN WELSH DULLES, THE CRAFT OF INTELLIGENCE 235–36 (1963).

3. *See* L. BRITT SNIDER, THE AGENCY AND THE HILL: CIA's RELATIONSHIP WITH CONGRESS 8 (2008).

4. *Quoted in* MICHAEL A. BARNHART, CONGRESS AND UNITED STATES FOREIGN POLICY: CONTROLLING THE USE OF FORCE IN THE NUCLEAR AGE 159 (1987).

5. *Quoted in* Loch Johnson, *The CIA and the Question of Accountability*, in INTELLIGENCE AND NATIONAL SECURITY: THE SECRET WORLD OF SPIES 178, 180 (Loch K. Johnson and James J. Wirtz eds., 1997). *See also* AMY B. ZEGART, FLAWED BY DESIGN: THE EVOLUTION OF THE CIA, JCS, AND NSC 193 (2000).

6. DAVID M. BARRETT, THE CIA AND CONGRESS: THE UNTOLD STORY (2005).

7. WEINER, *supra* note 1, at 156.

8. GEOFFREY PERRET, EISENHOWER 477 (1999).

9. WEINER, *supra* note 1, at 131.

10. Leory F. Aarons, *White House Tied to Ellsberg Break-In*, WASH. POST, May 5, 1973, at A1.

11. I interviewed John Rizzo four times, once in Cambridge, Massachusetts,

and three times in Washington, D.C., during 2010 and 2011. This quotation and all others from Rizzo come from these interviews, unless otherwise indicated.

12. SELECT COMMITTEE TO STUDY GOVERNMENTAL OPERATIONS, FINAL REPORT [CHURCH REPORT] (1976), http://www.icdc.com/~paulwolf/cointelpro/churchfinalreportIIIm.htm.

13. *Id.*

14. Greg Miller, *John Rizzo: The Most Influential Career Lawyer in CIA History*, L.A. TIMES, June 29, 2009.

15. WILLIAM DAUGHERTY, EXECUTIVE SECRETS: COVERT ACTION AND THE PRESIDENCY (2004); E-mail communication with John Rizzo (Apr. 20, 2011).

16. The Iranian operations were reported to Congress after they occurred. *See* Alfred Cumming, *"Gang of Four" Congressional Intelligence Notifications*, at 4 (Congressional Research Service, Mar. 18, 2011).

17. *See also* DAUGHERTY, *supra* note 15, at 193–212.

18. Intelligence Authorization Act of 1991, Pub. L. No. 102-88, 105 Stat. 429 (1991).

19. 50 U.S.C. § 413(b).

20. The description in this paragraph is drawn from DAUGHERTY, *supra* note 15; JAMES E. BAKER, IN THE COMMON DEFENSE: NATIONAL SECURITY LAW FOR PERILOUS TIMES (2007).

21. 50 U.S.C. § 413b(c)(3).

22. 50 U.S.C. § 413a(a)(1). *See also* Cumming, *supra* note 16.

23. The CIA reported the existence of the tapes and its plans to destroy them to the leaders of the intelligence committees, but it did not report their destruction. John Rizzo maintains that the failure to report this fact was an "unintentional oversight" by Porter Goss and says that he blames himself "for not following up to make sure [Goss] had informed the Hill." John Rizzo, *Mea Culpa*, LAWFARE, http://www.lawfare blog .com/2011/09/mea-culpa-john-rizzo/. The Bush-era CIA was also accused of not reporting to Congress a plan to train antiterrorist assassins. The plan never became fully operational, and Obama's Director of National Intelligence Dennis Blair concluded that it did not trigger a legal duty to report to Congress. *See* Joby Warrick, *CIA Assassin Program Was Nearing New Phase*, WASH. POST, July 16, 2009. Whether the CIA should have reported it to Congress as a matter of prudence is another question, a question that arises every day in the CIA as it tries to figure out how to comply with the very vague "potentially significant anticipated intelligence activity" standard.

24. Interview with senior CIA official, in Langley, Virginia (Aug. 10, 2010).

25. E-mail communication with William Danvers, Director, Congressional Affairs, Central Intelligence Agency (Apr. 6, 2011).

26. SNIDER, *supra* note 3, at 275.

27. Mark Danner et al., *Should the CIA Fight Secret Wars?* HARPER'S MAGAZINE, Sept. 1984, *available at* http://www.markdanner.com/articles/show/119;

Martin C. Ott, *Partisanship and the Decline of Oversight*, 16 INTERNATIONAL J. INTELLIGENCE & COUNTERINTELLIGENCE 69, 78 (2003).

28. Loch Johnson, *Covert Action and Accountability: Decision-Making for America's Secret Foreign Policy*, 33 INTERNATIONAL STUD. Q. 81, 100 (1989); DAUGHERTY, *supra* note 15, at 94.

29. Douglas Jehl & David Sanger, *Plan Called for Covert Aid in Iraq Vote*, N.Y. TIMES, July 17, 2005; Timothy Burger & Douglas Waller, *How Much U.S. Help?* TIME, Oct. 4, 2004; Seymour Hersh, *Get Out the Vote*, NEW YORKER, July 25, 2005.

30. *See* Judith K. Boyd, *Improving U.S. Intelligence Oversight of Intelligence Services: A Comparative Policy Approach*, 28 AM. INTELLIGENCE J. (2010).

31. 156 CONG. REC. S7887 (Nov. 15, 2010) (Statement by Senator John D. Rockefeller), http://www.fas.org/irp/congress/2010_cr/s111510.html.

32. NATIONAL COMMISSION ON TERRORIST ATTACKS, THE 9/11 COMMISSION REPORT: FINAL REPORT OF THE NATIONAL COMMISSION ON TERRORIST ATTACKS UPON THE UNITED STATES, 419–22 (2004).

33. ROBERT GATES, FROM THE SHADOWS: THE ULTIMATE INSIDER'S STORY OF FIVE PRESIDENTS AND HOW THEY WON THE COLD WAR 559 (1997).

34. *See* A. John Radsan, *Quis Custodiet Ipsos Custodes: The CIA's Office of General Counsel?*, 2 J. NATIONAL SECURITY L. & POLICY 201, 207 (2008).

35. *See* MICHAEL LIPSKY, STREET LEVEL BUREAUCRACY: DILEMMAS OF THE INDIVIDUAL IN PUBLIC SERVICE (1980).

36. Hearing on the Nomination of Scott W. Muller to Be General Counsel of the Central Intelligence Agency: Before the Senate Select Committee on Intelligence, 107th Cong. (2002), http://intelligence.senate.gov/muller.pdf.

37. Radsan, *supra* note 34, at 210. They must also inform the CIA inspector general, as I explain below.

38. Exec. Order No. 12333, § 1.6(b), as amended by Exec. Order No. 13470, 3 C.F.R. 218 (2009).

39. Radsan, *supra* note 34, at 237.

40. CIA INSPECTOR GENERAL, SPECIAL REVIEW, COUNTERTERRORISM DETENTION AND INTERROGATION ACTIVITIES (SEPTEMBER 2001–SEPTEMBER 2003), May 7, 2004 [hereinafter Helgerson Report], http://graphics8.nytimes.com/packages/pdf/politics/20090825-DETAIN/2004CIAIG.pdf.

41. Hearing on the Nomination of Scott W. Muller, *supra* note 36.

42. Helgerson Report, *supra* note 40, at 94.

43. John Rizzo, Speech before the American Bar Association's Standing Committee on Law and National Security (May 5, 2010).

44. *See* Transcript of Record, A.C.L.U. v. Department of Defense, 04 CV 4151 (AKH) (S.D.N.Y May 12, 2008) (referring to "the presidential authorization for the CIA interrogation and detention program," and later referring to this document as "general authority for the CIA's program"). *See also* Eighth Declaration of Marilyn A. Dorn, Information Review Officer, Central Intelligence Agency, in ACLU v. Department of Defense, 04 CV 4151 (AKH) (S.D.N.Y. 2007) (noting that item 61 is a "14 page memorandum

dated September 17, 2001 from President Bush to the Director of the CIA pertaining to the CIA's authorization to detain terrorists").

45. Senator John D. Rockefeller, Memorandum on Release of Declassified Narrative Describing the Department of Justice Office of Legal Counsel's Opinions on the CIA's Detention and Interrogation Program, Apr. 22, 2009, attached to Letter from Attorney General Eric Holder to Senator John D. Rockefeller (Apr. 17, 2009), http://intelligence.senate.gov/pdfs/olcopinion .pdf.

46. DEPARTMENT OF JUSTICE, OFFICE OF PROFESSIONAL RESPONSIBILITY, INVESTIGATION INTO THE OFFICE OF LEGAL COUNSEL'S MEMORANDA CONCERNING ISSUES RELATING TO THE CENTRAL INTELLIGENCE AGENCY'S USE OF "ENHANCED INTERROGATION TECHNIQUES" ON SUSPECTED TERRORISTS, 37 n.36, July 29, 2009 [hereinafter OPR Report], http://judiciary.house.gov/ hearings/pdf/OPRFinalReport090729.pdf.

47. For my take on these opinions, see JACK GOLDSMITH, THE TERROR PRESIDENCY: LAW AND JUDGMENT INSIDE THE BUSH ADMINISTRATION ch. 5 (2007).

48. Letter from Attorney General Eric Holder, *supra* note 45; Interviews with Rizzo, *supra* note 11.

49. Joby Warrick & Dan Eggan, *Hill Briefed on Waterboarding in 2002*, WASH. POST, Dec. 9, 2007.

50. *Id.*

51. *Id.*

52. Letter from Representative Jane Harman to Scott Muller, General Counsel, CIA (Feb. 10, 2003), http://www.cfr.org/terrorism-and-the-law/rep resentative-jane-harmans-letter-cia-general-counsel-muller/p15164.

53. Helgerson Report, *supra* note 40, ¶ 2.

54. Adam Goldman & Kathy Gannon, *Death Shed Light on CIA 'Salt Pit' near Kabul*, MSNBC, Mar. 28, 2010, http://www.msnbc.msn.com/id/36071994/ns/ us_news-security/t/death-shed-light-cia-salt-pit-near-kabul/; Dana Priest, *CIA Avoids Scrutiny of Detainee Treatment*, WASH. POST, Mar. 3, 2005; Jane Mayer, *Who Killed Gul Raham?* NEW YORKER, Mar. 31, 2010. *See also* Classified Response to the U.S. Department of Justice Office of Professional Responsibility Classified Report Dated July 29, 2009, Submitted on Behalf of Judge Jay S. Bybee, 28 n.29 (Oct. 9, 2009), http://www.fas.org/irp/ agency/doj/opr-bybeefinal.pdf.

55. *See* Helgerson Report, *supra* note 40, at 1–2.

56. *Id. Ex-CIA Inspector General on Interrogation Report*, DER SPIEGEL INTERNATIONAL, Aug. 31, 2009.

57. The best account of the history of the inspector general statute is Ryan M. Check & A. John Radsan, *One Lantern in the Darkest Night: The CIA's Inspector General*, 4 J. NATIONAL SECURITY L. & POLICY 247 (2010); *see also* L. Britt Snider, *Creating a Statutory Inspector General at the CIA* (Center for the Study of Intelligence, CIA, 2007), https://www.cia.gov/library/center-for-the-study-of-intelligence/kent-csi/vol44no5/html/v44i5a02p.htm. The CIA has had a non-independent inspector general, under the Director's control, since

1952, and the office was not always feckless. Allen Dulles asked his hand-picked inspector general, Lyman Kirkpatrick, to investigate the CIA's Bay of Pigs fiasco. Kirkpatrick's report was scathing. But it was largely ignored and not disclosed publicly until 1998. And its critical distance was exceptional. The congressional committee investigating the Iran-Contra scandal concluded that the non-independent CIA inspector general lacked adequate "manpower, resources, or tenacity." US Congress, House Select Committee to Investigate Covert Arms Transactions with Iran and the Senate Select Committee on Secret Military Assistance to Iran and the Nicaraguan Opposition, Report on the Iran-Contra Affair 425, House Report No. 100-433 and Senate Report No. 100-216, 100th Congress, 1st Sess. (1987), at 424.

58. *A Troubled Company*, Newsweek, Dec. 3, 1995.

59. Weiner, *supra* note 1, at 517.

60. Tim Weiner, *Veteran CIA Official Quits but Will Finish Investigations*, N.Y. Times, Oct. 3, 1997.

61. George Tenet, Statement on the Nomination of John L. Helgerson as CIA Inspector General (Feb. 28, 2002), https://www.cia.gov/news-information/press-releases-statements/press-release-archive-2002/pr02282002.html.

62. Hearing on the Nomination of John L. Helgerson to Be Inspector General, Central Intelligence Agency, Senate Select Committee on Intelligence, 107th Cong., 2nd Sess. (2002), http://intelligence.senate.gov/pdfs/107596.pdf.

63. Interview with John Helgerson, in Washington, D.C. (Jan. 18, 2011).

64. *See* Alfred McCoy, A Question of Torture: CIA Interrogation from the Cold War to the War on Terror (2006). These practices are alluded to on pages 9–10 of the Helgerson Report.

65. Interview with Helgerson, *supra* note 63.

66. Hearing on the Nomination of John Helgerson, *supra* note 62.

67. *Ex-CIA Inspector General on Interrogation Report*, *supra* note 56.

68. 50 U.S.C.A. § 403q(b)(3).

69. *Ex-CIA Inspector General on Interrogation Report*, *supra* note 56.

70. Walter Pincus & Joby Warrick, *Ex-Intelligence Officials Cite Low Spirits at CIA*, Wash. Post, Aug. 30, 2009.

71. This description is based on interviews with four CIA officials who were involved in the Helgerson investigation.

72. *See* OIG Report on CIA Accountability with Respect to the 9/11 Attacks, June 2005, https://www.cia.gov/library/reports/Executive%20Summary_OIG%20Report.pdf.

73. Helgerson also briefed a White House team led by Vice President Cheney. There were insinuations in the press that Cheney tried to pressure Helgerson to stop his review or change his conclusions. *See* Scott Horton, *Six Questions for Jane Mayer, Author of the Dark Side*, Harper's Magazine, July 14, 2008. But Helgerson viewed the White House briefing as an appropriate and important opportunity to educate the White House about what he had

learned about one of the government's most important counterterrorism programs. Cheney asked questions and sought clarifications, but he made no inappropriate requests, Helgerson says. Interview with Helgerson, *supra* note 63.

74. Leon Panetta, Statement on Release of Material on Past Detention Practices (Aug. 24, 2009), https://www.cia.gov/news-information/press-releases-statements/past-detention-practices.html. In my position as the head of the Office of Legal Counsel, I wrote a memorandum to Helgerson that outlined the Justice Department's views concerning what it viewed as "ambiguities or mistaken characterizations" in the report. *See* Memorandum from Jack L. Goldsmith III to John Helgerson, Special Review: Counterterrorism Detention and Interrogation Activities, June 18, 2004, http://www.washingtonpost.com/wp-srv/nation/documents/0614_04_Letter_to_Helgerson0001.pdf.

75. *See* Helgerson Report, *supra* note 40.

76. Department of Justice, Office of the Inspector General, A Review of the FBI's Involvement in and Observations of Detainee Interrogations in Guantanamo Bay, Afghanistan, and Iraq (2009), http://www.justice.gov/oig/special/s0910.pdf.

77. Department of Justice, Office of the Inspector General, Report to Congress on Implementation of Section 1001 of the USA PATRIOT Act (2002), http://www.justice.gov/oig/special/0207/index.htm.

78. *See* Department of Justice, Office of the Inspector General, A Review of the FBI's Use of Section 215 Orders for Business Records in 2006 (2008), http://www.justice.gov/oig/special/s0803a/final.pdf; Department of Justice, Office of the Inspector General, A Review of the Federal Bureau of Investigation's Use of Exigent Letters and Other Informal Requests for Telephone Records (2010), http://www.justice.gov/oig/special/s1001r.pdf; Department of Justice, Office of the Inspector General, A Review of the FBI's Use of National Security Letters (2008), http://www.justice.gov/oig/special/s0803b/final.pdf; Department of Justice, Office of the Inspector General, A Review of the FBI's Use of National Security Letters (2007), http://www.justice.gov/oig/special/s0703b/final.pdf.

79. *See, e.g.*, Department of Justice, Office of the Inspector General, Report to Congress on Implementation of Section 1001 of the USA PATRIOT Act (Aug. 2010), http://www.justice.gov/oig/special/s1008.pdf; Department of Justice, Office of the Inspector General, Report to Congress on Implementation of Section 1001 of the USA PATRIOT Act (Feb. 2010), http://www.justice.gov/oig/special/s1002.pdf.

80. Offices of the Inspector General for the Department of Defense, Department of Justice, CIA, NSA, and Office of the Director of National Intelligence, Unclassified Report on the President's Surveillance Program (July 10, 2009), http://www.fas.org/irp/eprint/psp.pdf.

81. Reducing Over-Classification Act of 2007, H.R. 4806, 110th Cong., 1st

Sess. (2007), http://frwebgate.access.gpo.gov/cgi-bin/getdoc.cgi?dbname= 111_cong_bills&docid=f:h553enr.txt.pdf.

82. Opinion of the Office of Legal Counsel, Inspector General Legislation, 1977 OLC LEXIS 8 (Feb. 21, 1977).

83. MILLER CENTER OF PUBLIC AFFAIRS, FINAL REPORT OF THE NATIONAL COMMISSION ON THE SEPARATION OF POWERS (1998), http://web1.millercenter .org/commissions/comm_1998.pdf.

84. Foreign Intelligence Surveillance Act of 1978 Amendments Act of 2008, Pub. L. No. 110-261, 122 Stat. 2467-69, 2471 (2008).

85. Anthony D. Romero, *Letter to the Editor*, N.Y. TIMES, July 11, 2008.

86. *Id.*

87. Josh Marshall, *Obama on FISA*, TPM, June 20, 2008, http://www.talking pointsmemo.com/archives/201032.php.

88. Interview with senior Justice Department official, Washington, D.C., Apr. 26, 2010.

89. *See* Dana Priest, *Wrongful Imprisonment: Anatomy of a CIA Mistake*, WASH. POST, Dec. 4, 2005; Letter from Senator Carl Levin to John Helgerson, Inspector General of the CIA (Oct. 24, 2005), http://www.chrgj.org/projects/docs/ cia/Doc%20125.pdf.

90. Letter from Michael Hayden et al. to President Barack Obama (Sept. 18, 2009), http://www.realclearpolitics.com/politics_nation/cialetter0918.pdf (stating less than twenty cases had been sent by the CIA's inspector general); Letter from Deputy Assistant Attorney General Benczkowski to Senator Richard Durbin (Feb. 7, 2008) (stating that twenty cases in total from the CIA and Department of Defense had been sent); Carrie Johnson, Jerry Markon & Julia Tate, *Inquiry into CIA Practices Narrows*, WASH. POST, Sept. 19, 2009 (twenty-four cases); David Johnston & Mark Mazzetti, *Hurdles Stand in Way of Prosecuting Abuses*, N.Y. TIMES, Aug. 25, 2009 (nearly twenty).

91. Johnston & Mazzetti, *supra* note 90.

92. Warren P. Strobel, *CIA Sacked Baghdad Station Chief after Deaths of 2 Detainees*, McCLATCHY, Aug. 25, 2009, http://www.mcclatchydc.com/2009/08/25/ 74345/cia-sacked-baghdad-station-chief.html.

93. 50 U.S.C. §403q(b)(5) (emphasis added).

94. Johnson, Markon & Tate, *supra* note 90; Letter from Benczkowski, *supra* note 90.

95. On Department of Justice efforts, see Johnson, Markon & Tate, *supra* note 90; Johnston & Mazzetti, *supra* note 90. On the legal standard, *see* the United States Attorneys' Manual, Rule 9-27.220, http://www.justice.gov/usao/ eousa/foia_reading_room/usam/title9/27mcrm.htm.

96. The first Helgerson quote is from Johnson, Markon & Tate, *supra* note 90. The second is from Strobel, *supra* note 92.

97. This is the standard for CIA Accountability Boards. See Exhibit B in OFFICE OF THE INSPECTOR GENERAL, CIA, PROCEDURES USED IN NARCOTICS AIRBRIDGE DENIAL PROGRAM IN PERU (2008), http://www.fas.org/irp/ cia/product/ig-airbridge.pdf; Strobel, *supra* note 92.

98. Paul Benson, *Sources: Report to Detail Alleged Abuse inside CIA Secret Prisons*, CNN, Aug. 23, 2009, http://articles.cnn.com/2009-08-23/politics/cia .prisoner.report_1_cia-inspector-general-cia-spokesman-secret-prisons?_ s=PM:POLITICS.

99. Strobel, *supra* note 92; Adam Goldman & Kathy Gannon, *Gul Rahman's Death in the Salt Pit*, Cleveland.com, Mar. 28, 2010, http://www.cleveland.com/ world/index.ssf/2010/03/gul_rahman_death_in_the_salt_p.html; Adam Goldman & Matt Apuzzo, *At CIA, Grave Mistakes, Then Promotions*, ABC News, Feb. 9, 2011, http://abcnews.go.com/Blotter/wireStory?id=12872190.

100. Joby Warrick & R. Jeffrey Smith, *CIA Officer Disciplined for Alleged Gun Use in Interrogation*, Wash. Post, Aug. 23, 2009; Adam Goldman, *CIA Officer Linked to Abuse Case Back at Work*, MSNBC, Sept. 7, 2010, http://www.msnbc.msn .com/id/39043456/ns/us_news-security/#.

101. Goldman & Apuzzo, *supra* note 99.

102. For my assessment, see Jack Goldsmith, The Terror Presidency: Law and Judgment Inside the Bush Administration, ch. 5 (2007).

103. I base this judgment on summaries of prior Office of Professional Responsibility investigations, *see* http://www.justice.gov/opr/reports.htm, as well as conversations with present and former Justice Department officials.

104. OPR Report, *supra* note 46.

105. Memorandum from David Margolis, Associate Deputy Attorney General, to the Attorney General, (Jan. 5, 2010), http://judiciary.house.gov/hear ings/pdf/DAGMargolis Memo100105.pdf.

106. Report of the Select Committee on Intelligence, United States Senate, Covering the Period January 3, 2009 to January 4, 2011 (Mar. 17, 2011), http://www.fas.org/irp/congress/2011_rpt/ssci.pdf.

107. Leon Panetta, Message on New Review Group on Rendition, Detention, and Interrogation (Mar. 16, 2009), https://www.cia.gov/news-information/ press-releases-statements/new-review-group-on-rendition-detention-and- interrogation.html.

108. Helgerson Report, *supra* note 40, at 36–37.

109. *See* Interview with Rizzo, *supra* note 11. Helgerson's team viewed all of the tapes (and written summaries of them), which were a basis for its conclusion that the waterboard was used in a way "different" from what the Department of Justice legal opinion had approved. Helgerson Report, *supra* note 40, at 37.

110. I did not advise the CIA on the tapes matter during my time in the Justice Department from 2003 to 2004, but Durham's team interviewed me in April 2009 on aspects of the program with no obvious connection to the tapes.

111. Holder did so after reading the Helgerson Report and the Justice Department ethics report, but without examining the prosecutors' original rationales for not bringing charges and without noting any newly discovered facts. Johnson, Markon & Tate, *supra* note 90.

112. *See* Statement of the Attorney General Regarding Investigation into the Interrogation of Certain Detainees (June 30, 2011), http://www.justice.gov/ opa/pr/2011/June/11-ag-861.html.

113. Peter Finn & Julie Tate, *Justice Department to Investigate Deaths of Two Detainees in CIA Custody*, WASH. POST, June 30, 2011. The burdens of the Durham investigation, combined with the burdens of the Senate, House, and many inspector general investigations, led to the creation of a deputy in the CIA General Counsel's Office—one of only two deputy slots—just to supervise investigations.

114. Statement of President Barack Obama on Release of OLC Memos (Aug. 16, 2009), http://www.whitehouse.gov/the_press_office/Statement-of-President-Barack-Obama-on-Release-of-OLC-Memos/; Leon Panetta, Statement on Release of Material on Past Detention Practices (Aug. 24, 2009), https://www.cia.gov/news-information/press-releases-statements/past-detention-practices.html.

115. Letter from the ACLU to the Freedom of Information Officer (Oct. 7, 2003), http://www.aclu.org/torturefoia/legaldocuments/nnACLUFOIArequest.pdf.

116. 5 U.S.C. § 552(b). Gerald Ford vetoed the law after Office of Legal Counsel Chief Antonin Scalia advised him it would violate the President's "exclusive" power to control national security information, and after CIA Director William Colby told him he could not "effectively and secretly conduct intelligence activities if a court after a *de novo* review can substitute its judgment for mine as to what information requires protection." Letter from William Colby, Director of the CIA, to President Ford (Sept. 26, 1974), http://www.gwu.edu/~nsarchiv/NSAEBB/NSAEBB142/092674%20CIA%20to%20Ford%20Memo.pdf; CHARLIE SAVAGE, TAKEOVER: THE RETURN OF THE IMPERIAL PRESIDENCY AND THE SUBVERSION OF AMERICAN DEMOCRACY 27 (2007). Congress overrode Ford's veto, however, and created an official back door into the President's previously impregnable secrecy system.

117. Freedom of Information Act, Pub. L. No. 89-554, 80 Stat. 383 (1966).

118. 120 CONG. REC. 17,019 (1974) (Statement of Senator Ted Kennedy).

119. Hunt v. CIA, 981 F.2d 1116, 1120 (9th Cir. 1992) (internal quotations omitted).

120. Exec. Order No. 13,292, 3 C.F.R. 196 (2003), § 1.1(c); Memorandum from Attorney General John Ashcroft to the Heads of All Federal Departments and Agencies (Oct. 12, 2001), http://www.doi.gov/foia/foia.pdf. Memorandum from Attorney General Janet Reno to All Heads of Departments and Agencies (Oct. 4, 1993), http://www.usdoj.gov/oip/foia_updates/Vol_XIV_3/page3.htm.

121. Telephone interview with Anthony Romero (May 2, 2011).

122. Clint Hendler, *Transparency Interview: Jameel Jaffer*, CAMPAIGN DESK, Mar. 4, 2009, http://www.cjr.org/campaign_desk/transparency_interview_jameel.php?page=all&print=true.

123. The quotations in this paragraph, and unless otherwise indicated all other quotations from Jameel Jaffer, are based on an interview with Jaffer, in New York, New York (Oct. 12, 2010).

124. Telephone interview with Anthony Romero, *supra* note 121. The ACLU's

membership grew from 275,000 in 2001 to over 500,000 by 2011, and its budget grew from $32.5 million in Fiscal Year 2001 to $110.7 million in Fiscal Year 2010. E-mail communication with Abby Adams, Senior Grant Writer, ACLU Foundation (May 17, 2011).

125. E-mail communication with Dan Metcalfe (May 11, 2011).

126. Scott Shane, *A.C.L.U. Lawyers Mine Documents for Truth*, N.Y. TIMES, Aug. 29, 2009.

127. The number of pages is based on an e-mail communication with Jameel Jaffer (May 4, 2011).

128. *See* sources in note 44.

129. Seth F. Kreimer, *The Freedom of Information Act and the Ecology of Transparency*, 10 U. PA. J. CONSTITUTIONAL L. 1011 (2008).

130. For definitive summaries, see Kreimer, *supra* note 129, and Seth F. Kreimer, *Rays of Sunlight in a Shadow "War": FOIA, the Abuses of Anti-Terrorism, and the Strategy of Transparency*, 11 LEWIS & CLARK L. REV. 1141 (2007).

131. A.C.L.U. v. Department of Defense, 351 F.Supp.2d 265 (S.D.N.Y. 2005).

132. For examples of these hearings, see Confirmation Hearing on the Nomination of Alberto R. Gonzales to be Attorney General of the United States: Before the Senate Committee on the Judiciary, 109th Cong. (2005); Confirmation Hearing on the Nomination of Timothy Elliot Flanigan to Be Deputy Attorney General: Hearing before the Senate Committee on the Judiciary, 109th Cong. (2005); Current and Future Worldwide Threats to the National Security of the United States: Hearing before the Senate Committee on Armed Services, 109th Cong. (2005); Detainees: Hearing before the Senate Committee on the Judiciary, 109th Cong. (2005); Iraq: Perceptions, Realities, and Cost to Complete: Hearing before the Subcommittee on National Security, Emerging Threats, and International Relations of the House Committee on Government Reform, 109th Cong. (2005); Material Witness Provisions of the Criminal Code, and the Implementation of the USA PATRIOT Act: Hearing before the Subcommittee on Crime, Terrorism, and Homeland Security of the House Committee on the Judiciary, 109th Cong. (2005); Reauthorization of the USA PATRIOT Act: Hearing before the House Committee on the Judiciary, 109th Cong. (2005); Review of Department of Defense Detention and Interrogation Policy and Operations in the Global War on Terror: Hearings before the Senate Committee on Armed Services, 109th Cong. (2005) (there were three hearings on this topic before the Senate Armed Services Committee in the spring and summer of 2005); Department of Defense Authorization for Appropriations for Fiscal Year 2005, Hearing before the Senate Committee on Armed Services, 108th Cong. (2004); Nomination of the Hon. Peter J. Goss to be Director of Central Intelligence: Hearing before the Senate Select Committee on Intelligence, 108th Cong. (2004); Review of Department of Defense Detention and Interrogation Operations: Hearings before the Senate Committee on Armed Services, 108th Cong. (2004) (five hearings before the Senate Armed Services Committee on this topic in the summer of 2004); Transition

to Sovereignty in Iraq, US Policy, Ongoing Military Operations, and Status of US Armed Forces: Hearing before the Senate Committee on Armed Services, 108th Cong. (2004).

133. Detainee Treatment Act, Pub. L. No. 109-148, § 1004(a), 119 Stat. 2680, 2740 (2005). The McCain Amendment also limited Defense Department interrogations to those found in the U.S. Army Field Manual. *Id.* § 1002(a).

134. Josh White, *President Relents, Backs Torture Ban*, WASH. POST, Dec. 16, 2005.

135. President's Statement on Signing of H.R. 2863 (Dec. 30, 2005), http://georgewbush-whitehouse.archives.gov/news/releases/2005/12/20051230-8.html.

136. Marty Lederman, *Senator McCain Lays Down a Marker*, BALKINIZATION, Jan. 4, 2006, http://balkin.blogspot.com/2006/01/senator-mccain-lays-down-marker.html.

137. Memorandum from Steven G. Bradbury, Principal Deputy Assistant Attorney General, to John Rizzo, Senior Deputy General Counsel, CIA (May 30, 2005), http://luxmedia.com.edgesuite.net/aclu/olc_05302005_bradbury.pdf.

138. Hamdan v. Rumsfeld, 548 U.S. 557 (2006).

139. *US Defense Dept: Top Terrorist Nabbed*, CBS NEWS, Sept. 10, 2009, http://www.cbsnews.com/stories/2008/03/14/terror/main3938934.shtml; *Profile: Abd al-Hadi al-Iraqi*, BBC NEWS, Apr. 27, 2007, http://news.bbc.co.uk/2/hi/middle_east/6601087.stm; Dafna Linzer, *CIA Held Al-Qaeda Suspect Secretly*, WASH. POST, Apr. 28, 2007.

140. *See* Memorandum from Steven G. Bradbury, *supra* note 137.

CHAPTER FIVE: WARRIOR-LAWYERS

1. *See* BOB WOODWARD, OBAMA'S WARS ch. 16 (2010).

2. Mark S. Martins, Remarks upon Promotion to Brigadier General at the Great Hall, Department of Justice (Sept. 30, 2009).

3. Attorney General Eric Holder, Remarks upon Promotion of Mark S. Martins to Brigadier General at the Great Hall, Department of Justice (Sept. 30, 2009).

4. General David Petraeus, Remarks upon Promotion of Mark S. Martins to Brigadier General at the Great Hall, Department of Justice (Sept. 30, 2009).

5. Willy Stern, *Wartime Legalities: A Top Military Lawyer Aims to Avoid "Victor's Justice" in Iraq*, HARV. MAG., Mar.–Apr. 2008; Petraeus, *supra* note 4.

6. Telephone interview with General David Petraeus (Nov. 12, 2010).

7. *Army Jag Corps: History*, U.S. Army, http://www.goarmy.com/jag/about/history.html.

8. FREDERIC L. BORCH, JUDGE ADVOCATES IN COMBAT: ARMY LAWYERS IN MILITARY OPERATIONS FROM VIETNAM TO HAITI 6 (2001).

9. General Curtis LeMay, who ordered the Tokyo firebombing, was never concerned about legal implications of air attacks. He stated in an interview in 1984 that he ordered the low-altitude bombing of Tokyo "without asking

anybody." Interview by Richard H. Kohn with General Curtis E. LeMay, in Washington, D.C. (June 15, 1984), *reprinted in* STRATEGIC AIR WARFARE 65 (Richard H. Kohn & Joseph P. Harahan eds., 1988). More generally, the Committee of Operations Analysts and the Joint Target Group, both of which aided in target selection in the Pacific Theater, appeared to consider only nonlegal criteria in forming their recommendations. *See* RONALD SCHAFFER, WINGS OF JUDGMENT: AMERICAN BOMBING IN WORLD WAR II 110–19, 121–23 (1985). In the European theater, commanders voiced concerns over the tactic of morale bombing, which decimated several German cities, but such concerns appeared to center on worries that such attacks violated American principles and morality, not that they were legally deficient. *See* Tami Davis Biddle, *Wartime Reactions*, in FIRESTORM: THE BOMBING OF DRESDEN 1945, 96 103–4 (Paul Addison & Jeremy A. Crang eds., 2006); SCHAFFER, *supra*, at 74–79.

10. Truman claimed in his memoirs that he wanted to use the bomb "in a manner prescribed by the laws of war." HARRY S. TRUMAN, MEMOIRS, YEAR OF DECISIONS 419–20 (1955). But as Gar Alperovitz has noted, despite this statement, "there is no evidence that legal issues were ever seriously considered in connection with the atomic bombings of 1945." GAR ALPEROVITZ, THE DECISION TO USE THE ATOMIC BOMB 529 (1995).

11. In their respective memoirs, both President Johnson and Secretary of Defense Robert McNamara discuss how they selected targets, but neither mentions legal considerations playing a role in their deliberations. *See* LYNDON BAINES JOHNSON, THE VANTAGE POINT: PERSPECTIVES ON THE PRESIDENCY, 1963–1969 (1971); ROBERT S. MCNAMARA & BRIAN VANDEMARK, IN RETROSPECT: THE TRAGEDY AND LESSONS OF VIETNAM (1996). When President Nixon took over as Commander in Chief, he gave the military full control over target selection, with the only proviso being to avoid massive civilian casualties. JOHN MORROCCO, RAIN OF FIRE: AIR WAR, 1969–1973, 133, 148 (1985).

12. Telephone interview with Frederic L. Borch, Regimental Historian and Archivist, The Judge Advocate General's Legal Center and School, Charlottesville, Va. (Aug. 4, 2010).

13. I conducted numerous interviews with Mark Martins, in person and over e-mail, in 2010 and 2011. All quotations by Martins are from these interviews unless otherwise indicated.

14. ANDREW J. BACEVICH, THE NEW AMERICAN MILITARISM: HOW AMERICANS ARE SEDUCED BY WAR 36 (2005).

15. *See, e.g.,* MICHAL R. BELKNAP, THE VIETNAM WAR ON TRIAL: THE MY LAI MASSACRE AND COURT-MARTIAL OF LIEUTENANT CALLEY (2002).

16. WILLIAM R. PEERS, THE PEERS REPORT (1970), http://www.law.umkc.edu/faculty/projects/ftrials/mylai/MYL_Peers.htm.

17. BORCH, *supra* note 8, at 51–52.

18. Interview with Petraeus, *supra* note 6.

19. BORCH, *supra* note 8, at 194–95; Interview with Borch, *supra* note 12.

20. For explanations of this term and the history of the rise of operational lawyers, from which I have learned much, see David Graham, *Operational Law—A Concept Comes of Age*, 1987 ARMY LAWYER 9; Marc Warren, *Operational Law—A Concept Matures*, 152 MIL. L. REV. 33 (1996); Marc Warren, *Teaching the JAG Elephant to Dance . . . Again*, U.S. Army War College Research Project, April 9, 2002, http://www.dtic.mil/cgi-bin/GetTRDoc?Location= U2&doc=GetTRDoc.pdf&AD=ADA404517; Stephen A. Myrow, *Waging War on the Advice of Counsel: The Role of Operational Law in the Gulf War*, 7 USAFA J. LEG. STUD. 131 (1996/1997); Steven Keeva, *Lawyers in the War Room*, A.B.A. J., Dec. 1991, at 52; Charles J. Dunlap Jr., *Law and Military Interventions: Preserving Humanitarian Values in 21st Century Conflicts*, Prepared for Humanitarian Challenges in Military Intervention Conference, Washington, D.C. (Nov. 29, 2001), http://www.duke.edu/~pfeaver/dunlap.pdf.

21. Interview with Colonel Jeff Bovarnick, in Newton, Massachusetts (Oct. 11, 2010). I benefited a great deal from Colonel Bovarnick's insights on this and many other matters in this chapter.

22. Warren, *Operational Law, supra* note 20, at 44.

23. Charles J. Dunlap Jr., *Lawfare Today: A Perspective*, YALE J. INTERNATIONAL AFFAIRS 147 (Winter 2008).

24. Charles J. Dunlap Jr., *Lawfare: A Decisive Element of 21st-Century Conflicts?* JOINT FORCE Q., 3rd quarter 2009, at 35, http://www.ndu.edu/press/lib/images/ jfq-54/12.pdf.

25. *Cf.* DAVID KENNEDY, OF WAR AND LAW 22 (2006) (noting that more broadly, both military violence and legal constructs can help "seize and secure territory, resources, or people, send messages about resolve and political seriousness, even break the will of a political opponent").

26. *Compare* OFFICE OF THE UNDER SECRETARY OF DEFENSE (COMPTROLLER), NATIONAL DEFENSE BUDGET ESTIMATES FOR FY 2011 63 (2010), http:// comptroller.defense.gov/defbudget/fy2011/FY11_Green_Book.pdf (total Department of Defense obligational authority in Fiscal Year 1977 was $107.6 billion), *with* OFFICE OF MANAGEMENT & BUDGET, BUDGET OF THE UNITED STATES GOVERNMENT, FISCAL YEAR 2003 101 (2002), http://www.gpoac cess.gov/usbudget/fy03/pdf/budget.pdf (U.S. Department of Defense total discretionary budget in 2001 was $302.6 billion).

27. DONALD RUMSFELD, KNOWN AND UNKNOWN: A MEMOIR 297 (2011).

28. *See* Memorandum from Rudy de Leon, former Deputy Secretary of Defense, on Significant Statutory, Regulatory and Judicial Changes 1974–2000 to Secretary of Defense Donald Rumsfeld (Apr. 9, 2001) (on file with author).

29. Memorandum from Secretary of Defense Donald Rumsfeld, on the Department of Defense Challenge (June 25, 2001) (on file with author).

30. In 2011, President Barack Obama proposed that the Senate consent to the Second Protocol. Julian E. Barnes, *Geneva Protections for al Qaeda Suspects? Read the Fine Print*, WALL ST. J., Mar. 14, 2011; Hans Nichols & Justin Blum, *Obama Reopens Debate on Military Trials of Detainees*, BLOOMBERG BUSINESSWEEK, Mar. 8, 2011. But as of this writing, no action has been taken in the Senate.

31. I am indebted in this paragraph to DUNLAP, *supra* note 20, and MICHAEL IGNATIEFF, VIRTUAL WAR: KOSOVO AND BEYOND (2000).

32. KENNEDY, *supra* note 25, at 45.

33. *Cf.* MICHAEL WALZER, ARGUING ABOUT WAR 9 (2004) (suggesting that justice has become a military necessity).

34. Keeva, *supra* note 20, at 52.

35. BORCH, *supra* note 8.

36. Keeva, *supra* note 20.

37. *NATO's Bombing Blunders*, BBC NEWS, June 1, 1999, 3:29 PM GMT, http://news.bbc.co.uk/2/hi/340966.stm.

38. WESLEY K. CLARK, WAGING MODERN WAR: BOSNIA, KOSOVO, AND THE FUTURE OF COMBAT 198, 278, 281 (2001).

39. Richard K. Betts, *Compromised Command*, FOREIGN AFFAIRS, July–Aug. 2001.

40. DUNLAP, *supra* note 20.

41. Interview with Petraeus, *supra* note 6.

42. Lawyers in the other services have mottos that express the same sentiment.

43. GREGORY FONTENOT ET AL., ON POINT: THE UNITED STATES ARMY IN OPERATION IRAQI FREEDOM 266 (2005).

44. David Petraeus, Undelivered Remarks Prepared for Harvard Law School (Feb. 27, 2011) (on file with author).

45. Interview with Petraeus, *supra* note 6.

46. I first heard the term used in this context by Colonel Renn Gade, who most recently served as the Staff Judge Advocate, U.S. Special Operations Command at MacDill AFB, Tampa, Florida. I am grateful to Colonel Gade for his many insights related to this chapter.

47. E-mail communication with Andru Wall (Mar. 22. 2011).

48. On the term "chronic obscurity," see ARTHUR M. SCHLESINGER JR., THE CYCLES OF AMERICAN HISTORY 423 (1999).

49. DEPARTMENT OF DEFENSE, DICTIONARY OF MILITARY AND ASSOCIATED TERMS (2011), http://www.dtic.mil/doctrine/new_pubs/jp1_02.pdf.

50. DON HIGGINBOTHAM AND HENRY Y. WARNOCK, GEORGE WASHINGTON AND THE AMERICAN MILITARY TRADITION 19 (2004).

51. Mark S. Martins, *Rules of Engagement for Land Forces: A Matter of Training, Not Lawyering* 143 MIL. L. REV. 3 (1994).

52. Tony Perry, *U.S. Air Support Troops Learn to Hold Back*, L.A. TIMES, Mar. 22, 2010.

53. *Id.*

54. *See* Kevin Baron, *New, Clarified Rules Issued for Afghan Fight*, STARS & STRIPES, Aug. 4, 2010; Rajiv Chandrasekaran, *Petraeus Reviews Directive Meant to Limit Afghan Civilian Deaths*, WASH. POST, July 9, 2010; John Vandiver, *Petraeus to Clarify, Not Alter, Warfighting Rules in Afghanistan*, STARS & STRIPES, July 8, 2010.

55. Interview by John Hawkins with former Secretary of Defense Donald Rumsfeld, RIGHT WING NEWS, http://rightwingnews.com/2011/03/the-donald-rumsfeld-interview/.

56. *See* Antonio Cassese, *The Italian Court of Cassation Misapprehends the Notion of War Crimes*, 6 J. INTERNATIONAL CRIM. JUST. 1077, 1077–79 (2008); Jed Babbin, *Petraeus Takes Charge: Clarifies ROE for Troops*, HUM. EVENTS, Mar. 15, 2007, http://www.humanevents.com/article.php?id=19838.

57. The information in this paragraph and the next are based on interviews with over a dozen soldiers and marines, lawyers and non-lawyers, from a wide range of ranks, who were deployed in Afghanistan and Iraq.

58. Thomas E. Ricks, *Target Approval Delays Irk Air Force Officers*, WASH. POST, Nov. 18, 2001; RUMSFELD, *supra* note 27, at 387–89; *cf.* Seymour M. Hersh, *King's Ransom: How Vulnerable Are the Saudi Royals?* NEW YORKER, Oct. 16, 2001, at 35. General Franks offers a different and somewhat confusing version of this event in his memoir. He says that he fired on the vehicle outside the mosque rather than the mosque not because of legal advice, but because, despite authorization from Rumsfeld and Bush to fire, President Bush had told him at an earlier meeting not to fire on Bin Laden if he was found in a mosque. TOMMY FRANKS, AMERICAN SOLDIER 292–94 (2004).

59. Ricks, *supra* note 58.

60. RUMSFELD, *supra* note 27, at 388.

61. Telephone interview with General Jack Keane (Nov. 17, 2010).

62. Interview with Petraeus, *supra* note 6.

63. Mark Bodwen, *The Professor of War*, VANITY FAIR, May 2010, http://www.vanityfair.com/politics/features/2010/05/petraeus-201005.

64. This is my highly reductionist summary of several lengthy official investigative reports. *See* Antonio M. Taguba, ARTICLE 15-6 INVESTIGATION OF THE 800TH MILITARY POLICE BRIGADE (2004), http://www.npr.org/iraq/2004/prison_abuse_report.pdf; George R. Fay & Anthony R. Jones, AR 15-6 INVESTIGATION OF THE ABU GHRAIB PRISON AND THE 205TH MILITARY INTELLIGENCE BRIGADE (2004), http://news.findlaw.com/hdocs/docs/dod/fay82504rpt.pdf; James R. Schlesinger, FINAL REPORT OF THE INDEPENDENT PANEL TO REVIEW DoD DETENTION OPERATIONS (2004), http://fl1.find law.com/news.findlaw.com/wp/docs/dod/abughraibrpt.pdf; A.T. Church III, REVIEW OF DEPARTMENT OF DEFENSE DETENTION OPERATIONS AND DETAINEE INTERROGATION TECHNIQUES (2005), http://www.aclu.org/images/torture/asset_upload_file625_26068.pdf; Staff of the Senate Committee on Armed Services, 110th Cong., INQUIRY INTO THE TREATMENT OF DETAINEES IN U.S. CUSTODY (Comm. Print, 2008), http://armed-services.senate.gov/Publications/Detainee%20Report%20Final_April%2022%20 2009.pdf.

65. MARK MARTINS, PAYING TRIBUTE TO REASON: JUDGMENTS ON TERROR, LESSONS FOR SECURITY IN FOUR TRIALS SINCE 9/11, at 135 (2nd ed., 2008).

66. David H. Petraeus, *The American Military and the Lessons of Vietnam: A Study of the Military Influence and the Use of Force in the Post-Vietnam Era* (Oct. 1987), unpublished Ph.D. dissertation, Princeton University, on file with Mudd Library, Princeton University.

67. COUNTERINSURGENCY, Field Manual 3-24, at 1-151, Department of the Army (December 2006) [hereinafter COIN Manual], http://www.fas.org/irp/doddir/army/fm3-24.pdf.

68. Robert M. Chesney, *Iraq and the Military Detention Debate: Firsthand Perspectives from the Other War, 2003–2010*, 51 VA. J. INTERNATIONAL L. 549 (2011).

69. COIN Manual, *supra* note 67, at 7-38–7-40; Appendix D-4–D-5.

70. Memorandum from General Stanley McChrystal, Commander, United States Forces–Afghanistan, to Secretary of Defense Robert Gates, Commander's Initial Assessment, Aug. 30, 2009, Annex F, at F-1, http://media.washingtonpost.com/wp-srv/politics/documents/Assessment_Redacted_092109.pdf?hpid=topnews.

71. *Id.*

72. Central Command, Combined Joint Interagency Task Force-435, at http://www.centcom.mil/jtf435.

73. Martins ultimately commanded troops totaling in the thousands for four months as JTF-435 commander (before Harward's confirmation and then between Harward's departure and the arrival of General Keith Huber to replace Harward) and for more than a year as the ROLFF Commander. This was unprecedented field command experience for a lawyer in modern combat operations. He also served as deputy commander for the other eight months comprising the two-year deployment.

74. *See* Commander's Initial Assessment, *supra* note 70, at F-1.

75. The process is described in Memorandum for US Military Forces Conducting Detention Operations in Afghanistan, July 11, 2010, http://www.politico.com/static/PPM205_bagrambrfb.html.

76. The description in this paragraph is based largely on Jeff Bovarnick, *Detainee Review Boards in Afghanistan: From Strategic Liability to Legitimacy*, THE ARMY LAWYER 9 (June 2010).

77. These illustrative examples are loosely based on two human rights reports, Human Rights First, *Detained and Denied in Afghanistan: How to Make U.S. Detention Comply with the Law* 6 (May 2011), http://www.humanrightsfirst.org/wp-content/uploads/pdf/Detained-Denied-in-Afghanistan.pdf; and Jonathan Horowitz, *New Detention Rules Show Promise and Problems*, OPEN SOCIETY FOUNDATIONS, April 20, 2010, http://blog.soros.org/2010/04/new-detention-rules-show-promise-and-problems/.

78. This paragraph is largely based on a memorandum that I received on May 23, 2011, that was prepared by William G. Doyne, Technical Leader, Latent Print Branch, U.S. Army Criminal Investigation Laboratory, who had extensive experience operating the JEFFs in Afghanistan. *See also* Thom Shanker, *To Track Militants, U.S. Has System That Never Forgets a Face*, N.Y. TIMES, July 13, 2011.

79. *See* Horowitz, *supra* note 77; *see also* Human Rights First, *supra* note 77.

80. For many examples drawn from the Iraq experience, see Robert Chesney, *Iraq and the Military Detention Debate: Firsthand Perspectives from the Other War, 2003–2010*, 51 VA. J. INTERNATIONAL LAW 549 (2011).

81. *See* Human Rights First, *supra* note 77.

82. *See* Commander's Initial Assessment, *supra* note 70, at F-1.

83. Yochi Dreazen, *Afghanistan's Judicial War*, NATIONAL JOURNAL, Jan. 6, 2011.

84. Secretary of Defense Robert M. Gates, Remarks at ISAF Troop Contributing Nation Session, NATO Headquarters, Brussels, Belgium (Mar. 11, 2011), http://nato.usmission.gov/mission/speeches/defense-secretary-gates-transition-in-afghanistan.html.

85. *See* COIN Manual, *supra* note 67; and Mark Martins, *Building the Rule of Law in Practice*, LAWFARE, Nov. 23, 2010, http://www.lawfareblog.com/2010/11/building-the-rule-of-law-in-practice/.

86. *See* COIN Manual, *supra* note 67, at D-9.

87. Dreazen, *Afghanistan's Judicial War*, *supra* note 83.

88. Mark Martins, *Building the Rule of Law in Theory*, LAWFARE, Nov. 16, 2010, http://www.lawfareblog.com/2010/11/building-the-rule-of-law-in-theory/.

CHAPTER SIX: THE GTMO BAR

1. *See* WILLIAM M. KUNSTLER, MY LIFE AS A RADICAL LAWYER (1996).

2. MARC A. THIESSEN, COURTING DISASTER: HOW THE CIA KEPT AMERICA SAFE AND HOW BARACK OBAMA IS INVITING THE NEXT ATTACK 241 (2010).

3. *Quoted in* BRANDT GOLDSTEIN, STORMING THE COURT: HOW A BAND OF YALE LAW STUDENTS SUED THE PRESIDENT—AND WON (2005).

4. Military Order of November 13, 2001, http://www.fas.org/irp/offdocs/eo/mo-111301.htm.

5. Michael Ratner, *How the Center for Constitutional Rights Launched the First Guantanamo Cases* (undated essay on file with author).

6. Telephone interview with Michael Ratner (Nov. 5, 2010). Unless otherwise indicated, quotations from Ratner are from this interview.

7. ARTHUR M. SCHLESINGER JR., THE IMPERIAL PRESIDENCY 287 (First Mariner Books, 2004) (1973).

8. Telephone interview with Ratner, *supra* note 6. See Campbell v. Clinton, 203 F.3d 19 (D.C. Cir. 2000) (Kosovo); Ange v. Bush, 752 F. Supp. 509 (D.D.C. 1990) (Iraq); Dellums v. Bush, 752 F. Supp. 1141 (D.D.C. 1990) (Iraq); Crockett v. Reagan, 558 F. Supp. 893 (D.D.C. 1982), aff'd, 720 F.2d 1355 (D.C. Cir. 1983) (El Salvador); Sanchez-Espinoza v. Reagan, 770 F.2d 202 (D.D.C. 1985) (Nicaragua); Conyers v. Reagan, 765 F.2d 1124 (D.D.C. 1985) (Grenada).

9. *See* BENJAMIN WITTES, LAW AND THE LONG WAR: THE FUTURE OF JUSTICE IN THE AGE OF TERROR, ch. 1 (2008).

10. *See* GOLDSTEIN, *supra* note 3.

11. Ratner, *supra* note 5.

12. Rasul v. Bush, 215 F.Supp.2d 55 (D.D.C. 2002).

13. Telephone interview with David Cole (Nov. 1, 2010).

14. Most famously Ex Parte Milligan 71 U.S. 2 (1866) and Duncan v. Kahanamoku, 327 US 304 (1946).

15. Youngstown Sheet & Tube Co. v. Sawyer, 343 U.S. 579 (1952) (steel seizure case); New York Times Co. v. United States, 403 U.S. 713 (1971) (Pentagon papers case).

16. WILLIAM H. REHNQUIST, ALL THE LAWS BUT ONE: CIVIL LIBERTIES IN WARTIME 225 (1998).

17. Arthur Krock, *In the Nation: Civil Rights in the Saboteurs' Trial*, N.Y. TIMES, JULY 21, 1942, at 18.

18. Telephone interview with Douglass Cassel (June 23, 2011).

19. Rule 37 of the Supreme Court of the United States, http://www.supreme court.gov/ctrules/2010RulesoftheCourt.pdf.

20. Korematsu v. U.S., 323 US 214 (1944) (Murphy, J., dissenting).

21. *See generally* GEOFFREY STONE, PERILOUS TIMES: FREE SPEECH IN WARTIME 305–7 (2004).

22. President Gerald Ford, Proclamation 4417, An American Promise (Feb. 19, 1976), http://www.digitalhistory.uh.edu/learning_history/japanese_intern ment/ford_proclamation_4417.cfm.

23. STEPHEN BREYER, AMERICA'S SUPREME COURT: MAKING DEMOCRACY WORK 189, 193 (2010).

24. Brief of Amicus Fred Korematsu in Support of Petitioners, Nos. 03-334, 03-343 (Jan. 14, 2004), http://www.jenner.com/files/tbl_s69NewsDocument Order/FileUpload500/88/Fred_Korematsu_amicusbrief0104.pdf.

25. BREYER, *supra* note 23, at 194, 190.

26. *See generally* MARGARET E. KECK AND KATHRYN SIKKINK, ACTIVISTS BEYOND BORDERS: ADVOCACY NETWORKS IN INTERNATIONAL POLITICS (1998).

27. Filartiga v. Pena-Irala, 630 F.2d 876 (2d Cir. 1980).

28. *See* Yale Law School, Lowenstein Clinic, *Past Project Highlights* (accessed June 30, 2011), http://www.law.yale.edu/intellectuallife/pastlowensteinhighlights .htm#AmicusUS.

29. Atkins v. Virginia, 536 U.S. 304 (2002); Sosa v. Alvarez-Machain, 542 US 692 (2004).

30. *See generally* Jeffrey Toobin, *Swing Shift*, NEW YORKER, Sept. 12, 2005.

31. *Id.*

32. *See* Brief of 175 Members of Both Houses of the Parliament of the United Kingdom of Great Britain and Northern Ireland as Amici Curiae in Support of Petitioners, Rasul v. Bush, 542 U.S. 466 (2004), http://www.jenner .com/files/tbl_s69NewsDocumentOrder/FileUpload500/79/AmiciCur iae_175_Members_Parliament_United_Kingdom_Northern_Ireland.pdf.

33. Brief of Diego Asencio et al., Rasul v. Bush, 542 U.S. 466 (2004), http:// www.jenner.com/files/tbl_s69NewsDocumentOrder/FileUpload 500/85/ amicicuriaeFormer_diplomats_amicus_brief.pdf.

34. Johan Steyn, "Guantanamo Bay: The Legal Black Hole," Twenty-Seventh F.A. Mann Lecture (Nov. 25, 2003), http://www.statewatch.org/news/2003/ nov/guantanamo.pdf.

35. International Committee of the Red Cross, *Guantanamo Bay: Overview of the*

ICRC's Work for Internees, http://www.icrc.org/eng/resources/documents/misc/5qrc5v.htm.

36. United Nations Press Release, *US Court Decision on Guantanamo Detainees Has Serious Implications for Rule of Law, Says UN Rights Expert* (Mar. 12, 2003).

37. Letter from Juan Mendez, President, Inter-American Commission on Human Rights, on Detainees in Guantanamo Bay, Mar. 13, 2002, http://www1.umn.edu/humanrts/cases/guantanamo-2003.html.

38. Brief Amicus Curiae of Retired Military Officers in Support of Petitioners, Rasul v. Bush, 542 U.S. 466 (2004), http://www.jenner.com/files/tbl_s69NewsDocumentOrder/FileUpload500/94/AmicusCuriae_Retired_Military_Officers.pdf; Brief for the National Institute of Military Justice as Amicus Curiae in Support of Petitioners, Rasul v. Bush, 542 U.S. 466 (2004), http://www.jenner.com/files/tbl_s69NewsDocumentOrder/FileUpload500/92/amicuscuriae_national_institute_of_military_justice.pdf; Brief for Former American Prisoners of War in Support of Petitioners, Rasul v. Bush, 542 U.S. 466 (2004), http://www.jenner.com/files/tbl_s69NewsDocumentOrder/FileUpload500/84/amicicuriae_former_american_prisoners_of_war.pdf.

39. Brief of the Military Attorneys Assigned to the Defense in the Office of Military Commissions as Amicus Curiae in Support of Neither Party, Boumediene v. Bush, 553 US 723 (2008), http://www.jenner.com/files/tbl_s69NewsDocumentOrder/FileUpload500/91/AmicusCuriae_Military_Attorneys.pdf.

40. E-mail communication with David Kennedy (Apr. 9, 2011).

41. *See, e.g,* Jake Tapper and Clayton Sandell, *JAG Lawyers: Prisoner Warnings Ignored,* ABC News, May 16, 2004, http://abcnews.go.com/WNT/story?id=131661&page=1.

42. Oral argument transcript, Rumsfeld v. Padilla, No. 03-1027, Apr. 28, 2004, http://www.jenner.com/files/tbl_s69NewsDocumentOrder/FileUpload500/352/03-1027_argument_padilla.pdf.

43. Hamdi v. Rumsfeld, 542 U.S. 507 (2004).

44. BREYER, *supra* note 23, at 200.

45. *See* Department of Defense, Consolidated Chronological Listing of GTMO Detainees Released, Transferred, or Deceased (Nov. 25, 2008), http://www.dod.mil/pubs/foi/operation_and_plans/Detainee/09-F-0031_doc1.pdf.

46. *See* WITTES, *supra* note 9, at 65–67.

47. *See* Hamdan v. Rumsfeld website, Case Briefs, http://www.hamdanvrumsfeld.com/briefs (last visited June 30, 2011).

48. BREYER, *supra* note 23, at 207.

49. Memorandum from Gordon England *re* Application of Common Article 3 of the Geneva Conventions to the Treatment of Detainees in the Department of Defense (July 7, 2006), http://jurist.law.pitt.edu/pdf/genevaconsmemo.pdf.

50. WILLIAM G. HOWELL AND JOHN C. PEVEHOUSE, WHILE DANGER GATHERS: CONGRESSIONAL CHECKS ON PRESIDENTIAL WAR POWERS (2007).

51. My own view is that the initiation of force in Libya was lawful, *see* Jack Gold-smith, *The Campaign against Libya Is Constitutional*, SLATE, March 21, 2011, http://www.slate.com/id/2288869/, but that while the matter is not certain, after sixty days the Obama administration probably violated the War Powers Resolution, *see* Jack Goldsmith, *Problems with the Obama Administration's War Powers Resolution Theory*, LAWFARE, June 16, 2011, http://www.lawfareblog .com/2011/06/problems-with-the-obama-administration%E2%80%99s-war-powers-resolution-theory-2/.

52. Authorization for Use of Military Force against Terrorists, S.J. Res. 23, 107th Cong. (2001).

53. See David Abramowitz, *The President, the Congress, and Use of Force: Legal and Political Considerations in Authorizing Use of Force against International Terrorism*, 43 HARV. INTERNATIONAL L. J. 71 (2002).

54. 147 CONG. REC. 17,105 (2001) (Statement of Rep. Peter DeFazio).

55. Uniting and Strengthening America by Providing Appropriate Tools Required to Intercept and Obstruct Terrorism Act of 2001, Public Law No. 107-56, 115 Stat. 272 (2001), codified as amended in scattered sections of Titles 18, 47 and 50 of the U.S. Code.

56. These efforts had few precursors in American history. The Civil War Congress in the 1863 Habeas Corpus Act required the courts to release certain persons detained in military custody who were not prisoners of war if they were held in states where the administration of the laws "con-tinued unimpaired." This was not a legal restriction on core presiden-tial military powers (because it excluded enemy soldiers), but it was an instance of Congress using law to push back against the President in the midst of war to protect civil liberties. Congress has also sometimes inter-vened in wars to narrow their scope. It did this most prominently when it tried to cabin and terminate the Vietnam War (and related military efforts in Laos and Cambodia), and also later when it placed restrictions on unilateral presidential interventions gone bad in Lebanon in 1983 and Somalia in 1993.

57. Interview with Senator Lindsey Graham, in Washington, D.C. (Sept. 29, 2010).

58. *Id.*

59. Kate Zernike & Sheryl Kay Stolberg, *Detainee Rights Create a Divide on Capitol Hill*, N.Y. TIMES, July 10, 2006.

60. Interview with Graham, *supra* note 57.

61. For explication of these details, see Jennifer K. Elsea, *The Military Commis-sions Act of 2006: Analysis of Procedural Rules and Comparison with Previous DOD Rules and the Uniform Code of Military Justice* (Congressional Research Service, 2007).

62. *See Detainee Provisions in National Defense Authorization Act*, at http://www .politico.com/static/PPM156_detainee_provisions.html; *see also* Josh Ger-stein, *W.H.: Defense Bill "Micromanages*," POLITICO, June 23, 2011, http://dyn .politico.com/members/forums/thread.cfm?catid=1&subcatid=56&thread id=5593506 (explaining origins of and context for this document).

63. Brief for Petitioners, Boumediene v. Bush, 553 U.S. 723 (2008), http://www.mayerbrown.com/public_docs/probono_Boumediene_Govt_Brief.pdf.

64. Boumediene v. Bush, 553 U.S. 723, 798 (2008).

65. James Oliphant, *Court Backs Gitmo Inmates,* CHICAGO TRIB., June 13, 2008.

66. Open letter from lawyers supporting Senator Obama for President (Jan. 28, 2008), http://online.wsj.com/public/resources/documents/habeasobama.pdf.

67. Michael Ratner, *On Closing Guantanamo: A Sisyphean Struggle,* HUFFINGTON POST, Jan. 23, 2009, http://www.huffingtonpost.com/michael-ratner/on-closing-guantanamo-a-s_b_160387.html (last visited July 4, 2011).

68. Peter Finn & Anne E. Kornblut, *How the White House Lost on Guantanamo,* WASH. POST, Apr. 24, 2011.

69. Memorandum for Respondents, *In re* Guantanamo Bay Detainee Litigation, http://www.justice.gov/opa/documents/memo-re-det-auth.pdf.

70. *Obama's National Security State: Interview with Michael Ratner,* INTERNATIONAL SOCIALIST REV., Nov.–Dec. 2010.

71. Finn & Kornblut, *supra* note 68.

72. Boumediene v. Bush, 553 U.S. 723 (2008) (Roberts, C. J., dissenting).

73. *See* Jack Goldsmith & Benjamin Wittes, *No Place to Write Detention Policy,* WASH. POST, Dec. 22, 2009.

74. This paragraph draws on the outstanding summary and analysis of the cases in Benjamin Wittes, Robert M. Chesney & Larkin Reynolds, *The Emerging Law of Detention 2.0: The Guantanamo Habeas Cases as Lawmaking* (Brookings Institution, May 2011), http://www.brookings.edu/papers/2011/05_guantanamo_wittes.aspx.

75. Al-Bihani v. Obama, 590 F.3d 866 (D.C. Cir. 2010).

76. ERIC A. POSNER & ADRIAN VERMEULE, THE EXECUTIVE UNBOUND: AFTER THE MADISONIAN REPUBLIC (2011); Aziz Huq, *What Good is Habeas?* 26 CONSTIT. COMMENT. (2010).

77. Katharine Q. Seelye, *Some Guantanamo Prisoners Will Be Freed, Rumsfeld Says,* N.Y. TIMES, Oct. 23, 2002. I say "most" in the text because of the dozens of Yemenis who remain at GTMO and who likely would have been repatriated by now if Yemen were a more stable country.

78. *See* Benjamin Wittes, *Updated Habeas Numbers,* LAWFARE, Aug. 2, 2011, http://www.lawfareblog.com/2011/08/updated-habeas-numbers-2/.

79. *See* Wittes, Chesney & Reynolds, *supra* note 74; Interviews with senior Obama administration officials, in Washington D.C.

80. Interviews with senior Obama administration officials, *supra* note 79.

81. E-mail communication with senior military lawyer (Nov. 4, 2010).

82. As noted in the previous chapter, the heightened detention standards in Afghanistan were also driven by COIN doctrine.

83. E-mail communication with senior military lawyer (Nov. 4, 2010).

84. *Boumediene,* 553 U.S. at 797.

85. *See* Memorandum in Support of Plaintiff's Motion for Preliminary, al-Aulaqi v. Obama, Civ. A. No. 10-cv-1469 (Aug. 30, 2010), http://ccrjustice.org/files/PI%20Motion.pdf.

86. *See* Opposition to Plaintiff's Motion for Preliminary Injunction and Memorandum in Support of Defendant's Motion to Dismiss, al-Aulaqi v. Obama, Civ. A. No. 10-cv-1469 (Sept. 24, 2010), http://www.lawfareblog.com/wp-content/uploads/2010/09/usgbrief.pdf.

87. *See* Center for Constitutional Rights, *Court Dismisses Targeted Killing Case on Procedural Grounds Without Addressing Merits*, http://www.ccrjustice.org/newsroom/press-releases/court-dismisses-targeted-killing-case-procedural-grounds-without-addressing-.

88. *See* Jack Goldsmith, *What ACLU and CCR Won in al-Aulaqi*, LAWFARE, Dec. 7, 2010, http://www.lawfareblog.com/2010/12/what-aclu-and-ccr-won-in-al-aulaqi/. The Obama administration had acknowledged this limitation in its briefs, but another administration might not have, and the matter is now addressed in a judicial opinion.

89. *See* Declaration of Jonathan Manes, The Joint Targeting Definitions and Process, Nasser al-Aulaqi v. Obama, No.p10-cv-1469 (JBD) (Oct. 8, 2010), http://ccrjustice.org/files/Declaration%20of%20Jonathan%20Manes%20 10-08-2010.pdf. As this book was in its final stages of completion, a federal court ruled that the CIA did not need to disclose records related to its targeted killing program in response to an ACLU request. ACLU v. Department of Justice, Case 1:10-cv-00436-RMC (Sept. 9, 2011), http://www .politico.com/static/PPM229_110909_acludrones.html.

90. John Brennan, Remarks at Harvard Law School (Sept. 16, 2011), http://www .lawfareblog.com/2011/09/john-brennans-remarks-at-hls-brookings-confer ence/.

91. Raphael G. Satter, *Group Threatens Legal Trouble for US Over Drones*, ASSOCIATED PRESS, May 9, 2011, http://abcnews.go.com/International/wireStory?id= 13563584.

92. Peter Beaumont, *Campaigners seek arrest of former CIA legal chief over Pakistan drone attacks*, THE GUARDIAN, July 15, 2011, http://www.guardian.co.uk/world/2011/jul/15/cia-usa.

93. See Ken Anderson, *Predators Over Pakistan*, WEEKLY STANDARD, Mar. 8, 2010, http://www.weeklystandard.com/articles/predators-over-pakistan. I am indebted to Anderson's essay, and his work on this topic more generally.

94. This point is based on conversations with Obama administration officials and is confirmed in JOBY WARRICK, THE TRIPLE AGENT: THE AL-QAEDA MOLE WHO INFILTRATED THE CIA 27 (2011).

CHAPTER SEVEN: THE PRESIDENTIAL SYNOPTICON

1. DAVID BRIN, THE TRANSPARENT SOCIETY: WILL TECHNOLOGY FORCE US TO CHOOSE BETWEEN PRIVACY AND FREEDOM? 11 (1998).

2. JEREMY BENTHAM, THE PANOPTICON WRITINGS (Miran Božovič ed., 1995).

3. MICHAEL FOUCAULT, DISCIPLINE AND PUNISH: THE BIRTH OF THE PRISON 200–207 (1977).

4. Jack M. Balkin, *The Constitution in the National Surveillance State*, 93(1) MINN. L. REV. 1, 4 (2008).

5. The latter term was coined, to the best of my knowledge, by the Norwegian sociologist Thomas Mathiesen. *See* Thomas Mathiesen, *The Viewer Society: Michael Foucault's "Panopticon" Revisted*, 1.2 THEORETICAL CRIMINOLOGY 215 (1997). I thank Stanford University English professor Blakey Vermeule for first bringing the synopticon idea to my attention.

6. *See generally* Steve Mann, Jason Nolan & Barry Wellman, *Sousveillance: Inventing and Using Wearable Computing Devices for Data Collection in Surveillance Environments*, 1(3) SURVEILLANCE & SOCIETY 331 (2003), *available at* http://wearcam .org/sousveillance.pdf.

7. FOUCAULT, *supra* note 3, at 201.

8. VICTOR DAVIS HANSON, CARNAGE AND CULTURE: LANDMARK BATTLES IN THE RISE OF WESTERN POWER 398–439 (2001).

9. There are scattered exceptions to this statement across American history. Congress, for example, gave modest guidance on the capture of prisoners of war during the War of 1812; it imposed subject matter restrictions on capture in the undeclared war with France in the 1790s; and it had a bit to say about military commissions during the Civil War. For a comprehensive account of congressional restrictions during wartime, see David J. Barron and Martin S. Lederman, *The Commander in Chief at the Lowest Ebb—A Constitutional History*, 121 HARV. L. REV. 941 (2008).

10. ARTHUR M. SCHLESINGER JR., THE IMPERIAL PRESIDENCY 470 (First Mariner Books 2004) (1973).

11. THE RECORDS OF THE FEDERAL CONVENTION OF 1787, at 422 (Max Farrand ed., rev. ed. 1966) (Statement of James Madison of Virginia, June 26, 1787).

12. *Cf.* Lawrence Lessig, *Fidelity in Translation*, 71 TEX. L. REV. 1165 (1993).

13. SCHLESINGER, *supra* note 10, at 473.

14. *See Ex CIA Chiefs Slowed Torture Memos Release*, MSNBC, Apr. 17, 2009, http://www.msnbc.msn.com/id/30270759/ns/politics-white_house/t/ ex-cia-chiefs-slowed-torture-memos-release/; Michael Isikoff, *"Holy Hell" over Torture Memos*, NEWSWEEK, Apr. 3, 2009; Mark Mazzetti, *Release of CIA Interrogation Memos May Open the Door to More Revelations*, N.Y. TIMES, Apr. 18, 2009; *Transcript: General Hayden on "FNS,"* FOX NEWS SUNDAY WITH CHRIS WALLACE, Apr. 20, 2009, http://www.foxnews.com/on-air/ fox-news-sunday/2009/04/20/transcript-gen-hayden-fns.

15. Barton Gellman, "Secrecy, Security and Self-Government: An Argument for Unauthorized Disclosures," Lecture at the Woodrow Wilson School, Princeton University (September 17, 2003).

16. Michael Hayden, Speech at Aspen Security Institute, Wye River, Md. (Oct. 2006) [hereinafter Wye River Speech].

17. Interview with Leonard Downie Jr., in Washington, D.C. (Sept. 8, 2010).

18. Wye River Speech, *supra* note 16; THE COMMISSION ON THE INTELLIGENCE CAPABILITIES OF THE UNITED STATES REGARDING WEAPONS OF MASS

DESTRUCTION, REPORT TO THE PRESIDENT OF THE UNITED STATES (May 31, 2005), http://www.gpoaccess.gov/wmd/pdf/full_wmd_report.pdf [hereinafter WMD REPORT].

19. ERIC LICHTBLAU, BUSH'S LAW: THE REMAKING OF AMERICAN JUSTICE 250 (2008).

20. Editorial, *Patriotism and the Press*, N.Y. TIMES, June 28, 2006.

21. Wye River Speech, *supra* note 16.

22. Michael Hayden, Keynote Address at book panel on GABRIEL SCHOENFELD, NECESSARY SECRETS: NATIONAL SECURITY, THE MEDIA, AND THE RULE OF LAW (2010), Hudson Institute, Washington, D.C. (May 25, 2010), www .hudson.org/index.cfm?fuseaction=hudson_upcoming_events&id=773; *see also* Wye River Speech, *supra* note 16.

23. Interview with Bill Keller, in New York, New York (Oct. 13, 2010)

24. LICHTBLAU, *supra* note 19.

25. *Id.*

26. *Tenet Is Open to Questions, Just Don't Ask Him about Iraq*, USA TODAY, Oct. 11, 2000.

27. See Memorandum appended to Memo from Donald Rumsfeld to the Deputy Secretary of Defense et al. on The Impact of Leaking Classified Information (July 12, 2002), http://www.fas.org/sgp/bush/dod071202.pdf.

28. WMD REPORT, *supra* note 18, at 381.

29. Barton Gellman, *Revealing a Reporter's Relationship with Secrecy and Sources*, NIEMAN REPORTS (2004), http://www.nieman.harvard.edu/reportsitem .aspx?id=100824. Gellman left the Washington Post the year after Downie retired and is now at Time magazine.

30. N.Y. Times Co. v. United States, 403 U.S. at 713, 728–29 (1971).

31. See Bill Keller, *Secrecy in Shreds*, N.Y. TIMES MAGAZINE, Apr. 1, 2011.

32. Arthur Brisbane, *Bill Keller Responds to Column on Swift Mea Culpa*, N.Y. TIMES, Nov. 6, 2006, http://publiceditor.blogs.nytimes.com/2006/11/06/ bill-keller-responds-to-column-on-swift-mea-culpa/.

33. Hayden, Keynote Address, *supra* note 22.

34. SENATE SELECT COMMITTEE ON INTELLIGENCE, REPORT ON THE INTELLIGENCE AUTHORIZATION ACT FOR FISCAL YEAR 2011 (Apr. 4, 2011), http:// www.fas.org/irp/congress/2011_rpt/srpt112-12.pdf.

35. Gabriel Schoenfeld, NECESSARY SECRETS: NATIONAL SECURITY, THE MEDIA, AND THE RULE OF LAW (2010); E-mail communication with Gabriel Schoenfeld (May 18, 2011).

36. *See, e.g.,* Scott Shane, *No Jail Time in Trial Over N.S.A. Leak*, N.Y. TIMES, July 15, 2011.

37. Marcus Brauchli, Richard S. Salant Lecture on Freedom of the Press, John F. Kennedy School of Government, Harvard University (Oct. 28, 2010), http://www.hks.harvard.edu/presspol/prizes_lectures/salant_lecture/ transcripts/salant_lecture_2010_brauchli.pdf.

38. United States v. Sterling, No. 1:10cr485 (LMB), July 29, 2011, http://www .documentcloud.org/documents/229733-judge-leonie-brinkemas-ruling- quashing-subpoena.html.

39. 28 C.F.R. § 50.10 (2010).

40. *See* Juhani Rudanko, James Madison and Freedom of Speech 110 (2004).

41. E-mail communication with Mark Martins (May 22, 2011).

42. Charles J. Dunlap Jr., *Law and Military Interventions: Preserving Humanitarian Values in 21st Century Conflicts* (Carr Center for Human Rights Policy, Workshop Paper, 2001), http://www.hks.harvard.edu/cchrp/Web%20Working%20Papers/Use%20of%20Force/Dunlap2001.pdf.

43. The full manual is available on the Federation of American Scientists' website, at http://www.fas.org/irp/world/para/aqmanual.pdf.

44. *See, e.g.,* Scott Horton, *Lawfare Redux,* Harper's Magazine, Mar. 12, 2010; David Rivkin & Lee Casey, *Lawfare,* Wash. Post, Feb. 23, 2007, at A11; John Fonte, *Democracy's Trojan Horse,* 76 National Interest 117 (Summer 2004).

45. *See Lawfare: The Use of the Law as a Weapon of War,* Lawfare Project, http://www.thelawfareproject.org/index.php?option=com_content&view=article&id=120&Itemid=74.

46. I am indebted here and elsewhere in this section to David Kennedy, Of War and Law (2006).

47. For a summary of the administration's legal arguments, see Marty Lederman, *The U.S. Perspective on the Legal Basis for the Bin Laden Operation,* Opinio Juris, May 24, 2011, http://opiniojuris.org/2011/05/24/the-us-perspective-on-the-legal-basis-for-the-bin-laden-operation/.

48. *See* Kennedy, *supra* note 46.; Dunlap, *supra* note 42.

49. Mark Martins, *Reflections on "Lawfare" and Related Terms,* Lawfare, Nov. 18, 2010, http://www.lawfareblog.com/2010/11/reflections-on-%E2%80%9Clawfare%E2%80%9D-and-related-terms/.

50. Andrew McCarthy, *Lawfare's Soft Targets,* Human Events, Mar. 10, 2008, http://www.humanevents.com/article.php?id=25408.

51. *The Torn Fabric of the Law: An Interview with Michael Ratner,* Mother Jones, Mar. 21, 2005, http://motherjones.com/politics/2005/03/torn-fabric-law-interview-michael-ratner.

52. Editorial, *The Lawfare Wars,* Wall St. J., Sept. 2, 2010.

53. This is a theme in Richard H. Pildes, *Conflicts between American and European Views of Law: The Dark Side of Legalism,* 44 Virginia Journal of International Law 145 (2003), which has influenced my thinking.

54. Those errors are recounted in the official Deputy Attorney General's Office review of the OPR Report, Memorandum from David Margolis, Associate Deputy Attorney General, to the Attorney General, On Objections to the Findings of Professional Misconduct in the Office of Professional Responsibility's Report of Investigation into the Office of Legal Counsel's Memoranda Concerning Issues Relating to the Central Intelligence Agency's Use of "Enhanced Interrogation Techniques" on Suspected Terrorists (Jan. 5, 2010) [hereinafter Margolis Memo], http://judiciary.house.gov/hearings/pdf/DAGMargolisMemo100105.pdf.

55. Donald Rumsfeld, Known and Unknown 587–601 (2011).

56. Margolis Memo, *supra* note 54.

57. Joby Warrick, *CIA Sets Changes to IG's Oversight, Adds Ombudsman*, WASH. POST, Feb. 2, 2008; Josh Marshall, *Transcript: Charlie Rose Interviews CIA Chief Gen. Michael Hayden*, TPM, Oct. 22, 2007, http://talkingpointsmemo.com/news/2007/10/transcript_charlie_rose_interv_1.php.

58. BENJAMIN WITTES, DETENTION AND DENIAL 146 (2010).

59. RUMSFELD, *supra* note 55, at 587–601.

60. Interview with Jameel Jaffer, in New York, New York (Oct, 12, 2010).

61. Statement of President Barack Obama on Release of OLC Memos (Aug. 16, 2009), http://www.whitehouse.gov/the_press_office/Statement-of-Pres ident-Barack-Obama-on-Release-of-OLC-Memos/; Jameel Jaffer & Ben Wizner, *Commentary: Accountability Is Needed for Bush-Era Torture*, McCLATCHY, Apr. 23, 2009, http://www.mcclatchydc.com/2009/04/23/66665/com mentary-accountability-is-needed.html.

62. *See* R. Jeffrey Smith, *In Obama's Inner Circle, Debate over Memo's Release Was Intense*, WASH. POST, Apr. 24, 2009; Michael Isikoff, *The Lawyer and the Caterpillar*, NEWSWEEK, Apr. 18, 2009; Siobhan Gorman & Evan Perez, *CIA Memos Released*, WALL ST. J., Apr. 17, 2009; Mike Allen, *Obama Consulted Widely on Memos*, POLITICO, Apr. 16, 2009, http://www.politico.com/news/stories/0409/21338.html; Siobhan Gorman & Evan Perez, *Obama Tilts to CIA on Memos*, WALL ST. J., Apr. 15, 2009. In the President's speech on the subject, he stated, "But at a time of great challenges and disturbing disunity, nothing will be gained by spending our time and energy laying blame for the past. Our national greatness is embedded in America's ability to right its course in concert with our core values, and to move forward with confidence. That is why we must resist the forces that divide us, and instead come together on behalf of our common future." Statement of President Barack Obama, *supra* note 61.

63. Dan Balz, *Confronting the Bush Legacy, Reluctantly*, WASH. POST, Apr. 22, 2009, http://voices.washingtonpost.com/44/2009/04/22/confronting_the_ bush_legacy_re.html.

64. Statement of President Barack Obama, *supra* note 61.

65. Jaffer & Wizner, *supra* note 61.

66. *See also* David Cole, *What to Do about Guantanamo?* N.Y. REV. BOOKS, Oct. 14, 2010.

67. Congress in the torture law "defined the prohibition on torture very narrowly to ban only the most extreme acts and to preserve many loopholes." JACK GOLDSMITH, THE TERROR PRESIDENCY 143 (2007).

68. As I detailed in THE TERROR PRESIDENCY, *supra* note 67, at 149–51.

69. *See* Scott Shane & David Johnston, *U.S. Lawyers Agreed on Legality of Brutal Tactic*, N.Y. TIMES, June 6, 2010; and Classified Response to the U.S. Department of Justice Office of Professional Responsibility Classified Report Dated July 29, 2009, Submitted on Behalf of Judge Jay S. Bybee, October 9, 2009, http://judiciary.house.gov/hearings/pdf/BybeeResponse090729.pdf. When I served in the Justice Department, I withdrew Jay Bybee's August 1, 2002, legal opinion that interpreted the torture law in the abstract, which

I believed was flawed, overbroad, and unnecessary. But I did not withdraw his opinion, signed the same day, that analyzed the legality of ten specific interrogation techniques. As I explained in THE TERROR PRESIDENCY, "I wasn't . . . confident that the CIA techniques could be approved under a proper legal analysis. I didn't affirmatively believe they were illegal either, or else I would have stopped them. I just didn't yet know. And I wouldn't know until we had figured out the proper interpretation of the torture statute, and whether the CIA techniques were consistent with that proper legal analysis." GOLDSMITH, *supra* note 67, at 155–56. In light of the CIA inspector general's report, I informed the CIA that I "strongly recommend" that it not use the waterboarding technique, not because I had concluded that it was unlawful (I had not), but because the inspector general report indicated that the "actual practice" of the technique "may not have been congruent with all of th[e] assumptions and limitations" in the Bybee techniques opinion. *See* Memorandum from Jack Goldsmith to Scott Muller (May 27, 2004), http:// www.aclu.org/torturefoia/released/082409/olcremand/2004olc28.pdf.

70. Adam Goldman & Matt Apuzzo, *At CIA, Grave Mistakes, Then Promotions,* ABC NEWS, Feb. 9, 2011, http://abcnews.go.com/Blotter/wireStory?id= 12872190.
71. *Id.* The quotation is presented in the AP story as a paraphrase of what Woolsey said.
72. Jaffer & Wizner, *supra* note 61.
73. Interview with John Rizzo, in Cambridge, Massachusetts (Nov. 8, 2010).
74. See American Enterprise Institute, *Video of Conference on CIA Interrogations and the Bin Laden Operation* (May 16, 2011), http://www.aei.org/video/101447.
75. *See* Jack Goldsmith & Cass Sunstein, *Military Tribunals and the Legal Culture: What a Difference Sixty Years Makes,* 19 CONSTIT. COMMENT. 261 (2002); Mark Tushnet, *Defending Korematsu? Reflections on Civil Liberties in Wartime,* 2003 WISC. L. REV. 273, 292 (2003).
76. THE FEDERALIST 51 (James Madison).
77. RICHARD HOFSTADTER, THE AMERICAN POLITICAL TRADITION 11 (1948).

AFTERWORD: AFTER THE NEXT ATTACK

1. *What Keeps the Counterterrorism Chief Up at Night,* NPR, Jan. 2, 2010, http:// www.npr.org/templates/story/story.php?storyId=122153001.
2. Giovanna Fabiano, *U.S. Counterterrorism Chief Returns to Dwight-Englewood, His Alma Mater,* NORTHJERSEY.COM, Apr. 12, 2011, http://www.northjersey .com/news/education/education_news/041211_US_counterterrorism_ chief_returns_to_Dwight-Englewood_his_alma_mater.html?mobile=1; Committee on Homeland Security and Government Affairs, United States Senate, The Lessons and Implications of the Christmas Day Attack: Watch-listing and Pre-Screening, 111th Cong. (Mar. 10, 2010) (Statement for the Record of Mr. Russell Travers, Deputy Director, National Counterterror-ism Center), http://www.dni.gov/testimonies/20100310_testimony.pdf.

3. Michael Leiter, "Looming Challenges in the War on Terror," Remarks Presented to the Washington Institute (Feb. 13, 2008), http://www.nctc.gov/press_room/speeches/wash-inst-written-sfr-final.pdf.

4. Travers, Statement for the Record, *supra* note 2.

5. See Susan Crabtree, *Intelligence Chief Says It Was a Mistake to Reduce No-Fly List*, HILL, Jan. 20, 2010.

6. SENATE SELECT COMMITTEE ON INTELLIGENCE, UNCLASSIFIED EXECUTIVE SUMMARY OF THE COMMITTEE REPORT ON THE ATTEMPTED TERRORIST ATTACK ON NORTHWEST AIRLINES FLIGHT 253 (May 18, 2010), http://intelligence.senate.gov/100518/1225report.pdf.

7. Hearing before the House Committee on Homeland Security, Understanding the Homeland Threat Landscape—Considerations for the 112th Congress (Feb. 9, 2011) (Testimony of Michael E. Leiter), http://www.nctc.gov/press_room/speeches/2011-02-09-SFR-NCTC-Director-Leiter-FINAL.pdf.

8. Interview with Michael Leiter (June 2, 2011).

9. *See, e.g.,* Center for Strategic and International Studies, Conference on the Changing Terrorist Threat and NCTC's Response (Dec. 1, 2010) (transcript of Michael Leiter's comments), http://csis.org/files/attachments/101202_leiter_transcript.pdf; Hearing before the House Committee on Homeland Security, *supra* note 7.

10. *See* sources cited in previous note.

11. HERMAN KAHN, ON THERMONUCLEAR WAR 535 (1960).

12. Conference on the Changing Terrorist Threat, *supra* note 9.

Index